Music for Today

At a summer workshop, Dr. Eriksen, author, works with selected voices of mixed ages.

Allyn and Bacon
Boston, London, Sydney, Toronto

MUSIC *for* TODAY
ELEMENTARY SCHOOL METHODS

Third Edition

ALETA RUNKLE
Elementary Vocal Music Consultant
Independence, Missouri

MARY LEBOW ERIKSEN
Westshore Community College
Manistee and Mason Counties, Michigan

LIBRARY OF CONGRESS CATALOGING IN PUBLICATION DATA

Runkle, Aleta.
  Music for today.

  Previous editions published under title: Music for
today's boys and girls; sequential learning through the
grades.
  Various bibliographies: p.
  1. School music—Instruction and study—United States.
I. Eriksen, Mary LeBow, joint author. II. Title.
MT3.U5R85 1976   372.8'7'044   75-35910

ISBN 0-205-05415-3

Acknowledgments

We should like to express our sincere appreciation to the students, elementary teachers, and administrators of the Independence and Detroit public schools, and all the hundreds of others throughout the country with whom we have shared rich experiences—many of which are recorded in this book. Their enthusiasm and cooperation through the years have been responsible for any successes that we have had in our music programs.

To Mrs. Mary Hahn and Mrs. Berneice Clark, who did the typing, to Mrs. Audrey Stubbart, who read the original manuscript and gave helpful criticism, to Dr. Guy Carter, Mr. Emory Parks, Mr. A. R. Meyer, and Dr. O. L. Plucker, present and former administrators in the Independence Public Schools, and to Mr. Alfred Bleckschmidt, former State Director of Fine Arts Education, Missouri, we extend special words of thanks.

To Mr. Patrick Burke, Director School–Community Relations, and Mr. Ken Raveill our special thanks for the pictures from the Independence Public Schools.

Contents

chapter 7   **Bicentennial Program Helps**   **283**

Appendixes

Preface

This book was originally written for those who plan to teach music in the elementary schools. The First Edition soon became popular not only with in-service teachers, consultants, and administrators, but also with university faculty who are preparing music education majors and elementary education majors to become skillful teachers.

One of the reasons most often given by these people for selecting this book is the fact that all the material in it has been "child-tested" in classrooms in *every regional division* of the Music Educators' National Conference. Specific experiences that have been successful in actual practice are described in detail. No inference is made, of course, that there is only one "best" way to present any given music activity. However, the material in the book does furnish an excellent "launching pad" for teachers to explore and expand their creative skills as they gain experience in the classroom.

Another reason this book has been so widely used is that it follows a program of *planned progress*—just as is done in other subject areas. For this reason, there are specific guidelines for three major growth levels: Music for 1) Early Childhood, 2) Middle Childhood, and 3) Later Childhood. Within these levels the chapters deal with specific music experiences.

The format is designed to give equal assistance to teachers in systems using the open concept philosophy and those in elementary schools with the grade-by-grade pattern. Teaching suggestions are given in order of difficulty for six levels of learning. These growth levels can give specific guidelines for those who have experimental groupings or are in an unstructured setting, while teachers with only one class can equate these levels with their particular needs. Levels 1 and 2 can be used for kindergarten, first, and second grades; levels 3 and 4 for third and fourth grades; levels 5 and 6 for fifth and sixth grades.

To assist all teachers in planning there are specific aids: 1) charts of sequential music activities, outlined to show their specific relationship to the musical experience for which they are designed; 2) skills defined in relation to the normal needs and characteristics of the learner; 3) Suggested Questions for Measuring Progress, which define specific criteria for evaluation at each level, and 4) twelve appendixes, which list specific materials and addresses where they may be obtained. In addition, at the conclusion of each chapter there is a list of Suggested Projects that can furnish material for assignments to university methods classes.

Aleta Runkle
Mary LeBow Eriksen

Introduction

Before beginning the detailed study of the elementary music program, it might be well to take a quick look at equipment you will need in order to have happy and successful experiences.

ESSENTIAL AND ENRICHMENT EQUIPMENT

At least one complete set of current basic music series (see Appendix A) which includes books for the pupils, large charts, teachers' books, and albums of recorded music for each level of experience. Many schools find it very desirable to have two or more sets of these basic music series.

A record player in good condition which will play 78, 45, and 33 r.p.m. records and which can be kept in your classroom.

Recordings in good condition (for use in listening experiences, singing games, other rhythmic movement, and activities using instruments) which are suitable to the level of experience of the children in your class.

At least one Autoharp (preferably with 12 or 15 bars) which is kept in tune and can remain in your classroom.

At least one set of individual chromatic resonator bells (a minimum of 20 tuned bars, with a mallet for each bar) which can be kept in your classroom.

At least one set of diatonic step bells (with a pair of mallets) which can be kept in your classroom.

A variety of rhythm instruments, including several types of drums, several sets of rhythm sticks, claves, guiros, cymbals, finger cymbals, tambourines, castanets, maracas, wrist bells, sleigh bells, sand blocks, wood block, tone blocks, cow bells, triangles, tugboat and train whistles, and jingle sticks.

A staff liner (with chalk), large paper rolls printed with a big music staff, large flash cards, large charts showing specific songs and rhythm drills printed by various publishers (see Appendix H).

A good piano kept properly tuned *every* two or three months.

An accurate metronome.

Films, filmstrips, transparencies, audiotapes, videotapes, and the equipment necessary to operate them.

A chromatic pitch pipe with note selector.

A tuning fork (an A 440 or a C 523.3 may be most useful in the classroom, but a B-flat 446.2 is also helpful).

Instruments such as the ukulele, guitar, and accordion.

Recorders, Tonettes, Flutophones, song flutes, and the *Melodica* (soprano, alto, and piano types).

Glockenspiels, xylophones, metallophones, drums, small percussion instruments, and other equipment designed especially for use in the Carl Orff *Schulwerk* are also desirable.

Slide projectors, opaque projectors, overhead projectors, film projectors, screens, television sets, radios (AM-FM), tape recorders, and at least three sets of earphones (for each record player, radio, or tape recorder) should be available in your school and easily accessible when needed.

You may want to explore the possibility of securing some of the above equipment through the assistance of federal funds. Your administrator should know the appropriate agencies to contact.

SCHEDULING MUSIC CLASSES

Within the last few years the scheduling of music classes in the elementary school has undergone many changes. The cause seems to relate to differing philosophies of education. Many schools have retained the traditional grade-by-grade organization. Others are experimenting with the open concept, team teaching, ability groupings, and ungraded curriculum. In some schools the classroom teacher on each grade level is responsible for his or her own music teaching. In others, music specialists are employed to teach each class once or twice a week, or perhaps to teach two sessions one week and three the next, alternating with another special teacher in physical education or art. Still other variations provide for music specialists with the older elementary children while primary teachers are responsible for music in their own classroom.

As music teachers heavily involved on the "front lines" of action in the elementary schools, the authors are very aware of this diversity of approach and structure. Because of this we have tried to plan this book to be flexible and yet specific enough to say meaningful things to *everyone* involved with music experiences with young children. Obviously, the matter of scheduling will be so individualized that it cannot be discussed in detail here. We hope that the ideas presented in the book can be adapted for the use of *all* teachers of music—no matter what the organizational setup! Above all, we believe that music should be *enjoyed*—by both students and teacher.

Music for Today

1

Overview

EARLY CHILDHOOD (AGES 5, 6, AND 7)

Educators have given much thought—and rightly so—to the characteristics of the learner and how these aspects will affect his accomplishment. Much has also been written and discussed about the child's total growth and how it can be enriched by appropriate and exciting experiences with music. Also, in the last few years, the amount of material for teaching music to children has greatly increased and improved. It is now possible to select excellent multimedia sources, new basic series of music texts, and colorful manipulative materials to help organize systematic instruction for individuals and small groups.

The information presented on the following pages is intended as a quick reference for planning. In general it will help to show the relationship of music experiences to what are considered the normal characteristics of elementary school children of various ages.

Developmental Characteristics*

PHYSICAL GROWTH AND SKILLS	*IMPLICATIONS FOR TEACHING MUSIC*
Growth at a slow rate; body lengthening out. Large muscles often bet-	Emphasis on fundamental and free movement to rhythms involving

* All material here and in other charts in this chapter, with the exception of "Implications for Teaching Music," adapted from *Your Child from Six to Twelve*, by U.S. Children's Bureau, U.S. Department of Health, Education, and Welfare, Washington, D.C. (1966).

1

ter developed than small ones. (Coordination of small muscles improves around age 7.)

large muscles. Action songs employing "finger play" to help develop coordination of small muscles.

Permanent teeth appearing.

Very active; sitting still is an effort; wriggling especially noticeable.

Variety of activity, providing frequent opportunity for getting up and moving about: marching, skipping, etc. with songs; playing informal instruments; phrase games.

Absorbed in running, jumping, chasing, and dodging games.

Rhythmic experiences involving entire body: creative, interpretive rhythms; singing games.

Tendency to tire easily.

Opportunity for frequent rest breaks in strenuous rhythmic experiences. Avoid prolonged activities.

Vision not yet fully developed; eye movements slow; likely to have trouble seeing small print, or making fine linear distinctions when music staff is not enlarged. Heart in stage of rapid growth.

Rote songs; occasional study of notation from large charts or chalkboard.

Strenuous activity periods should be brief.

SOCIAL PROGRESS

Thoroughly enjoys group play, but groups tend to be small. Boys and girls play together.

Group activities including singing games, playing informal instruments; phrase games.

Teacher's opinions and ideas very important.

Encouragement and sincere praise from teacher, giving guidance as well as approval.

Competition in school and at play.

Group activities to teach cooperation; individual activities to aid self-development.

Playing melodies and tonal patterns is much more stimulating when each student has his own tone bells or xylophone.

SOCIAL PROGRESS

Choice of friends seldom influenced by social or economic status. Interested in dressing and acting like his friends.

Awareness of differences between his home and those of others increasing.

INTELLECTUAL GROWTH AND ACTIVITIES

Short attention-span.

IMPLICATIONS FOR TEACHING MUSIC

Songs emphasizing personal worth of each individual and culture. Story records introducing people with varying backgrounds and situations.

Songs about home and community revealing natural differences among people and their modes of living.

Vary activity throughout music period. Guard against maintaining one type of experience too long.

Delights in imaginative, dramatic play.

Interpretive rhythms; dramatization of songs; creating and acting out of song stories.

Likes adventure programs.

Listening experiences that create feelings of excitement, mystery.

Enjoys beginning steps of reading.

Exploring new songbook, becoming aware of the printed page; reading aloud simple phrases from short songs.

Can grasp the basic ideas of addition and subtraction.

Understanding of basic concept that songs "swing" in twos, threes, and fours.

Increasing ability to take responsibility seriously.

Assume responsibility for behavior —self-discipline. Assist with passing out and collection of books, informal instruments, etc.

Planning Sequential Music Experiences

SINGING

Rote songs

Helps for uncertain singers
    for matching tones use:
        excerpts from familiar songs
        tonal drills
        tonal games
        imitation of sounds
           machines and motors
           animals and birds
           sounds of nature
               wind   rain   waves

Phrasing
    chant nursery rhymes
    sing familiar songs, discovering phrases (move arms in arc to feel scope of phrase). Give attention to correct breathing, keeping phrases smooth and unbroken.

indicate phrases by walking, skipping, etc. Turn at the end of each phrase and walk or skip in opposite direction.

Creative activities
    create appropriate motions to accompany songs
    sing conversation
    add new stanzas to a known song
    compose melody for a favorite poem
    create a new song—words and melody

Community sings

MUSIC READING AND READINESS

Tonal experiences

    melodic direction

lines on board
play tune with hand
study of syllables, num-
bers, letters

tonal patterns
    sing (from board, charts, flash
      cards)
    play on bells, piano, xylo-
      phone
    write on staff
    identify matching tonal pat-
      terns on board, in book

sing entire song using syllables,
    numbers, letters
        precede with chanting and
        clapping rhythm (both
        notes and words of song)

key feeling

Phrase feeling

Basic notation: dynamic markings
  treble clef   identical phrases
  staff   skips and steps
  measures   highest and lowest
  bars   notes of song
  rests   repeated or un-
  tie   usual rhythm
  slur   patterns
           octave

notes:
  whole
  half
  quarter
  eighth

Rhythm experiences
  beat
  meter sensing

Development of music vocabulary

RHYTHMS

Awareness of rhythm and meter
  chant rhythms—play on percus-

sion instruments
  names—e.g., Jerry
  animals—e.g., kangaroo
  objects—e.g., television

clap songs
  rhythm
  meter
develop feeling for steady beat,
  downbeat
chant words and notes of songs
  in rhythm
chant and clap rhythm patterns
  on charts
  on board
  in songs

Fundamental rhythms
  skipping, galloping, running,
  walking, hopping, marching,
  swinging, swaying, jumping,
  tiptoeing, etc.
      develop these skills by the
      use of songs
        percussion instruments
        (wood block, drum)
        Autoharp
        story records
        piano or piano record-
        ings
        orchestral selections
Creative and interpretive rhythms
  respond individually and as a
  class

Singing games and folk dances

LISTENING

Media for listening experiences:
  singing of teacher, guest artist,
  and other class members
  piano and other instruments
    invite musicians to demon-
    strate (students or adults)
  recordings
  tapes
  sound films
  experiments with sound
    objects—pencils, rulers, whis-
    tles, keys

percussion instruments
    develop discrimination of the unique tone color (timbre) of each

creative evaluation of sounds about us
    nature—rain, wind, birds, insects
    industry—machines, motors
    transportation—cars, planes, trains, buses, ships

Types of music
    program music
    descriptive
    narrative
      after listening quietly to music give creative response
    absolute
      respond with associations but avoid making up story

Listening skills to be developed
    sensitivity to mood
    awareness of tempo and dynamic changes
    discrimination of tonal beauty
    recognition and identification of solo instruments in compositions
    distinction between male and female voices in recordings of songs

Related information
    acquaintance with instruments of the orchestra
      place in categories
        blowing
        bowing
        striking

Attitudes
    listen expectantly, quietly, creatively
    become attentive, courteous members of listening audience

INSTRUMENTS

Percussion instruments
    use with songs
      children select instruments, matching tone color of instrument with desired sound effect
      introduce only a few instruments at a time
    create musical stories, using instruments for sound effects
      e.g., Jack and the Beanstalk climbing the beanstalk—xylophone
        giant walking—drum or tom-tom
    play rhythm patterns

Resonator bells, xylophone
    play short patterns from songs
    compose tunes

Autoharp
    child strums Autoharp in rhythm while teacher manipulates chord buttons

Keyboard instruments
    become acquainted with the piano keyboard
    study form
      use same instruments for identical sections
      different instruments for contrasting sections
        same   AA (ABA)
        different   B (ABA)

Suggested Questions for Measuring Progress

Have daily opportunities been provided for the children to explore the rhythm of the music by walking, running, skipping, taking "giant steps," swaying, tiptoeing, and other natural motions?

Do the children frequently explore the possibilities of "acting out" the music according to the way it makes them feel? Have they learned to listen attentively before deciding how to respond?

Do the children share the joys of all the sounds of the world around them—in nature, in technology, in their own names, in chants and poems, and in the sounds of different instruments?

Does each child—each day—have at least a ten-second, exciting opportunity to match the pitch of another singer? Is each child encouraged without being told, "Good!"—when his singing was really out-of-tune? Does the class respond with pleasure when pitches are matched beautifully?

If a good many individuals are still singing out-of-tune, is the class singing too much AS A GROUP? Is the tempo of the singing too slow? Are the songs performed expressively, musically? Are they worth sharing? Has a variety of accompaniments been provided for known songs? Are the accompaniments musically appropriate, or used as a powerful crutch?

Has the class discovered that some music is faster, and other music is slower? Have they experienced a marked contrast in speed in a single activity or composition? Have they learned the musical terminology needed to express their ideas about appropriate tempi for their own performances?

Does the class realize what is meant by "loud" and "soft" music? Do they confuse "loud" with "faster" and "soft" with "slower"? Have they had the opportunity to discuss their ideas about dynamics?

Can the children recognize which pitches are "higher" and which pitches are "lower"? Can they recognize which pitches "stay the same"? Has the class had many kinds of experiences that can lead to the discovery of the rise and fall of the melody (as shown on a large chart or in a book)?

Have the children discovered that some tones are longer than others? Can they differentiate between those tones which are "even" and those which are "uneven"? Can they identify the symbols used to indicate these differences in the DURATION of sounds?

Have all the children been successful in indicating the STRONG BEAT (through the use of "patschen," clapping, or similar activity)? Has individual remedial work been provided for those who find it difficult to hear and respond to the beat?

Can the class determine how many weak beats occur before the next strong beat? Can they conclude from this if the meter is organized in "TWOs, THREEs, or FOURs"?

Can most of the children read a simple rhythm pattern of quarter notes, eighth notes, half notes, whole notes, and their corresponding rests? Can they write (or construct with felt symbols) a simple pattern of this type when they hear it? Do they understand why the staff is not needed for the NOTATION OF RHYTHM PATTERNS? Do they realize that every note has two names: a rhythm name and a pitch name?

Through many opportunities to look at known songs on a large chart or book, has the class discovered that all notes have an exact pitch LOCATION ON THE STAFF? Have they developed skill through some kind of regular, systematic "ear training"— using so-fa syllables, numbers, or simple instruments?

Have the children had many experiences that can lead to the realization that the melody can go up, down, or stay the same? Do they understand that the pitches which look high, also sound high; the pitches which look low, sound low; and those which stay the same on the staff, sound the same?

Can the children perform many simple scale-wise and chord-wise tonal patterns? Have they been able to associate the sound of a "step" with the way it looks on the large chart? Can they recognize and perform the "skip" of an octave? a third? a sixth? Do they understand which part of each note on the staff indicates its exact pitch?

Are the children aware that music is put together in sections? Can they find identical portions? Can they recognize introductions and codas? Can they show where phrases begin and end, and distinguish between those which are alike and those which are different?

Have they had many opportunities to respond to FORM in music—through movement, through changing instruments, through changing colors, through drawing simple designs?

Does the class have a list of favorite music? Do they ever "make up" their own singing games, puzzles, or riddles? Can they sing about the things they saw on their way to school? Are many opportunities for expanding the child's natural creativity provided and encouraged?

MIDDLE CHILDHOOD (AGES 8 AND 9)

Developmental Characteristics

PHYSICAL GROWTH AND SKILLS	IMPLICATIONS FOR TEACHING MUSIC
Slow growth in height. Heart development slower, with increased strain.	Provide frequent rest breaks in rhythmic experiences. Alternate group and individual participation.
Permanent teeth continuing to appear.	
Growing interest in games requiring coordination of small muscles that are developing. Ability to write progressing, but fine muscle work is still difficult and taxing. Uses tools increasingly well.	Work at the piano keyboard; play song flutes.
Interested in many different kinds of play.	Enriched curriculum: singing, listening, rhythmic experiences; creating songs; dramatizing songs and rhythms; playing informal instruments; music reading.
Posture may become poor during this period.	Relaxed, happy singing relieves tension and fatigue, aiding mental alertness and improved posture. Stand at times to sing.

Vision maturing, nearing adult stage.

Singing from the book—both by rote and note; careful observance of the score; following notes in the book for the playing of instruments; writing and reading percussion scores.

SOCIAL PROGRESS

Gangs and clubs among own sex apparent. Group projects become absorbing, but no total capability of team play. Differences in play interest between boys and girls. Antagonism between sexes may appear.

Need for group music activities as a social experience: folk dances; playing of informal instruments; singing and acting out rounds.

SOCIAL PROGRESS

IMPLICATIONS FOR TEACHING MUSIC

Stronger emphasis on peer approval than on adult approval.

Providing opportunity for individual performance: playing piano or other instrument, singing solos, duets, trios; teacher and class planning together some music activities in the classroom.

INTELLECTUAL GROWTH AND ACTIVITIES

Interest in how things are made, produced, increasing.

Correlate music with units in science: tune water glasses to scale; demonstrate tuning fork; discuss length and quality of strings in relation to pitch.

Begins to be interested in what happened in the distant past. Interest in fantasy and make-believe on the decline during the latter part of this period.

Correlate music with units in social science—study Indians and their music: become acquainted with pentatonic and minor, use tom-toms and other Indian drums in rhythmic experiences; create dances.

Evidences dramatic interest.

Create dances; dramatize rhythms; act out song stories.

Understands basic mathematical facts.

Teach time signature, relationship of note values.

Enjoys comic books, cartoons, and adventure stories on TV.

Evaluate with class musical opportunities in the community, on radio, TV.

Planning Sequential Music Experiences

SINGING

Rote songs

Individualized singing experiences
Phrasing
    read text of song as verse-speaking choir
    discover phrases in new songs
    find phrases in instrumental compositions, move hand in small arc to describe phrase

Part singing
    rounds
    chants
    descants
    two-part songs

Study of form
    use songs to discover ABA and AB structure

Creative song experiences

Community sings

MUSIC READING AND READINESS

Study of syllables or numbers

Tonal patterns

Symbols of music notation
    time signature
    sharps and flats
    key and key signature
    letter names for lines and spaces

Rhythm problems
    feeling for the beat
        clap-tap rhythms
        play percussion instruments

    dotted rhythm patterns
    evenly divided beat
    understanding note values

Intervals

Awareness of score
    sequence
    melody patterns
    recognition of phrase and melodic direction
Reading new songs

Theory games

Form (design) of music

Music vocabulary

Scales
    major
    minor (natural)
    pentatonic

RHYTHMS

Awareness of meter and rhythm pattern
    chant and clap rhythms
        in songs,
        rhythm patterns
    develop feeling for steady beat, downbeat

Question and answer games
    clap (or play on percussion instrument) short original rhythm pattern
    student "answers" with original pattern in same meter and number of measures

Fundamental rhythms
    decrease emphasis second semester of third level

Creative and interpretive rhythms

Grand left and right

Singing games and folk dances
seek to perfect individual skills in fundamental rhythms when these are basic movements in singing games and dances

Marching

Acting out of rounds

LISTENING

Media:
songs
piano
recordings
orchestral instruments
filmstrips and recordings

Types of music
program music
e.g., suite
absolute music
e.g., dance forms (gavotte, minuet, etc.)
motivate listening by giving attention to:
mood
identification of solo instruments

Listening skills
recognize phrases in instru-
mental music and discover those which are identical

Related information
learn families of instruments in symphony orchestra
emphasize study of composers filmstrips and recordings biographies

Attitudes
maintain enthusiastic, attentive, courteous listening habits

INSTRUMENTS

Percussion instruments
use with songs, rhythm patterns
continue study of form
read and create percussion scores

Bells, xylophone, piano
play short patterns from songs
compose tunes
play chord roots in appropriate rhythm with songs
continue exploration of piano keyboard

Song flutes (Tonette, recorder, Flutophone)

Autoharp
strum and play chord buttons

Create introductions and codas for songs, using percussion and melody instruments

Suggested Questions for Measuring Progress

Have the children learned to sing a great many songs which are so appealing that they are willing to share them—even outside the classroom and in later years?

Can the majority of the class members sing well in tune, with pleasing tone quality? When the class sings as a group, can every word of the song be clearly understood?

Does the singing express musical mood and rhythmic swing—not mere accuracy? Do the children know how to establish an appropriate tempo for their singing, and do they get the opportunity to do so?

Can most of the children move to the rhythm of the music and interpret the phrase structure? Are opportunities for individual creative response provided along with group uniformity of movement?

Have the children had opportunities to interpret music through dramatization?

Can most of the class members play the Autoharp, tone bells, and other instruments with success and pleasure? Have opportunities been provided for each individual to explore each instrument?

Can all children make discriminating choices of percussion instruments based on the suitability of their timbre and capabilities of sustaining (or not sustaining) sounds?

Have opportunities been provided for the children to create introductions, codas, descants, and percussion scores?

Do most of the children understand that the term "chord" is related to the harmonic experiences they have enjoyed in music? Does the class realize that singing rounds and descants involves two or more melodies, and that this musical experience (polyphonic texture) is different from the harmony that results from chords?

Can the children distinguish phrases which sound exactly alike, those which sound entirely different, and those which sound similar? Has everyone in the class had the opportunity to discover that the music which sounds alike, also looks alike on the printed page; and that the music which sounds different, looks different?

Through their ability to interpret the printed page, do the class members show that they realize that every note has two names: one that shows pitch and another that shows duration?

Has the class developed a great many tonal pattern combinations in both the major and the minor modes? Can they recognize them "by ear"? Can they perform them on some kind of melodic instrument? How many can sing them in tune when they see them?

How many of the children can sense the strong beat, and determine how many weak beats there are in the meter? In terms of the printed page, how easily can the majority of the class members locate the strong beat?

Has everyone had the opportunity to listen often and to develop the skill of identifying "even" and "uneven" rhythm patterns?

Do most of the children recognize several instruments of the orchestra when they see and hear them?

Does the class look forward to exploring music again tomorrow?

LATER CHILDHOOD (AGES 10 AND 11)

Developmental Characteristics

PHYSICAL GROWTH AND SKILLS	*IMPLICATIONS FOR TEACHING MUSIC*
Period of rapid growth for some, plateau for others. Rapid increase in weight may begin for girls.	Party play games to relieve tension and overcome awkwardness; rhythmic activities stressing coordination and skill: marching drills, basic steps of the square dance, polka, schottische.
Permanent teeth continuing to appear.	
Willingness to work hard at acquiring physical skills, with emphasis on excellence of performance.	Increase challenges in classroom: two- and three-part singing, expanded listening opportunities, refinement of music reading skills. Provide opportunities beyond the classroom: extracurricular chorus; band and orchestra; music festivals involving group activities—singing, folk dancing.
Secondary sex characteristics may appear.	Possibility of voice change among boys. Distinguish between genuine

and "pseudo" and seek to help both.

Eye function reaches adult level at end of this period.

No limitation on activities involving this skill.

SOCIAL PROGRESS

Organized and competitive games more and more prominent. Team games very popular.

Plan short, competitive games among teams based on knowledge of music fundamentals: use flash cards, "spell-downs," musical bingo games, etc.

Emergence as an individual personality.

Explore opportunities for individual differences: accompaniment of singing by class on piano or social instrument such as ukulele; performances in class by: small vocal or instrumental ensembles; vocal or instrumental soloists (including piano); opportunities for class piano instruction.

Enjoys taking part in school, neighborhood, and community affairs, like "drives."

Increase teacher-pupil planning. If possible appoint assembly committees, work with them and school administrators in planning community sings in the building.

Teasing and antagonism between boy and girl groups.

Emphasize group activities: folk dances of many countries that develop a respect for the background of the dance; rhythmic experiences that stress skill.

INTELLECTUAL GROWTH AND ACTIVITIES

Interested in other people's ideas; able to discuss problems, to see different sides of questions.

Encourage understanding and study of music of other cultures and races. Promote feeling of patriotism, brotherhood.

Begins to be critical of own artistic products.

Provide increased opportunity for students' evaluation of their individual and group performance: encourage processes of self-evaluation as they sing or play; use tape recorder to give objective assistance.

Planning Sequential Music Experiences

SINGING

Rote songs

Part singing
    rounds
    chants
    descants
    chording
        sing chord roots as accompaniment to melody of songs—use syllables, letters, words
    aural harmony
        two-part songs
        three-part songs

Phrasing

Study of form
    ABA, AB song structure

Tonal quality

Attention to the changing voice

Creative experiences
    improvise harmony parts for songs
    compose chants and descants

Community sings

MUSIC READING AND READINESS

Theory problems
    chords
    keys and key signatures
        major
        minor
    syllables or numbers
    intervals

Rhythm problems
    dotted quarter rhythm pattern
    time signature
    feeling for the beat
    triplet
    syncopation
    $\frac{6}{8}$ rhythm

Awareness of score
    tempo and dynamic markings
    reading new songs

Tonalities
    minor modes
        natural
        harmonic
        melodic

Ionian mode
Aeolian mode
Dorian mode
Whole-tone system
12 tone row

Music vocabulary

RHYTHMS

Awareness of meter
    clapping rhythm pattern
    clapping meter

Question and answer games

Rhythm rounds
    use simple poem or chant (could create)
        notate rhythm and chant
        divide into groups for round; chant
        play with percussion instruments

Singing games and folk dances

LISTENING

Media
    songs
    piano
    recordings
    orchestral instruments
    filmstrips and recordings
    occasionally record on tape the singing of the class, providing opportunity for them to critically evaluate the performance

Listening skills
    discover principal themes in instrumental compositions

Maintain desirable listening attitudes

Evaluate music heard outside the classroom

Related information
    stress study of:
        orchestral instruments
        composers

Forms of music
    ballet
    concerto
    dance forms
    opera
    oratorio
    overture
    rondo
    string quartets, woodwind quintets, and other chamber music
    suite
    symphony
    theme and variations
    tone poem

INSTRUMENTS

Percussion instruments
    use with songs, rhythm patterns
    create percussion accompaniments and score
    strengthen understanding of note values
    play with instrumental recordings

Bells, xylophone, piano
    play patterns and melody of songs
    compose tunes
    play chord roots in appropriate rhythm with songs
    expand knowledge of piano keyboard
    play chords on resonator bells and piano

Autoharp
    use as accompanying instrument
    supplement study of chords
    play chords by ear
    tune Autoharp (select students)

Instruments: ukulele, guitar, accordion, etc. can be used to motivate interest and supplement chord study

Song flutes, recorders, Tonettes
    play songs from music book
    play descants or chants
    play rounds
        add resonator bells, Autoharp, and perhaps other social instruments for accompaniment

Suggested Questions for Measuring Progress

Are enough individuals vocally independent so that the class can sing two- and three-part harmony in tune? Can they interpret rounds and descants and other simple polyphonic forms intelligently?

Does the singing of the class as a group reflect an understanding of the expressive elements of the music? Are repeated opportunities offered for evaluation by the class members themselves? Can they listen critically to their own work and make sensible suggestions for improving it?

Is the development of visual and performance skills emphasized at the expense of the joys of exploration and discovery? Has the emphasis on fun crowded out the satisfaction of real accomplishment?

Are the children's performances and school programs an honest outgrowth of the learning that normally should take place, or are the pressures of public performance allowed to interfere with musical learning and increased powers of discrimination?

Are wholesome opportunities provided for competitive musical games that can promote greater skills and understandings? Do the class members volunteer willingly in the exploration of new materials?

Have effective planning and encouragement been successful with those individuals who don't sing well, or who do not like to sing because of a changing voice problem?

Do the children take any initiative in making suggestions for planning music experiences? Do they ever request a favorite song (or game or recording)?

Have frequent opportunities been given for creative use of instruments, movement, singing, or art work related to music? Has there been opportunity to explore the ways in which contemporary tonalities and rhythms differ from the traditional?

Can the class perform an audible beat without acceleration? Can they demonstrate the difference between beat, meter, and rhythm pattern?

When the class reads new material at sight do they "stop cold" at the first mistake? Can they show they understand that dotted notes are performed unevenly (and with precision)? Can they read simple syncopated rhythms—or at least recognize syncopation when they hear it? Can they read simple music written in compound meters? In "cut time"?

Is there evidence that some concepts about form are being clarified? Can they demonstrate visually the unity that results from identical segments, and the contrast that is necessary to all art forms? Do they read and understand "sequence"? Can they recognize some of the larger forms?

Can most of the class recognize and enjoy listening to instrumental and vocal music that is beyond the level of their own performance abilities?

How many children in the class take part regularly in some music study, activity, or musical organization in the community?

2

Singing

EARLY CHILDHOOD (LEVELS 1 AND 2)

Most children love to sing. It is so natural for them that they often want to sing whenever they hear any music. They sing with their records at home, with the radio and TV. For a while during their first school experiences they will sing along with the teacher, whether they know the song or not. At the very first you will probably want to use familiar songs, to give them this opportunity. Certainly they should be encouraged to join in the singing. However, if they are going to sing a new song accurately they must learn the tune. You might suggest that they "take turns" with you. It will require patience and diligence for you to help them remember not to sing when it is your "turn," but this is essential for their musical growth. Of course, after they have heard the melody a few times you will then want them to "help" you with it. Judged by adult standards, the tune may not always be clearly recognized in such singing, but this will come with time and experience.

For very young children songs should be short and repetitive. Children want to make a song their own very quickly. It's fun to go home and sing it to Mother that very day. They want to sing about the things that are important in their world—home, friends, pets, holidays, the rain and snow. Besides these, there will be other concepts that you will want them to learn; this can be done through songs. Becoming acquainted with community helpers, such as the mailman, fireman, policeman, and others, takes on extra meaning when you "sound" the siren or "whistle" for someone to stop! And numbers can be so interesting when you sing them: "One little, two little, three little Indians," or "One, Two, Buckle My Shoe."

"A Child's First Birthday Record" (Decca: VL-3711) includes an excellent song for counting ("One to Ten") and one for learning the alphabet ("ABC"). Rhythm Records also has a helpful record for reading readiness and number readiness (RRC-203).

One activity particularly appealing to very young children is the "acting out" of songs. Finger play songs, such as "Eency Weency Spider," constitute a large part of the repertoire, but story songs that can be dramatized also need to be included. In the familiar "Yankee Doodle," "Captain Washington" can lead a small "regiment" through the "streets" of the "city" as they march in parade. A "flag bearer" and a "drummer" might be part of this impressive group. Extending even beyond this type of dramatization is the song centered around a familiar story, such as "The Little Red Hen," or "Three Billy Goats Gruff." Here you may want to use a record. After the children have heard the story enough times to be fairly familiar with the tunes, they can sing along. Finally, they can act out the story, with a few being the principal characters and the others constituting the chorus. This type of activity can add great enthusiasm and zest to the singing experiences.

In addition to song stories your children will enjoy a series produced by Ginn and Co. and recorded by RCA, called "Dance-a-Story." The series includes:

At the Beach	LE-108	Little Duck	LE-101
Balloons	LE-104	The Magic Mountain	LE-103
The Brave Hunter	LE-105	Noah's Ark	LE-102
Flappy and Floppy	LE-106	The Toy Tree	LE-107

Basically, music can be related to every type of classroom activity. It can become a part of science experiences to sing about the changing seasons and health; songs can also be an interesting reinforcement in learning art, social studies, arithmetic, and reading readiness. For very young children music is not usually confined to a "set" time in the schedule. You will probably want to have one fairly long period daily when the children sing many songs, enjoy rhythms, or play instruments, but there may also be other times when you will want to sing. Creating a song when the snow first begins to fall, enjoying a song about "Mr. Rabbit" when such a story is read, or singing while waiting in line for the bus are but three examples of the opportunities to relate music to the children's life in your room. At times you may want to play a record when the youngsters are putting on galoshes or taking them off. You will find many opportunities for music throughout the daily session.

Most of the basic series include song books for early childhood (see Appendix A for specific titles). Any of these will provide you with good material. In addition, *American Folk Songs for Children in Home, School and Nursery School,* by Ruth Crawford Seeger, is very helpful (see Appendix J for information about this and other supplementary song materials).

ROTE SONGS

The joy we have in music comes to us through our ears. This is only natural, because music is an art made up entirely of *sounds.* For this reason, we teach many songs on these levels entirely "by ear." Songs that are taught "by ear" (by imitation) are called *rote songs.* Given sufficient opportunity to hear the songs again and again in a happy environment, most children will enjoy singing. Many children will want to sing the rote songs learned at school for their parents and friends.

Early Childhood (Levels 1 and 2)

TEACHING ROTE SONGS:
THE WHOLE SONG METHOD

Rote songs may be taught many ways, but three suggestions are offered here: the whole song method, the phrase method, and a combination of the two. The *whole song method* is preferred by many teachers. The following steps describe how this *method* can be used:

1. Create interest in the song with a brief introduction. Remember that too much talking is worse than none at all.

2. Sing the entire song once, while the children listen attentively.

3. Let the children discuss the song content briefly. Many teachers find it helpful to show attractive colored pictures to illustrate new words in the text of the song.

4. Sing the song again, using a light, clear voice. Be especially careful to enunciate all the words distinctly.

What a Surprise[1]

Francis Hilliard

Happily

We had a pump-kin yel-low; We gave it two big eyes.

We cut a round and ti-ny nose, A fun-ny mouth that smiles.

Now we'll hide be-hind the hedge, And wait un-til it's dark;

rit.   *a tempo*

Then when Dad-dy comes a-long, Up we'll jump. "Boo!" we'll shout. What a sur-prise!

[1] From *The Magic of Music* (Kindergarten), © Copyright, 1965, by Ginn and Company. Used with permission.

5. Sing the song several times. If there is a series of consecutive, related thoughts in the song, the repeated listening can be effectively motivated by having the children listen for a different thought each time. For example, let's look at the song "What a Surprise!"

6. By this time the class will have looked at a picture of a jack-o'-lantern (or a real one made from a pumpkin). Repeated opportunities to hear the song will have given the children the general outline of the story and its setting.

7. Ask the children to listen again, to discover which part of the pumpkin face was cut out first. Have them sing: "two big eyes."

8. Ask the children to listen again, to discover which part of the pumpkin face was cut out next. Have them sing: "tiny nose."

9. Sing the song once more, while the pupils listen for what was cut out after that. Have them sing: "mouth that smiles."

10. Ask the children to listen for what happened then. Encourage them to sing the answer, not to speak it. By the time the song has been repeated to this extent, some of the children can sing a good deal of it on their own. The addition of appropriate actions will help the class remember the words.

The final objective is to enable the children to sing the song accurately and pleasurably without the teacher's help. Not all of these things will come about in a single day. In fact, the second day the teacher may wish to begin with suggestion number 3, for a quick review of the material. This will give the children *many opportunities to hear the music.*

At first the teacher may need to help the class sing the first few notes, but as soon as the children gain confidence, the teacher should withdraw from the singing and encourage the boys and girls to sing independently. Do this as early in the year as you possibly can.

TEACHING ROTE SONGS:
THE PHRASE METHOD

Although the whole song method is often ideal in presenting short songs, the phrase method may be helpful at times with songs that are longer than usual or more difficult in content. Patriotic songs are good examples of this type.

A "phrase" is usually considered to be that portion of the song which the children can sing comfortably on one breath. In the text of the song, the words of the phrase are normally set off by some kind of punctuation mark. Many phrases in songs for young children are only four measures long, but they can be any length. A rote song may be presented by the *phrase method* as follows:

1. Create interest in the song with a brief introduction.
2. Sing the entire song once, while the children listen attentively.
3. Let the children discuss the song content briefly. If possible, have attractive colored pictures (or actual objects) to illustrate any new words found in the text of the song.
4. Sing the song again, remembering always to use a light, clear voice. Be especially careful to enunciate all the words distinctly. *Don't sing too slowly.* This will not only make the song more difficult to learn, but equally serious: *it's unmusical.* If you notice that the children can't sing the entire phrase comfortably on one breath, you will realize that the tempo is too slow or that changes need to be made in the phrasing.
5. Now sing the first phrase of the song, and let the children sing it after you in imitation.
6. Do the same for the second phrase. Ask the children to sing it for you. Now sing the third phrase, having the children repeat this. Follow this same procedure for the entire song. After the class imitates the last phrase, sing the entire song and have the class repeat it.
7. Correct inaccuracies as they occur, but if the class can't repeat the song accurately by themselves, you should sing the entire song correctly and then leave it until another time. In this way, the class will be more likely to retain the *sound* accurately because they have had an extra opportunity to hear it sung correctly.

One of the advantages of the *phrase method* is that it helps to develop independent group singing, because the teacher and the class "take turns." This makes it possible for the teacher to sing with the class as little as possible, and the children don't get the habit of depending on the teacher's voice. Any mistakes are easier for the children to find and for you to help them to correct.

Again, it is never necessary to go through the entire procedure the first time the song is presented. The skillful teacher realizes that every class reaches a point beyond which attention wanders. It is possible to push beyond this point, but it is questionable how much learning is being accomplished. This "saturation point" may not coincide with the end of the teacher's presentation of the new song. If it does not, the teacher should change to another kind of music experience, and work on the new song again at another time.

TEACHING ROTE SONGS:
WHOLE-PART-WHOLE METHOD

If a song is rather difficult, you may need to present it by the whole song method, then isolate the problem portions and teach them by the phrase method. Encourage the class to find for themselves the places where they ran into trouble. Some of the children will be able to answer the questions: *"Was it too high?" "Too low?"* or *"Was the note too short?"* or *"Too long?"* From the very first, always try to get the children to listen carefully to their own singing and to criticize it themselves. They can do it. This is how they learn.

TEACHING ROTE SONGS
BY RECORDINGS

Recordings of rote songs can always be used effectively in the classroom. The *whole song method* will, of course, be easier to use in these experiences. Children should have the opportunity to hear the record a number of times before they are expected to sing. Some teachers like to have the class sing softly with the record at first, *listening carefully* as they sing. Sometimes the children are told to "mouth" the words silently as they listen, until the song is learned. The final objective is the same as in any presentation: the accurate, *expressive* singing of the new song—independent of either the teacher or the record.

Each of the current basic series of music books is accompanied by a set of records for each grade level. These can be very helpful. There are also many other useful recordings.

No matter which system is used to teach the rote song, the effective teacher tries to present each new song differently. Each song is unique, and each child will have an individual experience in singing it. Whenever possible, try to avoid using a set routine in presenting any kind of music activity.

TEACHING ROTE SONGS
WITH MUSIC BOOKS

Sometime during the first or second levels, each child may have what will probably be a new experience for him—he will have a music book of his own! Earlier, he did much of his singing without a book.

Great enthusiasm can be generated by the advent of the new music book. Some time should be set aside at first for the children to browse through the book freely, enjoying the beauty of the illustrations and finding songs that look interesting.

At this point some teachers have the class sing a number of familiar songs from the book, giving the children a feeling of instant success in the new reading experience. Others will follow the children's lead in selecting a new song to be learned, and will teach it "on the spot" as soon as the class expresses interest in it. There is much to be said for this in terms of built-in, sure-fire motivation and pupil participation in planning desirable goals. However, be sure *you* are thoroughly familiar with every song in the new book before you undertake to do this kind of creative planning.

Some teachers feel more secure in planning to teach a new song of their own choice. Whichever approach you like, you will find that having a book in the hands of each pupil can be a big help. Pupils are not expected to read unfamiliar music "by note." However, the printed page gives many good clues to the children. They can discover:

1. That the words of the song are stretched out to go directly under the notes with which they are to be sung. Longer words are broken up into two or three syllables with a hyphen between, so that they fit the music properly.

2. That the notes of the music sometimes go up, sometimes down, and sometimes straight across, or "sideways." (*Melodic direction*)

Finding a favorite song in the new music book and singing it is an exciting experience for children.

At first, this is enough detail for the class to consider, but sometimes children who have had music lessons outside school or frequent music experience in the home will volunteer other facts about the printed page. They may suggest, for example, that *f* means loud, and *p* means soft. This kind of reference can be helpful and stimulating to the class, but its value lies in brevity and simplicity. Remember that experience with loud and soft music has to come first, and that unless the concept of dynamic changes is understood, the mere identification of dynamic symbols can be meaningless. However, a detailed study of the printed page is not the principal goal of music instruction on these levels. This study will usually come later, when vision and intellect are normally more mature. However, many children understand:

1. That some notes are black and solid (♩), and others can be "seen through" (♩).
2. That some notes have flags (♪♪) or beams (♫) on their stems, while others have no stems, flags, or beams at all (𝅝).

3. That the kind of note-heads, stems, flags, and beams that a note has, shows us whether it makes a shorter or longer sound than the other notes. These are the note values of the rhythm pattern.

It is not necessary, nor is it a good idea, to tell everything about notes to the class all at once or right at first. Always try to present the *sound* (and lots of it) before the *symbol.* In teaching rote songs, it is best to *use the book as an aid, but not as an end in itself.*

Even though the pupils have a music book in their hands, we are still going to teach most songs by rote. You may like to use the *whole song method,* the *phrase method,* or a *combination* of the two, but whichever method you use, the pupil's book can be a great help.

Teach as many rote songs as you can find time for. You will not need to perfect all of them, and you can use many of them for different purposes in developing reading readiness.

MIDDLE CHILDHOOD (LEVELS 3 AND 4)

Rote Songs in Preparation for Part Singing

Although unison singing is basic for these levels, by now the students ought to be able to explore further the concepts about harmony. This does not imply that unison singing is "laid on the shelf." Indeed, just the opposite is often the case. Whether the singing is done in one part or more, however, there are some basic problems in singing rote songs that are universal to all levels. These include enunciation, phrasing, and tempo.

ENUNCIATION

Every child, at an early age, should learn to speak and sing his words distinctly. Mispronunciation frequently adds to or creates a "muddy" effect in singing. Often it is lack of careful attention, or "laziness," that creates the problem. The meticulous teacher will keep his or her students alert to the need for careful diction.

PHRASING

The text of the song determines the length of the phrase. The punctuation frequently indicates where phrases begin and end. Teach the children to sing a complete phrase on one breath. During the year you can do much "choral reading" of phrases. Have the class read phrases together, pausing slightly after each one. This frequently helps to develop the "feel" for phrasing.

TEMPO (RATE OF SPEED)

When the entire class is singing together the children may tend to "drag" the songs—or at times they may "gallop" through them, destroying the natural rhythm. If you use recordings this device might occasionally prove helpful: After the class has progressed well into the song turn the volume button completely down, so they are unable to hear the voice on the record. After a brief interval turn it back up, to see if they are still at the same place in the song as the recording artist. The surprise element of this tactic is intriguing to the students and helps to keep them "on their toes." This "trick" can be tried several times in one song. It can be very useful in making the class aware of the necessity for an appropriate tempo.

It is not unusual for the teacher herself to have some difficulty in establishing a suitable tempo for singing. The class should always be made aware of the mood and ideas expressed in the text, because singing is—after all—one of the arts of communication. Whoever is responsible for setting the speed may find it helpful to conduct quietly in the air (before the group begins singing) and *think the words silently* to determine:

1. If the longest phrase cannot be sung comfortably with one breath, the tempo is too slow.
2. If the words cannot be articulated precisely and clearly, the tempo is too fast.

Much of the time, however, unmusical and inexpressive tempos are the result of singing too-slowly-one-note-at-a-time—perhaps accurately, but never beautifully.

In addition to the problems discussed here, there is another major one that confronts the teacher in preparing students for part singing. Before children are able to sing beautifully in harmony, they *must be able to hear the parts*. This means that while they are singing they must know whether their tone is in tune with the other parts. This ability is easier for some people than for others. However, it should be a natural outgrowth of well-planned singing experiences when the class can:

1. Sing in tune, and
2. Sing the rounds and songs with simple descants found in their music book.

Many children have had pleasure singing songs of this type in school and at camp. Whenever and wherever part singing is successful, these conditions must be present:

1. The group knows the song well, and enjoys singing it in unison, accurately and musically.
2. The group is divided in such a way that there are good singers on each part. Remember, some people can sing in tune only "by catching a ride with their neighbors," so they are not *independent* singers. If one part of the class consists entirely of dependent singers, quick success in this activity cannot be expected.
3. If there are some individuals who sing badly, too loudly, or out-of-tune, teach them to play a bell part or an Autoharp accompaniment. Remind them to *listen carefully* as they play.
4. When such accompaniment is used, remind the singers to *listen carefully* to the instrument while they are singing.

Careful listening is really the key to good part singing, and the better your musical "ear," the better you will be able to harmonize. For this reason, *all beginning part singing experiences should be done by rote*. Encourage your pupils to play and sing the descants in their music books, and to make up some of their own.

DESCANTS. The students can discover that a descant is an independent melody written above the principal melody of a song. Perhaps the class could learn, first, the principal melody of the

After repeated practice in a learning center, this student is now ready to accompany his class in a song (photo by Patrick Burke).

song by rote. Then, for study purposes, you could teach the descant to the entire class, or you might prefer choosing a few independent singers with light, high voices to learn this part. When you finally combine the two melodies you will want only a few singers on the descant—preferably those with light, high tones. The reason for this is that the top part "carries" more clearly than the others and can thus be heard more easily. At Christmastime or for some school program you may want to attempt this type of part singing as a special feature.

For variation you might have a few students play the descant on instruments (xylophone, recorder, or bells) while the rest sing the principal melody. If you have an instrumental student who is proficient enough to play the descant he might be invited to perform. (The flute, violin, or clarinet seem best suited to this type of activity.)

ROUNDS. Singing rounds (canons) is very useful at any level for developing melodic independence and an understanding of polyphonic texture. Always encourage the children to sing with a pleasing tone quality and to listen to the other parts. "Outshouting" each other or the "finger in the ear" technique should not be permitted, since it destroys the beauty of the sound and defeats the purpose of experiencing more than one melody at a time (polyphony).

Rounds can also furnish your group with excellent opportunities for hearing two-part harmonies (homophonic texture), if you will use them as described in this "game":

1. Be sure your class knows the round thoroughly and enjoys singing it. Take "Are You Sleeping?" for example.[2]

2. Alert the class to watch carefully so that when you give them the signal, they will *hold* the tone until you tell them to go on with the rest of the song.

3. When the second part enters on the word "Are," the first part is singing "bro-," the first syllable of the word "brother." This segment of the song looks like this on the staff:

First Part: Bro - ther   John

Second Part: Are   you   sleep-

You notice that there are three consecutive thirds, and our purpose is to get the class to *hear* them, *identify* them as harmonious, and *learn the terminology:* "thirds."

4. Have the class *hold* the words "Are" in the second part, the "bro-" (first syllable of the word "brother") in the first part.

5. Let them discover—by singing G, A, B, or playing those notes on the tone bells or piano—that G and B are three tones apart. We measure this interval in music by calling it a "third," because three different pitches are involved (G, A, and B—although only the G and the B are sung together).

6. Play the G and B together on the tone bells or piano, have the class sing the two tones together on "AH" (or any neutral syllable), and listen to the beautiful *harmony* that will result.

7. Have the class *hold* the words "you" in the second part, and "-ther" (second syllable of the word "brother") in the first part.

8. Have the class discover that the A and C are three tones apart; therefore this interval is also a "third."

[2] Found in Book 3 of *Exploring Music* Series, published by Holt, Rinehart and Winston,

9. *Listen* to the interval sung with a neutral syllable or played on the tone bells or piano.

10. Do the same by sustaining the place in the song where the second part sings "sleep-" (first syllable of the word "sleeping") and the first part sings "John." (B and D).

VISUAL RECOGNITION OF INTERVALS (THIRDS). Some teachers like to show the class how thirds look on the staff. If the lower tone is on a line, the upper will always be on the very next line above. If the lower tone is in a space, the upper will be in the very next space above. The note-heads are placed directly above each other to indicate that they are sung together. The stems go up on the notes sung by the first part, down on the notes sung by the second part.

It is a good thing to remember, however, that the most important thing is to give your pupils a good foundation in hearing two parts played and sung together harmoniously. Visual skills should be developed after a solid foundation of aural experience is provided.

LATER CHILDHOOD (LEVELS 5 and 6)

At every level singing should be a joyous experience for the child. This should reach a peak on the later levels—although there may be some problems with preadolescent voices. An enlarged repertoire of songs, increased experience with part singing, and a greater understanding of music symbols should enrich the students' knowledge and bring them added pleasure.

Many unison and part songs will still be learned by rote on these levels—at least in part. The class can listen to the teacher's voice or to a recording as they watch the song carefully in their books.

Frequently one hearing of this kind will be sufficient, although there may be need for special remedial work on difficult spots. If it seems necessary to repeat the song, the teacher would be well

Inc. (Key of F); Book 3 of *This Is Music for Today* Series, published by Allyn and Bacon, Inc.; Book 4 of *This Is Music for Today* Series, published by Allyn and Bacon, Inc. (appears as "Frère Jacques"—in Key of E); Book 2 of *Discovering Music Together* Revised Series, published by Follett Publishing Co. (Key of F); and in Book 2 of *The Spectrum of Music* Series, published by Macmillan Publishing Co., Inc.

advised to emphasize careful *listening* on the part of the class. Although there is no single procedure for teaching a song by rote, it is always best to let the class do as much as they can FOR THEMSELVES.

TWO-PART SINGING

EXPERIENCING HARMONY "BY EAR." All early experiences in part singing are begun by rote because it requires the ABILITY TO HEAR the part that is being sung IN RELATION TO THE OTHER PART. Of course, the greater skill the class has in sight-reading the easier part singing will become.* However, there never has been any good part singing without a successful background of experience in ear training.

Here are some suggestions for part singing by ear:

1. For two-part harmony, your class must have at least TWO INDEPENDENT singers. This may seem to be a remarkable minimum, but not all children are independent singers. The class that is conditioned to depend on the teacher's voice to "lead them" has greater difficulty than it deserves. On the other hand, some children seem to be "born harmonizers" because HEARING HARMONY is very easy for them.

2. If your class is skillfully divided into two groups with about an equal number of leaders and followers, select a good song such as the one shown here. You will notice the parts move in thirds—that is, the second part is just three scale degrees from the melody and follows in the same direction. When the melody moves up, the second part also moves up. When the melody moves down, so does the second part.

When the Chestnut Leaves Were Falling[3]

English Version by Luther Wilde   Spanish Folk Song

* See the material on sight-reading, pages 67–124.

3. Ask the class to watch the direction in which the parts move on the staff and listen to BOTH PARTS at once. Sometimes two class members can play the parts on the tone bells, if they have had an opportunity to practice. It takes a little skill to play both parts together on the piano, but many pupils and their teachers can. It is easier, of course, if both hands are used—perhaps using only the index finger of each hand. *Remember:* this is a typical presentation of a new rote song using the books as visual aids—but most important: it is a HOMOPHONIC experience, and should strengthen SKILL IN VERTICAL LISTENING.

4. Emphasize the need for good tone quality and for singing "phrase-wise" rather than "punching" the notes.

5. Encourage the students to observe carefully the direction of the notes as they sing. As they learn to move their voices with the notes they will improve their skill in *reading* part songs.

In addition to harmonizing two-part songs, the students will enjoy continuing with rounds and descants. After sufficient successful experience in this activity, encourage the children to attempt singing their own harmony to a familiar song. It would be best to begin with a select few who have shown a flair for "sticking" to a

---

³ From *The Magic of Music* (Book 5), © Copyright, 1968, by Ginn and Company. Used with permission. Another good song in thirds is "Saturday Night," which appears in Book 5 of *Discovering Music Together* Revised Series, published by Follett Publishing Co., in Book 6 of *This Is Music for Today* Series, published by Allyn and Bacon, Inc., in Book 6, *The Spectrum of Music* Series, published by Macmillan Publishing Co., Inc. (appears in both books as "Ev'rybody Loves Saturday Night"), and in Book 6 of *Exploring Music* Series, published by Holt, Rinehart and Winston, Inc. (appears as "Everybody Loves Saturday Night").

Using Orff instruments, a group of upper level students plays a descant for the song "Poor Wayfarin' Stranger" (photo by Patrick Burke).

part. Emphasize that *listening* is the key to success in this activity. One must *hear* the *total* effect to be sure that his tones are blending properly. These first efforts may not be very musical; it is natural for errors to occur. However, after repeated practice it would be best to discontinue this type of activity if the errors are still uncorrected. The students must have some opportunities to experiment if they are going to develop skill and independence in making up harmony, but constant singing off key contributes nothing to anyone's musical development.

Three-Part Singing

After the class has become reasonably skilled in singing two-part songs they will enjoy adding another part. The same methods used in two-part singing apply here. However, there are a variety of techniques you might want to use to give assistance in singing the third or lowest part. Usually this part is rather limited in range and tends to center around the basic chord roots. You might try grouping the children who are going to sing this part. Then assign to two or three students (depending on the number of chords in the song being studied) the bells with the tones of the chord roots. Hearing these tones at the appropriate places will give real assistance to the singers. Variations of this technique could include playing the chord roots on the Autoharp or piano.

ROOT TONE CHORDING.   A different type of part singing may also have a great appeal to students in later childhood. This is the experience of singing chords. Here is one approach that might be used, with the song "Down in the Valley":[4]

Down in the Valley

3. Build me a castle, forty feet high,
   So I can see him as he rides by.
   As he rides by, dear, as he rides by,
   So I can see him as he rides by.

[4] Found in Book 5 of *Discovering Music Together* Revised Series, published by Follett Publishing Co.; Book 5 of *Exploring Music* Series, published by Holt, Rinehart and Winston, Inc.; Book 5 of *The Magic of Music* Series, published by Ginn and Co.; Book 5 of *Silver Burdett Music Series,* published by General Learning Corporation; Book 5 of *The Spectrum of Music* Series, published by Macmillan Publishing Co., Inc.; Book 6 of *This Is Music for Today* Series, published by Allyn and Bacon, Inc.; and in "Enjoying Music" (Book 2) from *New Dimensions in Music* Series, published by American Book Co.

1. Have the class sing "Down in the Valley."
2. This time play the Autoharp with the class as they sing the song again.
3. By this time the boys and girls know that the Autoharp is a chording instrument. Tell them that they can now learn the "Autoharp part," and sing the chords.
4. Explain how to make chords.
   a. Place the syllable or number scale on the chalkboard in a vertical "ladder" style.

Syllable	Number	Chord
DO	1	I
TI	7	VII
LA	6	VI
SO	5	V and V$_7$
FA	4	IV
MI	3	III
RE	2	II
DO	1	I

   b. Now place the Roman numeral I on the chalkboard. Ask the class which number of the scale they would guess to be the first tone in this chord. (DO or 1 is the answer.) Continue by saying that RE or 2 would be the first tone in the II chord; MI or 3 would be the first tone in the III chord, and so on.

   c. Then show the class that, basically, a chord is constructed by choosing every other number or syllable above the first tone. Build the chord by "skipping."

   For example, when using syllables I begins with DO. MI and SO above DO make up the other two tones of the I chord—DO, MI, SO. II begins with RE. FA and LA above RE make up the other two tones of the II chord—RE, FA, LA.

   Or, when using numbers I begins with 1. 3 and 5 above 1 make up the other two tones of the I chord—1, 3, 5.

II begins with 2. 4 and 6 above 2 make up the other two tones of the II chord—2, 4, 6.

d. Put the I chord and the V chord on the chalkboard.

SO 5   RE 2   (these are fifths)

MI 3   TI 7   (these are thirds)

DO 1   SO 5   (these are roots)

I   V

e. Erase MI (3) and SO (5) from the I chord and replace with short lines. Erase TI (7) and RE (2) from the V chord and replace with short lines.

——— ———

——— ———

DO (1)   SO (5)

Explain that the lines will show that two more tones belong in each chord, but today the class will sing only the root tone.

f. Hold up the forefinger of one hand and suggest that, when you give that signal, the class should sing DO (1). Hold up all five fingers and tell the class to sing SO (5) when you give that signal.

g. Practice the I and V chords with the class, giving the appropriate signal for each.

h. Do a "trial run" of the chords for "Down in the Valley" in this order:

I I I V V V V I I I I V V V V I

(Most texts use the V_7 chord instead of the V in this song. If students wonder what the 7 means, simply say it indicates there are four tones in the chord instead of three. In order to "find" that fourth tone we just do one more "skip" above when we are building the chord.)

i. Now divide the class into two groups. Let one sing the melody for "Down in the Valley," the other the chords. (It would be well to make the melody group smaller than the other. Select a few good singers for this part. Then you (or one of your students) can lead the group singing the chords. Be sure to put *some* strong singers on this part also. Practice the melody group alone briefly, stressing that they must keep the tempo moving.)

j. After one or two times through the song, alternate the groups. The melody group will now sing the chords. The rest will sing the melody. Teachers should sing with the group only when it needs help. If a student is leading the group, you may also need to help him.

k. When this procedure has been mastered suggest that the students sing the *words* of the song in the proper rhythm on the tones DO (1) and SO (5). For example, the group singing the chords would sing the words "Down in the valley, the valley so" on F. Then they would sing, "low ——— Hang your head o-ver, hear the wind" on C. This is an easy type of two-part singing.

Some time later, after the class seems to be quite independent in singing harmony, you might attempt chording with three tones. The only difference between this and the basic method outlined above is that DO, MI, SO, or 1, 3, 5, will be sung whenever the tonic chord (I) is indicated, and SO, TI, RE, or 5, 7, 2, will be sung whenever the V or V₇ chord appears. Before, only the root of each chord—DO or 1 for the I chord, and SO or 5 for the V chord—was sung by the students. (If IV or any other chord is used the previous material will explain what to do.) This type of chording will necessitate dividing the class into four groups. Be sure that some strong singers are put on each part.

To illustrate the teaching method, let's use the song "My Boat Is Sailing."[5] Divide the class into the four singing groups—the melody, low, middle, and high chord tones. In measure 1, when those in the melody group say, "sail," the full chord DO, MI, SO, or 1, 3, 5, should be heard also. In measure 2, when the syllable "sail" is again sung, the chord SO, TI, RE, or 5, 7, 2, should be

---

[5] From Book 6 of *Growing with Music* Series, by Harry R. Wilson, Walter Ehret, Alice M. Snyder, Edward J. Hermann, and Albert A. Renna, © Copyright, 1966 by Prentice-Hall, Inc., Englewood Cliffs, N.J. Reprinted with permission. Also found in Book 3 of *Exploring Music* Series, published by Holt, Rinehart and Winston, Inc. (appears as "Hawaiian Boat Song"—in key of A♭).

sung by the three harmony groups. Proceed with the rest of the song in a similar manner.

Some songbooks have such chord markings as I, IV, V_7, and so on. Others indicate the chords by letters—G, C, D_7. The only thing to remember is that the letter name of the key is I, IV is the fourth tone of the scale, and V the fifth tone. For example, in the key of G:

My Boat Is Sailing

Hawaiian Melody
Words by Helena Hargrave

Scale	Chord	Tonal Syllables		Numbers	Pitch Names
G	I	DO, MI, SO	or	1, 3, 5	G, B, D
F♯	VII	TI, RE, FA	or	7, 2, 4	F♯, A, C
E	VI	LA, DO, MI	or	6, 1, 3	E, G, B
D	V	SO, TI, RE	or	5, 7, 2	D, F♯, A
C	IV	FA, LA, DO	or	4, 6, 1	C, E, G
B	III	MI, SO, TI	or	3, 5, 7	B, D, F♯
A	II	RE, FA, LA	or	2, 4, 6	A, C, E
G	I	DO, MI, SO	or	1, 3, 5	G, B, D

COMMUNITY SINGS

Early and Middle Childhood
(Levels 1, 2, 3, and 4)

In many schools, a number of classes meet together once or twice a month for a "community sing." In schools where there is only one room of each level, the first, second, and third levels may meet together for their own sings; and the fourth, fifth, and sixth for their own. Some schools have the entire student body sing together at "assemblies" and "community sings," and find that a tradition of beautiful singing is often the outcome. The most successful combined "sings" are the result of careful preparation, and a suitable repertory of songs must be selected and learned by the children of all the levels involved.

No matter how the "sing" is organized, some teachers like to begin with well-known action songs, to ensure as much participation as possible. Often, for contrast, this is followed by a quieter number such as a lullaby or a religious song. The use of informal instruments and the piano will add variety and interest to the singing, and it is a good plan for the teachers to take turns in directing the group.

Later Childhood (Levels 5 and 6)

In later childhood the children can often help in planning these "sings." Perhaps a committee made up of representatives from each class could plan one a month, or one every other month. Some teacher should probably be an advisory member of the group, to give careful guidance and to serve as a resource person. In these assemblies you might provide opportunities for individual and small group performances. A soloist might be featured, or children in the elementary band or orchestra could appear as ensembles. (An important by-product in learning could be achieved as students become familiar with such words as "solo," "duet," "trio," and "ensemble.") Student song leaders could be responsible for directing one or two songs, and certain boys and girls could accompany on the piano. The possibilities are limitless in the hands of creative teachers.

THE ELEMENTARY CHOIR

Some schools provide additional opportunities for group singing through an elementary choir. This is frequently an extracurricular activity offered to older students. When administrators and teachers consider the possibility of organizing such a group a number of questions confront them:

1. Who should be invited to become members? Should it be a select choir offering unique opportunities to the gifted—or should anyone with a good attitude be welcome? Should auditions be held to determine membership?

2. Will this be a performing group? If so, where shall they perform and how frequently?

3. Will it be a "pop" ensemble, folk-singing group, or "traditional" choir? What music will constitute the repertoire—songs from the students' regular song book, octavo music, or other materials?

4. Will there be accompanying instruments other than piano—brass, guitars, accordion, etc?

5. When will the rehearsals be held? After school? During school hours? Once a week? Will the choir be in session the entire school year?

These are only a few of the major questions to be answered by the director, administrator, and classroom teachers as they evaluate the possible benefits of an elementary choir. No one can answer these questions for another. Each school system must assess its own needs, opportunities, and circumstances to determine what is right for its children. However, a few guiding principles relating to some of these questions may be helpful. 1) If the decision is to make this a select choir, try to find some responsible tasks for the eager volunteers who can't sing in tune at all, but who have good attitudes. Perhaps one such person could be the librarian or the arrangements chairman (setting up chairs, getting the room prepared, etc.). It is difficult to refuse membership to such a child. If possible, work out something that will give him a feeling of belonging to the group—even if he isn't one of the singers. 2) Even with elementary school children the performance objective is strong motivation for rehearsing. One or two opportunities during the year (presenting a Christmas program, singing for the P.T.A., appearing in other area elementary schools, performing for Golden Age Clubs or in nursing homes, etc.) will provide a genuine stimulus for learning and perfecting songs. (Guard against exploitation, however, either by the school or the community.) One of the most natural opportunities that should not be overlooked is the school assembly. Here the choir can perform for its peer group. This gives great satisfaction to the choir members and permits the other students to hear children's voices in a quality performance. 3) Rehearsing more than once a week could be burdensome, but rehearsing less frequently could destroy interest. The schedule that usually works out best is to meet once or twice a week, preferably during the regular day's activities, during the major part of the year.

An elementary choir can often spark the children's interest in vocal music more than any other single influence. It is certainly worthy of careful consideration.

HELPING THE UNCERTAIN SINGER

Probably the greatest help for the child who can't "carry a tune" is to make the music class SO interesting that he becomes totally involved in the experience. This directs his attention away from himself, freeing him from the inhibitions that are a part of his problem.

In addition to being genuinely enthusiastic the teacher must be creative. Examine every song to see what body movements would be appropriate and exciting, what particular rhythm instruments would enhance the singing, what elements of drama could be introduced, and what opportunities for individual participation are inherent in the song. Even though they may need to take "turns," give all of the children over a period of time many opportunities to be a part of all of these exciting activities.

Without question this type of climate is the greatest motivator and aid in helping the uncertain singer. However, there are some specific techniques that can assist the children in hearing and singing more accurate tones. If these techniques are handled in a manner that makes it seem like fun for the child, then they can be very beneficial.

Early Childhood (Levels 1 and 2)

REMEDIAL TONAL GAMES

One of the most effective ways to help children "find their singing voices" is to select parts of songs that are already familiar to the children. These small segments of known songs can be used as individual *games*. For example, let's consider the well-known song "Down by the Station."[6]

Down by the Station

Traditional Song of the South

[6] From *The Magic of Music* (Kindergarten), © Copyright, 1965, by Ginn and Company. Used with permission. Also found in Book 2 of *Exploring Music* Series, published by Holt, Rinehart and Winston, Inc.; and in Book 1 of *Growing with Music* Series (appears as "Pufferbillies"), published by Prentice-Hall, Inc.

I can see the en-gi-neer Pull a lit-tle le-ver.

Choo! Choo! Woo! Woo! Off they go!

(Repeat ad lib., gradually diminishing in volume.)

After the song is well-known to the children and they enjoy singing it with appropriate actions, you can play a game of "matching whistles." Not all train whistles sound alike. Members of the class can tell you that some sound low, some high, and some in-between. The teacher may want to sing "Woo! Woo!" on D (as in the song), and ask individual children to try to match her whistle. If a child is not able to discover whether his response was too high, or too low, or just right, encourage the class to help him decide. Part of his trouble may be due to his *ear* more than his voice. Many teachers make good use of the better singers in these games. Often pupils can match other children's voices more easily than the teacher's voice.

Two suggestions may be helpful: 1) *Know the individual child.* Keep trying to determine what his capabilities are from day to day. When he doesn't sing well, don't tell him it's good; but tell him something that will help him to keep trying. He needs self-confidence in singing as much as anything else. 2) *Keep the class busy helping.* A helpful attitude on the part of those who are not singing will not only benefit the uncertain singer, but it will aid in the development of the important concepts of *high and low in music.* In order to keep the class involved and alert, this activity should move fast. Don't stop to do much talking. The children's interest can be stimulated by surprises and a vital presentation.

Using excerpts from a familiar song can be very helpful in remedial tonal work but there are other approaches that you will want to explore also. Here are some suggestions:

1. Make it a routine practice to have all the children sing individually every day, even if it is only two notes like "Yoo-hoo," or let them practice making the voice go up and down like the siren on a fire engine.

2. Without question, there will be some children in your room who sing considerably better than average. Identify them as early as possible, even if you have to make a secret list of their names. Remember, in remedial work *everyone* should participate individually, the good ones as well as the weak ones.

3. Single out one of the good singers to "answer the telephone when it rings." No matter how modest your voice, you can sing some kind of "ding-a-ling-a-ling." Let the good singer answer. Move as fast as you can from good singers to weaker ones, back and forth, keeping the class alert by reminding them "you can never tell when *your* telephone may ring."

The most important thing, at first, is to do some simple remedial work such as this *every day*—even if only for two or three minutes. Don't take too much time to talk, and above all, go quickly from child to child. Be sure no one—including the teacher—looks pained or cross. Who would care to telephone such a person? Unless the atmosphere is pleasant and brisk, not much will be accomplished. What is worse, the attitude may be transmitted that singing is not a very desirable thing to do.

Of course, you can't keep the simple "yoo hoo," the sound of the fire engine siren, and the telephone game going indefinitely. It's true that creative children sometimes expand the telephone game into quite a production, but this happens only when they are *ready*. You may have a class who has had little successful experience from which to be creative. Therefore, you will need additional devices for doing remedial work.

Remember, the most effective remedial devices are taken from rote songs that the children already know and enjoy. For example, let's consider the well-known song "The Muffin Man."[7] This song provides some interesting musical questions and answers, and your group can make up some different words. It is important that the

[7] Found in Book 1 of *Growing with Music* Series, published by Prentice-Hall, Inc.; and in Book 2 of *Discovering Music Together* Revised Series, published by Follett Publishing Co.

words fit the beat of the music, and that both questions and answers be *SUNG, not spoken.* Here are some suggestions:

> Do you know the ice-cream man? Yes, I know . . . etc.
>
> Do you know what time it is? Yes, I know . . . etc.
>
> Do you know what day it is? Yes, I know . . . etc.
>
> Do you know your teacher's (principal's, custodian's) name? Yes, I know . . . etc.
>
> Do you know this boy's first name? (Point to one of the children)
>
> Do you know this girl's last name? (Point to one of the children)

Later, the children can make up some of their own questions and sing them for each other. Children who can't sing the entire question or the entire answer should be encouraged to try a small pattern, like: "Yes, I know . . ." Some children will be able to make up a little pattern of their own and to sing the actual name the question calls for. There is almost an unlimited number of possibilities for playing this question-and-answer game. Be sure the children remember the importance of keeping it *musical* as well as fun.

It's also fun to play games of musical "Hide and Seek." Instead of finding real places to hide, the children stay in their seats and "look" for imaginary places. Some teachers choose the child to be "It" by finding a voice that can match a simple pattern like the "Yes, I know . . ." in the song "The Muffin Man." Instead of singing: "Yes, I know . . .," the teacher sings: "Who is 'It'?"

The pupil who can sing in tune accurately: "I am 'It,' " continues the game by singing to the same tune: "Where is John?" (or any other name of his choice). John will answer with the same tune: "In my lunch box" (or any other place he thinks of). If John can't sing accurately, the teacher will choose a helper quickly from among the better singers to "tag" John.

The purpose of the "tag" is to have the helper stand close to John and sing with him. Even the uncertain singer should have a chance to be "It." The helper will probably have to sing with him when he is "It," and ask the question: "Where are you?" of still another child. Each uncertain singer should have a chance to sing about the place he is "hiding"—no matter how well or poorly he sings. He should not feel penalized.

Encourage the children to think up surprising places to "hide" and new ways to play the game. There are many possibilities for children to make up little tunes of their own.

It is best to *begin individual work the very first week of school.* By the end of the first month—if you have spent a minute or two every day going quickly from child to child—the class will be conditioned to respond routinely to the idea of singing alone and in small groups. When you want a "model singer" simply call the child's name, or the names of individuals to form a small "model group." Simply say, "Joe and Mary and Tom and Grace, sing it for us. Everyone listen carefully, so we can be ready when our own turn comes!" If the singing is good, say so. If not, correct it.

If the singing of the small "model group" is incorrect, the chances are that the song is too difficult and you may wish to select something easier. Before you go on, however, try to correct the mistakes made by the "model group," even if you have to find only one child who is singing it right; or sing it for the class yourself, or play the record if you have one.

The important thing is to *leave the correct sound in the children's ears.* If, week after week, most of them are unable to repeat the correct tones, the songs are probably too difficult. Sometimes it is possible to figure out what is causing the difficulty and overcome it. But there is also the possibility that the children are just not ready for that level of difficulty. One of the pleasures of teaching music is that there is *no one song* that is indispensable, so we can accomplish our purposes just as well with some other song that may be easier for the class.

Middle Childhood (Levels 3 and 4)

INDIVIDUALIZED SINGING ACTIVITIES

Singing experiences should still include opportunities for some individual work daily. A pleasant atmosphere is important, to encourage children to explore the multiple possibilities of *many songs.* One of the most effective and natural ways to help children enjoy individual singing experiences is to select parts of known songs like "Old MacDonald Had a Farm."[8] If your class is inexperienced, you may want to select five or six of the most reliable singers to stand together in a group and sing the "E-i-e-i-o" when the time comes. It is important that the group sing its special part without pause, and that the rest of the song *be kept going without a break—at a suitable lively tempo.*

When the class and the small group can sing the song well in rhythm, arrange for as many individual pupils as possible to take turns singing the "E-i-e-i-o" by themselves. It is again important that the song be kept swinging along in a brisk tempo so that the individual singing *does not interrupt the flow of the rhythm.*

It is also important that *everyone* get a chance to sing a simple pattern of this sort. In this song you will find three such patterns in each stanza, and each time the words are sung with the same melody.

Of course some of your pupils will sing better than others. There may be some who can't sing very well in tune. Skillful teachers avoid placing these uncertain singers in embarrassing situations. They can be helped by learning to play the "E-i-e-i-o" pattern on the tone bells, xylophone, or piano while others take their turns singing. These instruments should be used by the good singers and the uncertain ones alike, so that no child feels embarrassed by his own singing. Many pupils can be helped to carry the tune by singing softly while playing a simple pattern on a melody instrument.

Another song that is useful for giving children an opportunity to sing a short pattern alone is "Three Blind Mice."[9] Just as children enjoy being "It" in a singing game, they will also enjoy individual singing activities of this type. Try to give your students frequent chances to sing alone. Where this kind of activity has become a routine part of the school day, children learn to use their voices expressively without self-consciousness: a facility demonstrated happily in many countries of the world today.

Later Childhood (Levels 5 and 6)

By this stage of development the problem of the inaccurate singer becomes more acute. Hopefully, this type of singer is in the minor-

---

[8] Found in Book 3 of *Discovering Music Together* Revised Series, published by Follett Publishing Co.; Book 3 of *This Is Music for Today* Series, published by Allyn and Bacon,

ity. And yet, this very fact complicates the problem. The few boys and girls who cannot sing in tune are painfully embarrassed to be in a music class with their peers. The game approach of earlier years is not effective at this point. How to deal with this problem is of great concern to many teachers.

Some teachers have been successful in working privately with these children individually or in small groups. They try to find ten or fifteen minutes during the day (as often as two or three times a week if possible) and work with them in an area where they are alone. The teacher's attitude is one of complete helpfulness directed toward the purpose of assisting the student to be more comfortable and at ease in the class as well as improving his personal skills.

Techniques include attempts at matching tones on the piano, singing the highest and lowest possible tones the student can manage, and working on simple, familiar melodies with a narrow range.

In the classroom the teacher can frequently invite the uncertain singers to play rhythm instruments as accompaniment for songs. Giving them specific assignments such as the responsibility for passing out the music books, being in charge of the record player, or taking care of the position of the chairs can often assist with the development of a proper attitude.

TONE QUALITY

Early and Middle Childhood
(Levels 1, 2, 3, and 4)

THE YOUNG CHILD'S VOICE

Singing voices of young children are normally light and free. Every class has some children who can sing well, and others who need remedial help. Many factors influence the tone quality of a child's voice. His physical growth and development, emotional temperament, and home life are but a few. Perhaps greater than any other is his individual response to the entire experience of singing. Nor-

Inc., and in Book 2 of *The Spectrum of Music* Series, published by Macmillan Publishing Co., Inc.

[9] Found in Book 4 of *This Is Music for Today* Series, published by Allyn and Bacon, Inc.

mal, healthy boys and girls who genuinely enjoy singing have a vibrancy and vitality of tone that has a unique beauty. The goal of the teacher should be to make the music class so pleasurable that each child will express himself freely. You should encourage a full-bodied tone from your students, guarding against a forced or displeasing quality on the one extreme, or a breathy, sterile, un-supported tone on the other.

Later Childhood (Levels 5 and 6)

From the children's first music classes until now, their teachers have been concerned with tone quality in singing. You should continue to help your boys and girls develop an easy, lilting quality. Happy singing in an atmosphere of freedom is one of the first requisites. By this time there are additional aids that you can give them. By now you can talk with them about proper breathing habits. (This should have been already quite well established by careful attention to phrasing.) Awareness of proper phrasing is the framework for breath control, but a few words about the dia-phragm and its function as a control center might be helpful. Continue to stress good diction and "clean" enunciation.

One method that excites the attention and interest of students in the effort to refine their tone quality is the use of the tape recorder. Children are charmed with the sound of their own voices. Of course, the newness of the experience may at first dull their powers of perception, but soon they will be listening with a more critical ear. They need to make an honest evaluation of their own performance, both as a group and as individuals. Record their singing of a selection, then appraise it critically and record again. After a few times with one song, switch to another. Provide oppor-tunities for individuals to hear themselves in solo roles also.

THE CHANGING VOICE

The changing voice is a normal part of individual growth. Both girls' and boys' voices mature, but the change is more obvious in the boys' voices. Boys' voices can drop in range a full octave or more as they mature. Because individuals differ, changing voices are different. The age when the change will begin varies with the individual, just as the time it takes for the voice to mature differs from one person to another. While this is entirely normal, it is not always easy to handle in group learning situations.

Some teachers are very skilled in dealing with changing voices, and are able to organize effective performing groups. For many of us, however, the changing voice constitutes one more variable to plan for in an already complex schedule. Because there are no apparent patterns of voice change that apply to all individuals at a given age, planning seems more difficult than it actually is. The key to effective planning is to emphasize individual and small group experiences.

The children's voices you will be working with fall into three simple groups:

1. the unchanged voices,
2. the changing voices, and
3. the changed voices.

Plan flexibly for each group, and you will have a more effective means of meeting individual needs. This division into groups is by no means arbitrary. There are times when a child's voice seems to be changing, and then the individual may resume singing in the unchanged voice. Sometimes an individual voice may seem to go from unchanged to changed almost overnight, with little or no time spent in the "changing voice" group. It is important that you "test" voices frequently in small informal groups. One authority has written much about exactly how to do this, and his suggestions are excellent and easy to use.[10]

Some unchanged voices are the most beautiful and brilliant just before the voice change. On the other hand, some changed voices are low and out-of-tune. Some individuals have difficulty singing in tune at any age. The voice may never be in tune, even when mature. The problem in this case is not a matter of the changing voice, but a matter of the individual's vocal inability to match pitches.

The vocal aspects of the voice change are nowhere nearly so intricate as some of the emotional overtones can be. The individual whose voice is *NOT* changing needs reassurance just as much as

---

[10] Irvin Cooper, clinician, composer, professor, authority on the changing voice. Author of *Letters to Pat, Tunes for Teen Time,* and many others published by Carl Fischer, Inc.

the one whose voice has dropped hopelessly below the range of the group. An understanding teacher will be able to foresee these needs, and help to provide for them. Much depends on the quality of the relationship you have with your students.

The following suggestions may help you plan individual and small group experiences for your singers:

1. Encourage each individual to make the most of what he has, and to keep track of the fun as it is happening. Using tone bells or the piano, let small groups of individuals take turns trying to discover which bells or keys they can match with their voices. Individual "logs" can be kept showing the date and the names of the tones that were matched. Sometimes changes seem to occur almost overnight. Other individuals find a gradual change happening week by week. Variation in normal growth patterns can be exciting. Individuals can then be encouraged to transcribe the pitch names of the bells or the piano keys onto a staff. Many teachers have used this personalized device to teach individuals to read music in the bass staff (F clef) and to help keep them singing during the voice change.

2. Select song materials with easy descants and ostinatos that fit the range the individual can sing comfortably.[11] Encourage experienced individuals to create their own. Let those who are having trouble singing use tone bells to play the ostinatos and descants.

3. Provide as many chording and other part song experiences as you can. They will be easier for the changing voices than unison singing. Put the unchanged voices on the parts that have the widest range, and put the changing voices on the chording parts and ostinatos.

4. Whenever any individual feels uncomfortable because the music is too high or too low, the singer should feel free to drop out and then try to "catch on" at another point in the song.

5. It is very helpful if there is someone available who has good functional keyboard skills so that melodies

---

[11] For specific titles and sources, see Appendix A and Appendix E.

and simple chordal accompaniments can be transposed to a different key to match the voices. The Autoharp can also be useful for such simple transpositions.

CREATIVE SONG ACTIVITIES

Early Childhood (Levels 1 and 2)

Encouragement and a happy environment are conditions needed for successful creative song activities. The children are ready for these experiences when they can sing reasonably in tune. Encourage the children to sing about some of these adventures:

1. Sing about what you saw on the way to school.
2. Sing about the things you need to buy at the supermarket, and choose another to sing what the checkout man might say.
3. Sing about all the ways in which you can help mother, and choose someone to sing what mother might say.
4. Sing about your trip this summer (or what you will do on your next vacation).
5. Sing a question to the girl of your choice as to what color dress she is wearing, and have her sing her answer.

These short sentences may be sung to any tune the child makes up. The more tunes with which he has become familiar in the past, the more material he will have with which to create his own melodies. Some teachers like to record these musical sentences with a tape recorder.

Just as children's performance varies from individual to individual in reading or in arithmetic, so also does creative ability. Some children can and will make up tunes to go with well-loved poems and stories. Others may not make any contribution to this kind of activity all year long. If any kind of creative activity is to be successful, we must accept each child's uniqueness—whether he responds or not.

We need to remember that creative activity is essentially an individual experience. Desirable group activity, however, can stimulate the individual child to express himself in his own way. Some children will be able to make up many tunes by themselves. Our purpose, however, is to give *every child* in the class as good an opportunity as possible to explore and develop *his own creative powers* through successful experiences in music.

Here are some suggestions for helping the class make up songs of their own, using favorite poems. You may find a tape recorder useful in this kind of activity, whether you know how to write the music down or not. These suggestions may seem quite rigid, but they can serve as a foundation from which to launch similar, freer activities.

1. Have four lines of a favorite poem on the board, with the words divided into syllables and hyphenated. Use chalk in three different colors, and have the first and third line of the poem in the same color. Leave plenty of space between each of the four lines.

2. Have the class recite the poem together, then ask the class how the words make them *feel,* because we want the music we are going to make up to express that same mood. (Because the favorite poem is already well-known, we take it for granted that all of the unfamiliar words have been previously explained.)

3. Tell the class that the first and third lines of words are in the same color just to remind us of our plan. All composers have a plan for writing music (which is called *form*). Just to get a start, this plan is for a song in which the first and third phrases will be alike. When the music is complete, the first and third lines of words will become the first and third phrases of the music.

4. Now read the poem *rhythmically* to emphasize which words and which syllables are accented. This rhythmic reading may sound funny at first, and it is certainly not the way to recite poetry properly, but we want to exaggerate the accent deliberately, so that the beat of our music will fit the words of the poem just right.

5. Have the class read the first line of poetry rhythmically as you mark the accent at the board. For example:

"The | sun one | morn-ing rose | late from his | sleep,"

(Notice that sometimes the words tell us which direction the tune can go.)

6. Let the children hum their tunes to themselves (all at the same time) as you say the words rhythmically to the first phrase. Now start the tape recorder. Call on several individuals to sing their own tunes with the words to the first phrase (one at a time, of course).

7. Let the class decide which tune they like best for the first phrase. Use the tape recorder to play back the tune.

8. Have the class sing the tune as selected for the first phrase, and record it on the tape.

9. Refer to the *form* on the board and sing the same tune with the words of the *third line* of poetry, because in this song we have decided that the first and third phrases were to sound just alike.

By this time our song is already half finished! If the activity has taken a lot of time you may wish to continue the remainder another day. At any rate, the next thing to consider is the second phrase—for example:

10. Have the class sing the first and third phrases again (or listen to them played back on the tape recorder).

11. Read the words of the second line of poetry *rhythmically*. We really have two choices in planning this tune: It could be a very different kind of tune— going up where the other two phrases went down, or it could be a tune that starts out like the first and third phrases but ends differently.

12. Turn the tape recorder on "record" again, and continue the activity as suggested in item 6.

13. Have the class sing the *third phrase* with the words and record it on the tape.

14. Read the words of the fourth line of poetry *rhythmically.* In planning our tune now, we have to take into consideration how we planned our second phrase. We may decide to have the second and fourth phrases sound something alike, but the fourth, or last phrase, should really sound like the end of the song when we get there.

15. Have the class repeat the first three phrases of their song before they decide on a fourth phrase. Complete the fourth phrase in the same manner as before.

Ask your music teacher to listen to the tape and write the song out on the staff for your class. They will enjoy seeing how it looks. Some of the children may want to draw a picture to illustrate their song.

Middle Childhood (Levels 3 and 4)

ENCOURAGING CREATIVITY

A balanced music curriculum provides opportunities for children to explore a wide variety of music activities; melodic and rhythmic, vocal and instrumental.

Creative song activities combine many of these experiences, and can include:

1. Brief musical "sentences" describing anything that interests the children on these levels;
2. Original words for familiar songs;
3. Original melodies for familiar poems;
4. Songs in which both the words and music are original.

Most children this age enjoy working in groups and experimenting in new areas. These characteristics can be put to good use in creative song activities.

Often students like to paint pictures, write or tell stories about their songs, or make simple instruments for their own use. These are excellent ways in which children can *discover relationships* in learning experiences, but they should not constitute the entire program. Our purpose, which is to *make music,* should not be obscured by merely *talking about* music.

Creative music activities can flourish if you are:

1. Willing to accept the individuality of each child;
2. Willing to encourage *contributions* from all children;
3. Willing to be more interested in creative *process* than in *product,* and
4. Willing to teach from *any occasion* that arises naturally and spontaneously.

The joy the children have experienced on earlier levels in composing songs should be retained and increased now. By now they have had many opportunities to create new stanzas for familiar tunes and have acquired some skills in originating their own melodies. Their vocabulary has broadened and their range of interests has expanded. The alert teacher will find creative experiences with her students to be most rewarding.

Later Childhood (Levels 5 and 6)

CREATING NEW SONGS

Children are by nature creative. One plan was outlined for younger children in creating a song with the aid of a tape recorder. Older students need the opportunity to try to notate the song for themselves (with some assistance perhaps) rather than depend on the tape recorder entirely. If so, these suggestions may be helpful:

1. Place a poem the class has selected on the board or a large chart. Have the class read it aloud and discuss its meaning and mood.
2. Reading the poetry aloud should be continued until it is decided where the natural accents of the words fall. Divide the words into syllables, hyphenate them (just as in any good song book), and mark the places where the accents fall.
3. Say the first phrase together. Invite the children to sing some tunes for these words. Only one child should sing at a time. Several may respond in turn.

4. Write down each melody that is sung for the first phrase. (If you have difficulty doing this with notes, indicate the movement of the music by lines.)

Then let the children decide which of these melodies they want to use. (If the children have forgotten the tunes you will find the tape recorder very helpful.)

5. Proceed in a similar manner until all phrases have a melody.

6. Sing the entire song.

7. Play the first phrase and ask some student to place the proper rhythm pattern for it on the chalkboard. (If the first phrase is unusually short you may want him to write two or three.) For example:

Rhythm Pattern:

Words: Win - ter's   here,———   Snow is   on   the   way.

8. Proceed in a similar manner until the rhythm patterns for all the phrases are on the board.

9. Play the first phrase (or sing it) and see if the class can sing the melody with syllables or numbers. Then ask a student to put the correct syllables (numbers) under the rhythm pattern for the first phrase. For example:

so   mi   so   mi   fa   so   fa   mi   re
5   3   5   3   4   5   4   3   2

10. Proceed in a similar manner until the syllable (number) patterns for all the phrases are on the board.

11. Put a treble clef and a key signature on the staff on your felt board, then ask a child to put in the correct notes for the first phrase. He will look at

the syllables (numbers) that have been written
under the rhythm pattern to decide on what line
or space he should put each note. He will look at
the rhythm pattern to decide whether a note
should be a quarter, eighth, or half.

Win - ter's   here,___   Snow is   on   the   way.

12. Proceed in a similar manner until all the phrases are
on the staff.

13. Sing the song (using words, syllables, or numbers)
and clap the pulse (heavy beat or "one" beat).
Place measure bars directly in front of the word,
syllable, or number receiving the strong beat.

14. Put the proper time signature on the staff. For
example:

Win - ter's   here,___   Snow is   on   the   way.

15. The children may want to copy the song and put it
in a music notebook or scrapbook. They may also
want to illustrate it with pictures drawn during art
period.

As a further opportunity to develop creativity the teacher might
invite the piano students in the class to compose a simple accompaniment for the song. Selecting the accompaniment to be used
could be done in the same manner as in suggestion 4 above.

SUGGESTED INDIVIDUAL
AND SMALL GROUP PROJECTS
FOR METHODS COURSES

Here are some suggestions for those who wish to plan a variety of
supplementary music activities related to singing experiences (similar suggestions will be found at the end of each chapter of this
book):

Early Childhood (Levels 1 and 2)

1. Plan a community sing incorporating seasonal, action, quiet, and religious songs. Use appropriate informal instruments. Give opportunity for some solo and small group performance.

2. Make a list of short melody patterns (tonal patterns) taken from well-known early childhood songs to illustrate "tunes that go up." Make another list to illustrate "tunes that go down." Use these patterns for remedial work with uncertain singers. Develop creative singing games with these same patterns, in which the pupils sing to one another in imaginary telephone conversations.

3. Compile a list of poems that could be used in creating songs. Include a wide range of interests—seasonal and holiday, home and school, family and friends, pets, community helpers, etc.

4. Write out a plan for the school year based on seasonal and holiday songs found in the students' music books. Describe in detail related listening, rhythm, singing, and creative activities, and show how you can use simple informal instruments—rhythmic, melodic, and harmonic.

5. Write out another plan of this type based on the social studies units used in your school on the first or second level. Include all the activities mentioned above.

Middle Childhood (Levels 3 and 4)

1. Select any holiday and create a story about it, using songs from the students' music books that describe activities appropriate to the celebration of the holiday.

2. Write descants for "Home on the Range" and "Silent Night."

3. Plan some music activities to be correlated with a specific social studies unit.

4. Partner songs such as "Three Blind Mice" and "Are You Sleeping?" can be sung at the same time when

the class is divided into two groups. Make a list of as many such song combinations as possible.

Later Childhood (Levels 5 and 6)

1. Choose several songs that are particularly suitable for a descant or "barbershop" treatment and write the harmony parts.

2. Create melodies and accompaniments for a number of poems that would be appropriate for students on these levels.

3. To give your students further experience with the classification of the adult voice, invite friends or school patrons to sing for your class during the year. If possible try to have one from each "category"— soprano, contralto, etc. Make a list of people in your community who might be available for such a service.

4. Choose five folk songs and in each one write a part for the boy with a changing voice. (Keep it within a range limited to the interval of a fifth.)

5. Write chord indications for a guitar or ukulele for five songs that do not have such markings.

3

Music Reading and Readiness

The very essence of music is *sound,* and many music experiences should properly be "EAR" experiences. Music should never be approached as one of the visual arts. However, any study of music that does not include SOME attempt to develop reading skills is not really fair to the learner. Although not every child will become adept at reading unfamiliar music at sight, many experiences with the staff can increase his or her independence and discrimination. Reading skills provide the child with limitless opportunities for enjoying musical accomplishment both now and in the future. Helping children to develop these skills is well worth the effort required. The key is in making this effort both ENJOYABLE and musical.

Two world-famous musicians, the late Zoltán Kodály (Hungarian composer and educator) and Carl Orff (German contemporary composer), seem to have discovered this secret. Because their philosophy and techniques seem to be so successful with young children around the world, this chapter will include some of their basic concepts. The explanation of the Kodály and Orff techniques will be sequential in nature, coinciding with the philosophy of the authors that learning over a period of time can best be accomplished in this manner.

KODÁLY AND ORFF CONCEPTS

At the very beginning of this discussion of Kodály and Orff, it is important to emphasize that the concepts of both composers are based on total ENJOYMENT and involvement with the music in every way—using body movement (hand signals, playing instruments, clapping, stamping, snapping fingers, etc.), the voice in singing and speech exercises, the mind in disciplined concentration, and the spirit in creative sensitivity. Thus the WHOLE person is immersed in the musical experience. Although this thought may not be constantly reiterated here, it is well to remember that it is the undergirding principle of all teaching of music to children.

In this presentation the authors have selected specific features from both Kodály and Orff and combined them.

This discussion is not intended to be all-inclusive. Rather, it is an attempt in abbreviated form to blend varied ideas, suggestions, and techniques that have come from many sources. There are many excellent workshops and university courses devoted exclusively to the teaching of Orff and Kodály techniques. Many books on the subject and much suitable music are also available. For specific titles of these materials, see Appendix B.

Information about Kodály techniques can be obtained from the:

> Organization of American Kodály Educators
> c/o Christine Kunko
> School of Music
> Duquesne University
> Pittsburgh, Pa. 15219

This organization publishes the *Kodály Envoy,* and can furnish information concerning conferences, workshops, and materials.

Information about the American Orff Schulwerk Association can be obtained by writing to:

> Mrs. Ruth Pollack Hamm,
> Executive Secretary,
> P.O. Box 18495
> Cleveland Heights, Ohio 44118

This organization publishes *The Orff Echo* and can arrange for back issues. Supplementary articles are also available, as well as information on conferences, workshops, and instruments.

Two other excellent sources of information are the publications *Keeping Up with Orff* and *Keeping Up with Kodály*. Write to:

> Prof. Arnold Burkhart
> Music Dept.
> Ball State University
> Muncie, Ind. 47306

Professor Burkhart was one of the original founders and the first president of the American Orff Schulwerk Association. He also edits and publishes *Keeping Up with Music Education*.

Following the presentation of Kodály and Orff concepts some practical suggestions are given. These represent "child-tested" procedures and techniques that have proved successful for many teachers. The discussion will be sequential, proceeding from the simple, introductory steps to the more advanced ones. This implies that the entire process could be spread out over a number of years.

Rhythm Syllables

This approach suggests the use of rhythm syllables for recognition of note values by sight and sound, and hand signals to indicate pitches—using a pentatonic approach in the early stages. In this approach the rhythm concepts are introduced before the tonal. Through stem, or stick, notation the children become acquainted with the quarter, eighth, and half notes. They say, "tah" for the quarter, "tee" for the eighth, and "tah-ah" for the half. They learn that the quarter rest takes as much QUIET time as the "tah" for the quarter note. (Most teachers use some type of hand motion to indicate the rest—such as "throwing away" the rest with the hands, but remaining *silent* on rests.)

tah tah tee tee tah | tah tah tah (rest; not spoken)

There is great value in MOUTHING the word "REST," or even whispering it. "Throwing it away" is excellent. It is hard to teach concepts of SILENCE through SOUND. A rest is a symbol that says, "Be quiet" (in both rhythm and tone). The symbol does

Mr. Dale Jones directs the attention of his special education students to the "pretend" symbol for a rest (photo by Patrick Burke).

NOT indicate a different kind of sound, but rather the ABSENCE of sound.

Much motivated drill is needed to help the children FEEL the rhythm as well as say the "tahs" and "tees." Clapping, tapping, stepping, or playing a rhythm instrument make the learning fun. Many times you may clap a short rhythm pattern and ask the children to be your "echo." Children should also be given opportunities to write rhythm patterns frequently. You might clap a pattern and ask a child to write it on the board—or have the class write it at their desks. Creatively varying the procedure of the drill can keep excitement high.

Tonal Syllables and Hand Signals

After the class has developed reasonably good rhythmic skills, the tonal concepts should be introduced. One of the best ways to accomplish this is to teach the children a SHORT song based only on the two syllables SO and MI.

For example:

1. "Play" the tune with your hands as you sing, then ask the class how many different tones they hear.
2. Repeat the song, having them "play" the tune with you.
3. Suggest to the children that even as they have special names (Jim, Jane) so these music sounds have special names.
4. Sing the song with the syllables SO and MI, "playing" the tune with the proper SO and MI hand signals:

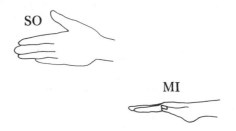

5. Have the children sing the syllables with you, using the hand signals.
6. Ask the class which was higher—SO or MI.
7. Write the words on the board, indicating the pitch levels:

8. Have the children sing the song from the board, first with words, then with tonal syllables, using hand signals.
9. After a few days of varied practice at recognizing the sounds of SO and MI, place the song on the board with stem notation:

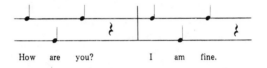

How are you? | I am fine.

10. Have the children read the rhythm with "tahs," then sing the words followed by tonal syllables with hand signals.

11. Next, write the notes on two lines. Suggest to the children that you are going to put a head on each stem and make it a note.

12. Have them sing the song using tonal syllables and hand signals:

How   are   you?   I   am   fine.

After continued practice with placing SO and MI in varying combinations on the staff, teach another song introducing the syllable LA. A favorite with teachers is the familiar "Rain, Rain, Go Away." (The children do not see the music yet. It is pictured here as a convenience for the teacher.)

Rain, rain,   go   a - way.   Come a - gain an - oth - er   day.

Rain, rain,   go   a - way.   All   the   chil - dren   want   to   play.

1. Teach this as a rote song first with words, then with tonal syllables and hand signals:

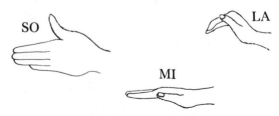

2. See if the class can discover that the new tonal syllable, LA, is higher than SO.

3. After the song is well-learned, place it on a two-line staff on the board:

4. Have the children clap the rhythm using the "tah" and "tee" syllables.

5. Repeat the song using the tonal syllables and hand signals.

Two-Line Staff

Give the children experience with several other songs using the three syllables SO, MI, and LA appearing on a two-line staff, then introduce the complete staff with the song "Rain, Rain, Go Away." It would be helpful to place SO and MI on lines.

1. Have the class read the rhythm with "tahs" and "tees."

2. Ask them to find identical tonal patterns.

3. Sing these with tonal syllables and hand signals.

4. Assist the children—if necessary—in singing the entire song with tonal syllables, using hand signals.

Continue the practice of rhythm syllables and tonal syllables over a period of time, giving the children MUCH opportunity to experience the sight and sound of each type. Constantly vary the approach by using game techniques and other FUN methods that are appealing to children.

Although the rhythm and tonal syllables form the heart of this approach, many other concepts such as high-low, up-down, fast-slow, and loud-soft are presented as well as such symbols as the repeat, key sign, and others. Ostinatos are also introduced and experienced. However, the discussion in this material will be largely confined to the presentation of the rhythm and tonal syllables.

A thorough review of the tonal syllables MI, SO, LA, and the quarter, eighth, and half notes with appropriate rhythm symbols should precede the introduction of a new rhythm symbol, the dotted half ($\downarrow$. "tah-ah-ah") and two new tonal syllables, RE and DO. As usual, the best way to present the new syllables is through a known rote song. No doubt the class already knows the familiar "Old McDonald Had a Farm." Sing it with words, inviting the children to join you, then sing for the class the phrase "E-i-e-i-o" with tonal syllables and hand signals.

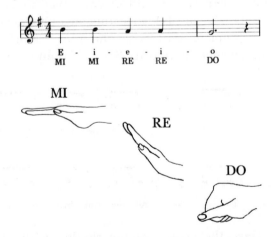

1. Place the notes on the staff for "E-i-e-i-o."
2. Have the class clap the rhythm and chant the rhythm syllables. (They will discover a new note,

the dotted half note. Tell them the rhythm syllable for this is "tah-ah-ah.")

3. Practice the rhythm several times, clapping, tapping, etc., while chanting the rhythm syllables.
4. Sing, "E-i-e-i-o" again with tonal syllables and hand signals. Have the class tell you what new tonal syllables they heard. (RE and DO)
5. Ask the class which way the tune goes on this phrase.
6. Have the class sing the phrase with tonal syllables and hand signals, maintaining the correct rhythm.
7. Give several children an opportunity to play the tune on the bells while the other members of the class sing the tonal syllables using hand signals.
8. Challenge the class to find other places in the song using the MI, MI, RE, RE, DO tonal patterns. Sing them with words and tonal syllables.

Following this introduction of the tonal pattern, continue stress on RE and DO by reading SHORT, simple songs incorporating these tonal syllables. Have the class read the rhythm first with "tees" and "tahs," then discover the new tonal syllables. Be sure the students know the appropriate hand signals. Game-oriented drills (such as "playing" a song with hand signals for them to identify the song) will reinforce their learning.

Pentatonic Scale

When the children have achieved a fair mastery of the two new syllables, RE and DO, they are ready to be introduced to the pentatonic scale in its entirety. "Playing" the tonal syllables of the scale (DO, RE, MI, SO, LA) with hand signals, playing the scale on the bells or piano, singing the scale with hand signals, or a variety of other approaches should be satisfactory if the scale is identified at the same time. Some educators at this point prefer to call this scale simply the five-tone scale, while others challenge their children with learning the term "pentatonic," explaining that the scale has five tones.

Continue reading songs in the pentatonic scale. Perhaps it would be best to limit this at first to songs in the key of C. When it becomes evident the children are quite confident, try new songs in the key of G or F. Point out that the sharp or flat helps to locate DO for us.

Encourage the students to create pentatonic accompaniments on the bells. One of the advantages of reading in the pentatonic scale is that any one of the five tones can be played or sung at any time with the melody and create desirable harmony. Since the tonal syllables for these five tones are DO, RE, MI, SO, LA, you can choose these five bells in whatever key your song is in. Then the child can be totally creative and free to play any of the five bells at any time he or she chooses. There is no possibility of discordant "mistakes." Pleasant sounds will result no matter what tonal or rhythmic pattern the student creates. This gives him a feeling of instant success and satisfaction.

In the key of C the DO, RE, MI, SO, LA bells are C, D, E, G, A; in the key of G they are G, A, B, D, E; and in the key of F they are F, G, A, C, D.

Encourage the children to create introductions, codas, and ostinatos. These may be either melodic or rhythmic.

Although it would be wise to limit reading songs for some time to those based on the pentatonic scale, there is one new tonal syllable that can be introduced—high DO. Since the children are already familiar with low DO, it should be a simple matter to sing high DO, giving the proper hand signal.

High DO

Select a few songs containing high DO, then motivate the children to discover this new syllable in the song. After singing it with the new hand signal, proceed to read the song in the usual manner:

1. Read the rhythm with rhythm syllables.
2. Look for tonal patterns that are alike. Sing them with tonal syllables using hand signals.
3. Attempt singing the entire song with tonal syllables.

Review the rhythm syllables for the quarter, eighth, half, and dotted half notes, then introduce a new one—the dotted quarter

Mrs. Anne Thompson and her pupils sing "high DO" using hand signals (photo, courtesy of Mrs. Ollie McFarland).

note. The rhythm syllable for this is "tah-ee." The dotted quarter sounds like a quarter and an eighth tied together.

The pupils' book will no doubt have several interesting songs that contain this note and yet are simple enough to read with rhythm syllables. A familiar example is "America":

My	coun -	try	'tis	of	thee
tah	tah	tah	tah-ee	tee	tah

Some DAILY reading involving the pentatonic scale (including high DO) and the quarter, eighth, half, dotted half, and dotted quarter notes will be most effective in developing the students' skills. Caution should be exercised, however, in not making the reading period too LONG. It is better to work at it consistently day by day than to concentrate on reading for most of a music period at infrequent intervals. Try always to keep the instruction varied and INTERESTING!

After the students have had much experience reading pentatonic songs in the keys of C, G, and F major, it would be well to introduce the concept of the major scale. This could be done in a variety of ways. The favorite "Do Re Mi" song from *The Sound of Music* presents the two missing syllables—FA and TI. Once this has been learned and enjoyed as a rote song, some song from the students' book based on the scale could be used for study purposes. Such questions as these could direct the study:

1. How many hand signals do we need to show all the tonal syllables of the major scale? (8)
2. What tonal syllables in the major scale are the same as those in the pentatonic? (DO RE MI SO LA)
3. How many hand signals do we need to show all the tonal syllables in an octave? (8)

Major Mode

The same reading techniques that have been employed previously are now used in the study of songs in the major mode. As the students develop their skills in this mode (scale) they should also continue to read some songs in the pentatonic scale to keep the sound in their ears. By this time they will have quite a basic understanding of the use of rhythm syllables, tonal syllables, and hand signals. They have but to transfer this knowledge to other musical learnings—such as the minor mode, dotted eighth, sixteenth, triplet, and syncopated rhythms. Perhaps the only one of these that may need some discussion here is one type of syncopated rhythm:

♪ ♩ ♪ ♩ ♩

Some educators prefer using the rhythm syllables:

♪ ♩ ♪ ♩ ♩
tee tah tee tah tah

Others have found a special device more helpful to them:

♪ ♩ ♪ ♩ ♩
syn - co - pa - tah tah

Either way is appropriate. Whichever syllables seem to help the students most should be used.

Keeping in mind the approach of rhythm first, then tonal patterns and syllables, all of the basic concepts can now be applied to any new song that is to be studied. A complete list of rhythm syllables and tonal syllables with hand signals is given here as a quick reference for you. A variety of tonal patterns based on the pentatonic scale in the keys of C, G, and F are pictured in Appendix K.

|	tah	⊓ (tee tee-ry)	tee tee - ry
⊓	tee tee	⊓⌐	tee - ry tee
♩	tah - ah	♩.	tah - ee
♩.	tah - ah - ah	⌐ · ⌐	teem - ry
o	tah - ah - ah - ah	⌐ ·	ry - teem
♪ | ♪	syn - co - pa	³⊓⊓	tri - ple - tee
♪ | ♪ | |	syn - co - pa - tah - tah	𝄽	(whisper "REST" first, eventually silence)
⊓⊓	tee - ry tee - ry	𝄾	st

Rhythm and Tonal Syllables

Beyond the basic concepts presented here, there are many desirable aspects of the Kodály and Orff techniques that make them a favorite with educators. Probably the most outstanding of these is the creative philosophy that provides not only the setting but the tools for rich musical experiences. Much experimentation with rhythm patterns, tonal patterns, and the combination of these in making up new songs not only provides an excellent background for reading but is an integral part of the process itself. In addition, creativity helps to obliterate age differences, making it possible for pupils to share meaningfully in ungraded situations and other purposeful groupings.

High DO

TI

LA

SO

FA

MI

RE

DO

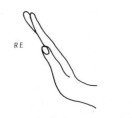

Hand Signals for Tonal Syllables

SUGGESTED SEQUENCE OF DIFFICULTY

Early Childhood (Levels 1 and 2)

Many music educators in addition to Kodály and Orff believe that a good deal of aural experience should precede the presentation of visual symbols. It is certainly a necessary part of children's musical growth to experience pitch and rhythm sounds in order to be able to interpret what they see. Some teachers like to use musical "games" as a device for developing reading readiness in the early stages.

Two types of "games" for young children are those which develop senses of *key feeling* and *phrase feeling.*

DEVELOPING KEY FEELING
(MAJOR, MINOR, PENTATONIC)

Music is traditionally built around a keytone, or "home tone." Nearly all children's songs end on the "home tone," and when we hear the last note of the song we usually have a feeling of rest or repose because the tune has come "home" to its keynote.

This response to "key feeling" is so natural that we sometimes take it for granted. Several times during the year, however, we should remind the children in some simple way that the keytone can be heard and *anticipated.* There are many ways to do this, but these suggestions might serve as a suitable motivation:

1. Have the class sing a well-known song, stopping on the next to the last note. For example:

Little Jack Horner

English Nursery Rhyme

Melody by J. W. Elliott
Acc. by Dustin Harriman

Have the class sing: "what a good boy am," and stop. It is important that *everyone remain absolutely quiet.*

2. Have the children cover their eyes while the teacher counts to ten.

3. Now see if the class can sing *the last note of the song.*

Simple games of this kind help to develop tonal memory and *a sense of key feeling.* The lack of a sense of key feeling (a feeling for the "key center," or the "home tone") is one of the things that also handicaps the out-of-tune singer. The effective teacher will want to make as many opportunities as possible for this kind of activity.

During the year the children should also develop a *sensitivity* to the minor and pentatonic tonalities through experiences in singing and listening. The song "My Rocket Ship"[1] is a good example of appealing music written in the minor mode. This song "comes home" to the E-G-B chord, and the "Blast off" and "ZIP" end on E, the key tone (or tonic) of the key of E minor.

Pupils can sense the difference in the sound of the minor tonality, even though they are not expected to study the key

[1] Reprinted from *The Sunflower Song Book,* by June M. Norton. Copyright © 1935, 1956 by June M. Norton. Used with permission of The John Day Company, Inc., publisher. Also from *This Is Music for Today: Kindergarten and Nursery School,* published by Allyn and Bacon, Inc.

signature. When the song is well-known many children will be able to sing, "Blast off!" in tune, and play a sweeping glissando on the bells. The B$_7$ chord shown with the word "Blast" provides a musical opportunity to "launch" an effective game to develop *minor key feeling* (see the suggestions for "Little Jack Horner," pages 81-82).

My Rocket Ship

Music and Words by June Norton

Pentatonic music has been enjoyed for so many generations, and there are so many universal favorites, that we often are unaware of the tonality. For example, the delightful counting song "Band of Angels"[2] looks as though it is written in the traditional key of F major. However, the music is made up entirely of five tones: C, D, F, G, and A.

These five pitches provide rich experiences for experimentation at the keyboard. Children can play the song readily by ear after they know how to sing it, using only the black keys.

Band of Angels

South Carolina Spiritual

1. There was one, there were two, there were three lit - tle an - gels,
2. There was ten, there were nine, there were eight lit - tle an - gels,

There were four, there were five, there were six lit - tle an - gels,
There were sev'n there were six, there were five lit - tle an - gels,

There were sev'n, there were eight, there were nine lit - tle an - gels,
There were four, there were three, there were two lit - tle an - gels,

[2] From *Thirty-Six South Carolina Spirituals,* by Carl Diton. Copyright 1930 by G. Schirmer, Inc. Used by permission. Also from Book 2 of *Exploring Music* Series, published by Holt, Rinehart and Winston, Inc., Book 1 of *The Spectrum of Music* Series, published by Macmillan Publishing Co., Inc. (appears in both books as "The Angel Band"), and from Book 1 of *This Is Music for Today* Series, published by Allyn and Bacon, Inc.

DEVELOPING PHRASE FEELING

Phrase feeling is one of the things that makes a difference between a musical performance and a mechanical one. These levels are not too early to begin the development of musicality. Resourceful teachers keep reminding children to listen to their own work, and to express an opinion of the beauty of the performance. Each time they sing or move to music they are taught to ask themselves: "How can we make it more beautiful?"

Playing simple "phrase games" is one way to develop a feeling for the phrase. At first, it is probably easiest to do this through the known rote song. Here is a suggested procedure:

1. Be sure the song is well-known to the class before you start the game.

2. Sing the song without using the words. Sing it on "ta-da-da"[3] or any sound that makes it possible to omit the words and have the class *concentrate on the music.*

3. While the better singers sing the song with "ta-da-da," or some other neutral syllable, have the rest of the class *move their arms in a large arc* with each phrase.

4. After moving to each phrase, have the class *count how many phrases* there are in the song. (By counting the number of phrases, the children will now be able to refer to them as the "first" phrase, the "second" phrase, and so on, and thus identify them by name.)

5. The purpose of the game is to lead the children to discover which phrases are EXACTLY ALIKE.

For example, let's look at this well-known song to illustrate how "phrase games" can be played:

Rock-a-Bye Baby

Old Song
Acc. by Dustin Harriman

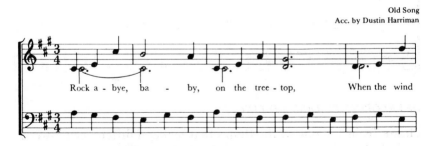

---

[3] The neutral syllable "loo" is often used, but this is not recommended because it is vocally difficult for inexperienced singers. The "oo" is a closed vowel, and often sounds pinched and thin. Also, the initial consonant "l" is often improperly articulated by undesirable jaw movement. "Ta-da-da," however, is easy to sing and sounds well.

1. Have the class sing the entire song all the way through with the words, just as it's written.

2. Explain how the game will begin: Some of the children (it might be well to choose the better singers) will sing the tune on "ta-da-da" (or any good neutral syllable), so that we can all *concentrate on the music.*

3. As part of the class sings, the rest will move their arms in a large arc each time they hear a phrase sung. For example, they will make one large arc while "Rock-a-bye, baby, on the tree top" is being sung on a neutral syllable. (They can begin with both hands in their laps, bringing the arms up in front of the face, stretching them up over the head, and then bringing the arms down to the sides—each arm describing a semicircle. The hands go up over the head together, but on the way down, the right hand moves smoothly to the right while the left hand is moving smoothly to the left, each making a big curve. At the end of each phrase, both hands have come to rest in the lap again, ready to start a new phrase if one is heard.)

4. During the singing of "when the wind blows, the cradle will rock," they will describe another large arc to indicate the second phrase.

5. During the singing of "when the bough breaks, the

cradle will fall," another large arc will be described to indicate the third phrase.

6. Complete the same process during the singing of the fourth phrase: "and down will come baby, cradle, and all."

Ask the class how many phrases they heard. Sometimes the children will not realize how many phrases there are until the teacher chooses four children—one to walk across the front of the room during the singing of each phrase.

When the class is able to distinguish easily that this song has four phrases, they are ready for the next part of the game: *to listen for the phrases that are exactly alike.*

The easiest way to accomplish this is to get the class to "take turns" singing the phrases with the teacher. Since the first and third phrases in this song happen to be the ones that are exactly alike, they will be the ones you will want the class to sing. For example:

1. Have the class sing the first phrase on a neutral syllable, or use only the better singers if the entire class can't sing well enough. Those who aren't singing should be moving their arms in large arcs in time with the singing of each phrase.

2. The teacher should sing the second phrase (or have a small selected group do it).

3. Have the class (or the group that sang the first phrase) sing the third phrase.

4. The teacher (or the small selected group) should sing the fourth phrase.

Given enough opportunities of this kind, most children will be able to decide which phrases are *exactly alike.* They will do this entirely "by ear." Later on they will discover that the phrases that *sound alike* also *look alike.* For this reason, these "games" are an important part of "reading readiness" in music.

Follow up this experience with similar ones. Try another song in which the *first and third phrases* are again exactly alike. Then select another song, in which the *second and fourth phrases* are exactly alike.

In selecting songs for "phrase games," avoid those in which there are phrases *similar* to the ones which are exactly alike.

"Looby Loo" is not a good choice for this reason. Notice that the second phrase, "here we go looby light," is very similar to the two identical phrases, "here we go looby loo" (the first and third phrases of the refrain). Phrases that are similar may cause confusion at first. Given repeated opportunities, however, most children can find similar phrases and discover how they differ from the identical ones. This skill simply requires a little more experience.

Sometimes people do not agree on exactly how long a phrase is in any given song. As an example, your class may feel that "London Bridge" has four phrases, and they may want to sing it:

> *"Lon-don Bridge is fall-ing down,*
> *Fall-ing down, fall-ing down.*
> *Lon-don Bridge is fall-ing down,*
> *My fair la-dy!"*

However, some children who are accustomed to singing four measures comfortably on one breath find the song sounds more musical to their ears if it is sung in two phrases, like this:

> *"Lon-don Bridge is fall-ing down, fall-ing down, fall-ing down.*
> *Lon-don Bridge is fall-ing down, My fair la-dy!"*

Whether your class feels this music in two phrases or in four phrases is not really the most important consideration. It is very important, however, that they develop the concept that music moves in *groups of notes* and that they learn to sing it (and later read it) *phrasewise*.

NOTE VALUES. Many teachers like to review the whole, half, quarter, and eighth notes by using this simple parody:[4]

TUNE: MULBERRY BUSH

> *First you have a hollow note,*
> *hollow note, hollow note,*
> *First you have a hollow note*
> *and this you call a whole note.*

(Clasp hands together, making a big circle with your arms.)

> *Next you put a stem on it,*
> *stem on it, stem on it,*
> *Next you put a stem on it,*
> *and this you call a half note.*

(Touch fingertips of left hand to inside crook of right elbow. Extend right arm.)

---

[4] This parody is used so widely that the original source is unknown to the authors.

> *Then you fill the center in,*
> *center in, center in,*
> *Then you fill the center in,*
> *and this you call a quarter note.*

(Circle your left arm over your head. Touch fingertips of left hand to inside crook of right elbow. Extend right arm.)

> *Then you put a flag on it,*
> *flag on it, flag on it,*
> *Then you put a flag on it,*
> *and this you call an eighth note.*

(Assume position for stanza three. Bend fingers of right hand backward for the flag.)

After each stanza you may want to invite a student (or several students) to draw the note on the chalkboard.

SIGNIFICANT READINESS
AND READING EXPERIENCES

Middle Childhood (Levels 3 and 4)

CHOICE OF SONGS
FOR EARLY EXPERIENCES

In order for the first independent reading experiences to be successful, you should choose songs that:

1. are short,
2. have mostly quarter notes and half notes,
3. have some phrases that are identical (or very similar), and
4. have mostly steps and easy skips in the tune.

It is far better to choose a song that is too easy, than to choose one that defeats and discourages the class.

When presenting new songs for the class to *sing on sight, remember:*

1. Don't stand in front of the group. If you do, the class will look at you instead of at the book.
2. Keep a steady, audible beat going.
3. Encourage the class to *keep singing* steadily through

to the end. A good sight-singer doesn't allow himself to be defeated by his mistakes, but keeps going in time with the beat, and tries to get back "on the track." Mistakes can be analyzed and corrected after the song is finished, but silence does not result in musical achievement.

4. Use the Autoharp for skips in the melody that give trouble.

5. Join in and help the class if they are floundering. If necessary, let them read only those parts of the song they can handle successfully—even if you have to have one of the more experienced children read the difficult parts by himself. It is better to permit the class to learn parts of the song *by rote* than to defeat them with material they are not ready to read.

6. If your class has trouble too often, look for easier songs and give some extra time to developing reading readiness activities.

The fourth level music books in the current series have many excellent reading songs for your use.

RECOGNITION OF SEQUENCE

One valuable assistance in sight reading is the recognition of *sequence*. When a tonal pattern or brief melody is repeated, beginning on a different pitch, this repetition is called a *sequence*. As your students become increasingly aware of this they will find their reading process of many songs greatly accelerated. One particular advantage in this recognition of sequence is that reading by the phrase method rather than the note-by-note process is encouraged. To illustrate let's consider the first part of the song "The Galway Piper."[5]

The Galway Piper

Irish Folk Song

1. Ev - ery   per - son   in   the   na - tion,——
2. When the   wed - ding   bells   are   ring - ing,——
3. When he   walks   the   high - way   peal - ing,——

---

[5] From Book 4 of *Exploring Music* Series, by Boardman and Landis, Copyright © 1966, published by Holt, Rinehart and Winston, Inc. Used by permission of Holt, Rinehart and Winston, Inc.

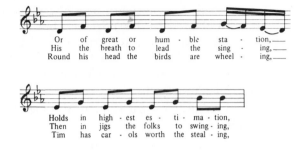

From observing the printed page, the class can discover that the music on the first staff is repeated on the second staff *on a slightly lower pitch.* By developing the skill of looking ahead to see what's coming, children can understand that they should sing the *same melodic contour and rhythm* from the notation on the second staff as they sang from the first staff, but that IT WILL SOUND ONE STEP LOWER THE SECOND TIME.

As is the case in many examples of *sequence,* the music on the third staff *begins exactly* like the music on the first staff. Try to give your class many opportunities to discover and experience SEQUENCE in music. This recognition can also help to develop concepts about FORM.

DEVELOPING RHYTHMIC FEELING

THE BEAT. Be sure that everyone in your class has plenty of opportunity to *discover and respond to* the beat of the music. Many teachers like to have the children bounce and catch a ball. This is a good practice because it is an activity that is natural to children, and it involves using the large muscles of the entire arm.

It is probably most effective when used to express music with *two beats* to the measure: *BOUNCE,* catch. By using an imaginary ball you can attempt *three beats* to the measure: *BOUNCE,* catch, catch; or *four beats: BOUNCE,* catch, catch, catch. Obviously this is more difficult.

However, there is real value to having the children *move in time with the beat* and to discover that music has at least one *STRONG BEAT* in each measure and *that strong beat can be heard and felt.* (The strong beat can also be *seen*—directly after every measure bar—but this visual skill is not always presented to children at this level.)

METER. These experiences can help children understand the term

"METER," which implies an organization of beats into measures. Through experience in hearing the *STRONG* beat and moving in time to it, children can discover that it is followed by one or more weak beats. Those pupils who can strum the Autoharp can show that they understand how the *beat* sounds by performing it.

For a number of complex reasons, some children cannot hear or feel the beat even after much experience with the class. In the case of those whose arms do not come *DOWN* (bounce) on the *STRONG* beat, try using a tom-tom to see if you can match their movement. Sometimes this will help them.

Most pupils normally can respond to the *beat* of the music and can distinguish between simple music that moves in:

TWOS: STRONG, weak   (*or* BOUNCE, catch)
THREES: STRONG, weak, weak   (*or* BOUNCE, catch, catch)
FOURS: STRONG, weak, weak, (*or* BOUNCE, catch, catch,
           weak   catch)

Some teachers like to have the children try to clap *exactly* on the strong beat, and whisper the number of the weak beats. This has the advantage of alerting the children to the *sound* of the beat. This is absolutely vital to a later understanding of the notation.

DEVELOPING A FEELING
FOR TONALITY

THE PENTATONIC SYSTEM. Many old and new songs are built on a PENTATONIC system (five tones).* To explore the sound of the pentatonic scale, play only the black keys on the piano, or the chromatic resonator bells. Your class may enjoy experiences in exploring tonality. This brief plan is suggested:

Play the old familiar song "Loch Lomond" by ear, using only the black keys of the piano (or the chromatic resonator bells). Can the class discover the place in the song where one white key finally has to be played?

> *"Oh you take the high road, and I'll*
> *take the low road,*
> *and I'll be in Scotland a-fore ye.*
> *For me and my true-love will (NE)-ver*
> *meet again*
> *on the bonny, bonny banks of Loch Lomond."*

* See pages 75-78 on the pentatonic scale.

Does the class realize that many Scottish folk songs (as well as Oriental folk music) are built on a PENTATONIC tonal system?

Many of the folk songs of our own nation are also pentatonic, for example:

"All Night, All Day"

"Cindy"

"Lonesome Valley"

"Sourwood Mountain"

"Swing Low, Sweet Chariot"

"This Train"

Students can test known songs using only the black keys. There are many such songs. Perhaps your class can test and find several. They may discover that some old favorites have been changed a little, and are not entirely pentatonic as they were originally.

STRUCTURE OF THE MAJOR SCALE. Children on these levels generally are familiar with the "scale ladder" and recognize that the distances between MI and FA, TI and DO, are smaller than those between other tones of the scale. With a rich background of both aural and visual skills they may be expected to examine in detail the structure of the major scale. You might plan to present the information in this manner:

1. Choose the eight tone bells of the C major scale (C, D, E, F, G, A, B, C) from your tuned resonator bells and place them in correct order on a desk. (You may prefer to use a standard xylophone for this.)

2. Invite one of the children to play all eight bells, beginning with low C.

3. Ask the class to identify the scale they have just heard (the major scale).

4. Have the class sing the major scale using syllables, numbers, and letters.

5. Next, place the major scale on the board, being careful to make the spaces between MI and FA (3 and 4) and TI and DO (7 and 1) smaller than the spaces between the other pitches.

DO	1	C
TI	7	B
LA	6	A
SO	5	G
FA	4	F
MI	3	E
RE	2	D
DO	1	C

Explain that the term "ladder" was used when the students first became acquainted with the scale to indicate that their voices climbed or descended in much the same manner as a person would in going up or coming down a ladder step by step. Then, show that the first step is from DO to RE. The second is from RE to MI. Ask the class what seems different about the relationship of MI and FA on the ladder. They can quickly detect the narrow difference and comment about this. Challenge them to discover another such place in the scale. When they have identified TI, DO:

1. Have a student play the C scale on the bells or xylophone.
2. Ask the class to sing the scale with syllables, numbers, and letters.
3. Draw a staff on the board and ask a student to put middle C (the bottom tone of the scale) in its correct position on the staff.

Invite seven other children to place the remaining tones of the scale on the staff.

AWARENESS OF MINOR TONALITY. The boys and girls became acquainted early with music composed in the minor mode. Continue to help them experience the unusual "color" of minor music. Encourage them to describe the mood to you. Some children will use adjectives such as "lonely," "sad," "dark," or "quiet," but many pupils will also understand that the minor mode can express feelings of frenzy, gaiety, excitement, etc. Assist the class in their evaluation of the mood and develop with them a vocabulary of appropriate terminology. Since many children have a preconceived idea that all minor music is sad, you need to help them discover that it can often be merry. However, there is a basic difference in the sound of major and minor. Creative activities can provide good opportunities for you to explore this distinction with your students. Help them to develop a recognition of major and minor songs when they are played or sung. One device that will help is the piano or Autoharp. Play some major and minor chords to see if the students can identify them; they will enjoy the challenge. Also, show the class how minor chords can be created by lowering the third of a major chord. For example, play G, B, D on the piano or bells. After the students have identified it as a major chord, play G, B♭ , and D to see if they can detect the change from major to minor. Then explain what you have done. Encourage several of the children to play these two chords on the piano with your help. Use other major chords, inviting the students to make minor chords of them. Find as many ways as possible to make this study of the minor mode fascinating to your class.

THEORY GAMES

"MYSTERY WORD." To introduce words that you want the children to have in their music vocabulary, or to review such words already presented, this game may be helpful. Announce at the beginning of the music class that you have a "mystery word" for the day. Point to the symbol that you are going to use—for example, the G (or treble) clef—and tell the students that you will say the name of the symbol several times during the music class. Point out that you will not call special attention to it, but that you will just mention it casually as you talk about the music. (This encourages the pupils to be alert during the music period.) At the end of the period see how many know the name of the symbol.

RIDDLES. Some children like to make up riddles about various words to be included in their music vocabulary. For example:

> Every child has a staff.
>
> It goes to school with him by day.
>
> It goes home with him after school.
>
> It is with him every hour.
>
> What is it?

Answer:

His *hand* (five lines and four spaces).

TREASURE HUNT.[6]   Adapt this game to drill on whatever features of music reading you may be studying:

> Suggest that the first item in a specific song that you want the children to find in the treasure hunt is a measure containing DO MI SO (1 3 5). When you give the signal "GO," the students are to open their books and begin the search. As soon as someone finds the measure he is to stand.
>
> When several are standing the class will check with the first "explorer," to see if he is correct. Continue with SO LA SO (5 6 5) patterns, and so on. The children might search for:
>
> > Time signatures
> > Treble clef
> > A measure of quarter notes
> > A measure of eighth notes
> > A dotted half note

The possibilities are numerous. This is another interesting way of varying drill in music reading.

MUSIC BASEBALL.[7]   Here is how this game can be played:

> Clear the room and arrange it as a baseball diamond. Designate first, second, third, and home bases. (These might be chairs placed in proper places.)
>
> Divide the class into two teams. By guessing a correct number or note name—or other device—decide which team comes to "bat" first. Have a player come to home base. The "pitcher" from the other team asks a question on music theory, such as:
>
> What is a staff?
>
> What is the purpose of the treble clef?
>
> What is a sharp?

[6] Mrs. Doris Ream, former teacher in the Independence Public Schools, contributed this game.

[7] Mrs. Stanley Oleksy, classroom teacher at the Tom D. Korte Elementary School in Kansas City, Mo., created this game.

How does a flat change a note?

What are the lines that divide the staff into measures called?

A flannelgraph could be used to demonstrate the symbols discussed.

If the player gives the correct answer he proceeds to first base. The second batter then "receives" a question from the pitcher. If he answers correctly, the first player goes on to second base and the batter goes to first.

When four questions are answered correctly the first player "comes home," making a score.

Any player missing a question is "out." When three "outs" are made the other team comes to bat. Keep a record of the "runs" and "outs." The team scoring the most "runs" in nine "innings" (or whatever number of "innings" you play) wins the game.

IDENTIFYING SONGS FROM THE SYLLABLE OR NUMBER LADDER. Use a syllable or number ladder at times to assist students in developing tonal skills. For example:

DO	1
TI	7
LA	6
SO	5
FA	4
MI	3
RE	2
DO	1
TI	7
LA	6
SO	5

As an interesting drill ask students to sing various syllables and numbers as you point to them on the "ladder." Such intervals as DO MI SO (1 3 5), RE FA LA (2 4 6), and others can be used. To vary this, "play" a song on the ladder occasionally. At the conclusion see if the students can name the song.

For example, take the song based on the bugle call "Taps." Begin with low SO. *In the rhythm of the bugle call* point to the following syllables:

SO	SO	DO
SO	DO	MI
SO	DO	MI
SO	DO	MI
SO	DO	MI
DO	MI	SO (high SO)
MI	DO	SO (low SO)
SO	SO	DO

IDENTIFYING SONGS FROM PHRASES. At times you can have your students identify songs by phrases that you place on the board. For example, take "America":

Read the phrase with rhythm syllables (tah, tah, tah/tah-ee, tee, tah), then ask the class to sing the syllables or numbers to the phrase. See if anyone knows the name of the song.

RECOGNIZING BASIC TONAL PATTERNS. One activity that might help the students understand that DO or 1 is not always on the same line or space of the staff involves the use of colored charts. An explanation of the procedure should make this clear.

> Cut sixteen large squares of oak tag suitable for syllable or number patterns. Divide them into four sets of four cards each. Number the backs of the cards in each set—1, 2, 3, 4. The cards in each set will picture these syllable (number) patterns:
>
> | | | | | | | | | | | |
> |---|---|---|---|---|---|---|---|---|---|---|
> | DO | RE | MI | FA | SO | (1 | 2 | 3 | 4 | 5) | |
> | DO | MI | SO | | | (1 | 3 | 5) | | | |
> | SO | LA | SO | | | (5 | 6 | 5) | | | |
> | SO | MI | LA | SO | | (5 | 3 | 6 | 5) | | |
>
> Thus there will be four cards that say DO RE MI FA SO (1 2 3 4 5), four that say DO MI SO (1 3 5), etc. Each set, however, will be in a different color. (The four cards in set number one might be green, those in set number

two might be red, etc.) In each set, also, DO (1) will be in a different location. (In the four cards in set number one, DO (1) might be on the first line; in set number two, it might be in the first space, etc.) *Any* syllable patterns and colors can be used.

Examples of 16 Charts

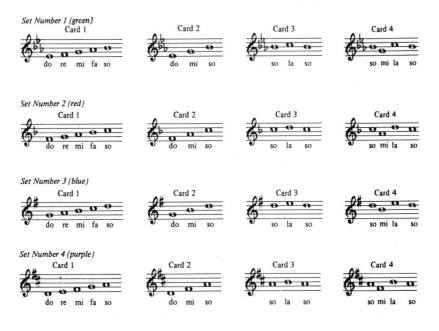

Do not mark syllables or numbers on charts. They are placed here for your help only.

READING PROBLEMS

Later Childhood (Levels 5 and 6)

Students on these levels should have many opportunities to attempt reading new songs. All of their singing, rhythmic, and listening experiences of the past should have brought them to a level of skill that makes this possible. They should be able to recognize:

1. identical phrases, different phrases, and similar phrases;

2. basic tonal patterns they have played, sung, and looked at;

3. melodic contour: UP (by steps or skips), DOWN (by steps or skips), and STRAIGHT ACROSS (repeated pitches);

4. how intervals SOUND and LOOK (see pages 113-115);

5. how the meter is organized into strong and weak beats in the measure and shown by the UPPER FIGURE of the time signature;

6. how the "one-beat" note is shown by the LOWER FIGURE of the time signature and how the note values are related to the value of the "one-beat" note through these rhythm patterns:

   a. extending the "one-beat" note to *sound* LONGER (and exactly how much longer);

   b. dividing the "one-beat" note into two or four EQUAL parts to *sound* "EVEN," or smooth;

   c. dividing the "one-beat" note into TWO UN-EQUAL parts to *sound* "UNEVEN," or jerky;

   d. dividing the BEATS UNEQUALLY so that the "one-beat" note is extended for at least half its value to *sound* "UNEVEN," or jerky;

   e. *seeing* that all dotted notes *sound* "UNEVEN," or jerky.

When your class has had enough experience to develop the above skills, syllables and numbers may still be used to read unfamiliar songs that have difficult melodic and rhythmic patterns. However, many opportunities can be offered to try to read simpler songs with the words right away. If the class has difficulty with any specific part of the song, *the syllables or numbers* can be used to help solve *tonal problems*—just as *chanting* the words can be used as a device to help solve *rhythm problems*. If a simple chordal accompaniment is played on the Autoharp or the piano, it can strengthen the experience by providing a *homophonic framework* for singing pitches accurately.

After the class can read simple, new songs with success, plans can be made to provide *experiences in depth* in:

7. understanding key signatures
8. reading in the minor tonalities
9. performing (through accurate reading) these rhythms:
   a. syncopated patterns
   b. the triplet eighth-note patterns
   c. the triplet quarter-note patterns
   d. $\frac{6}{8}$ meter and its common patterns

LEARNING INTERVALS

An interval is a measurable distance between two pitches. To present this concept to your students you might begin with a familiar analogy. Every morning they come from home to school—two locations. Frequently in their conversation they "measure" the distance from home to school in terms of blocks. One might say he walks four blocks to school, while another may ride eight or ten blocks on his bike. In music it is also possible to measure distances.

After this brief introduction place a staff on the board with two notes on it.

Example:

Pointing to the G, tell the students that you will call this *1*. This note is on a line. The space just above G has no note on it but you must count it anyway as you would one of the blocks between home and school because you are measuring *distance*. Therefore, this space is *2*. Next, of course, is B, which will be *3*. The distance we have measured between G and B is three. Therefore, this interval is called a *third*. Counting in the same manner (the first note is always 1), acquaint them with other intervals such as the fourth, fifth, and octave (interval of an eighth).

Examples:

Fourth   Fifth   Octave

Be sure that your students know that intervals can be counted *down* the staff as well as up. Using the examples just given, here is how they would look in reverse:

We speak of a "fourth up" or a "fifth down," etc.

Activities to reinforce this learning could include:

1. Singing of intervals with syllables, numbers, or letters. Examples:

Third:	DO	MI
	1	3
	G	B

Fourth:	DO	FA
	1	4
	G	C

Fifth:	DO	SO
	1	5
	G	D

Octave:	DO	DO
	1	1(8)
	G	G

2. Playing of intervals on tuned resonator bells, xylophone, or piano.

3. Melodic dictation: Teacher plays intervals on bells, xylophone, piano, or sings them while students write them on the staff on the chalkboard or on manuscript paper at their desks.

4. Identification (by individual students or competitive teams) of measures of intervals written on the chalkboard.

USING TUNED RESONATOR BELLS TO LEARN CHORDS

One particularly effective aid in teaching chording is the use of the tuned resonator bells. This instrument is so fascinating to children that they are immediately receptive to any instruction that uses it.

Let's consider how chording might be done with the song "Clementine."[8]

1. Have the class sing "Clementine."

2. Choose seven students to play the bells. Give the G, B, and D bells to three and ask them to stand at the front of the room. The other four children should take the D, F♯, A, and C bells. Suggest that they stand at one side of the room, near the front.

3. Encourage the students with the bells to "experiment" with them. Show them how to strike the metal bars and permit them to practice. (It is important that the action of the striking be similar to drawing one's finger away from a hot stove. If the mallet is left on the bar after striking it, the tone is deadened.)

4. Tell the class that you will now sing the song alone while the bells play the accompaniment. Explain to the students not playing that you want them to listen and to enjoy the total effect. Ask them to listen intently to the harmony.

5. As you sing point to each chord group when it is time for them to play. For example, above the first part of the word "cavern" is the letter G. Point to the boys and girls holding the G, B, and D bells as you sing "cav—."

Clementine

Music and Words by Percy Montrose

1. In a cav - ern, in a can - yon, Ex - ca - vat - ing for a
2. Light she was, and like a fair - y, And her shoes were num - ber

mine, Dwelt a min - er for - ty - nin - er, And his
nine, Her - ring box - es with - out top - ses, San - dals

---

[8] Found in Book 5 of *Silver Burdett Music Series,* published by General Learning Corporation; Book 5 of *This Is Music for Today* Series, published by Allyn and Bacon, Inc.; and in Book 4 of *The Spectrum of Music* Series, published by Macmillan Publishing Co., Inc.

When you sing "mine" indicate to the boys and girls with the D, F♯ , A, and C bells that they should play.

6. After you have sung one or two stanzas ask the class if they can find anything in the song that helped to determine which chord should be played and at what time. The class can discover the letters above the staff and read all the letters used during the song.

7. When the class understands that these letters are chord markings, ask how many *kinds* of chords there are in the song. When the students discover that there are two different kinds, ask them to name them. (G and D_7.)

8. Help the students discover that a chord usually has three or more tones. Call attention to the fact that the G and D_7 chords differ—one has three tones, the other four. Ask them to look at the markings for the two chords in the book and see if they can detect a difference there. The 7 will immediately be apparent to them. Some teachers do not involve the class in detailed theory at this point. However, others include a review of how to build chords by skipping and simply explain that a seventh chord has four tones.

9. Sing the song again, inviting the class to join with you while the bells play.

10. Now ask the students standing in the chord group of three to "spell" their chord. (Each student will give the letter name of his bell.) It is best to have the three students positioned in proper order—G, B, and D. Have the class spell the chord. Identify this as the G major chord.

11. Invite some student to draw the chord on the chalkboard. Sometimes a student will place the notes in this manner:

This gives the teacher an opportunity to explain that the notes must all be sounded at once to be a chord; therefore the notes must be written in this manner:

12. Ask the students in the chord group of four to spell their chord. (Be sure the one with the F♯ bell *says* "sharp.") Have the class spell the chord and ask them what was different about it besides the fact that there were four tones. When someone calls attention to the fact that there was a sharp have him specify *what* sharp. (*f* sharp.) Identify the chord as D₇ and have a student draw the notes on the chalkboard.

13. Now ask the class to look at the song in their books to find some indication that F♯ might be one of the bells used. (They should be able to find the F♯ in the key signature.)

14. Ask the class to look once again at the chord markings in the song. Which chord is used at the beginning and at the end? When they discover that it is G explain that important people are sometimes called "key" people because of the position they hold. It is the same with music. The chord that appears at the beginning or end of a song is the "key" chord because the song is based on it. Thus it holds a very important position. Establish with them that this song, then, is in the key of G and G has one sharp—F♯.

15. As other students replace those playing the bells challenge them to arrange themselves in proper chord order. Have them read the letters on their bells so that the class may "check" them to see if they are correct. Then have all the students spell the chords. Keep emphasizing that the song is in the key of *G* and that G has one *sharp*, which is F-sharp.

16. Interspersed with this procedure should be frequent opportunities for the boys and girls to sing

the song with bell accompaniment. Encourage student "directors" to come to the front and "lead" the chord groups.

You may find it best not to attempt this entire plan in the first music lesson, but to extend it over two or three days. This, of course, will depend upon the interest of the students, the time you have to give to the music class that day, and other factors. The Autoharp, guitar, accordion, or ukulele could be used in combination with the tuned resonator bells after the first few lessons. You and your students will enjoy experimenting with these instruments.

METER SENSING

Another way to strengthen reading skills while learning a rote song is to help the children become increasingly aware of the time signature and its meaning. Basically, they have to experience the meter through repeated practice before they really know what it means. To emphasize this point and make the purpose clear let's look at the song "The Spanish Guitar."[9]

The Spanish Guitar

[9] From Book 5 of *Discovering Music Together* Revised Series, published by Follett Educational Corp., 1970.

1. Have the students learn the song.

2. After singing the song a few times suggest that the boys and girls clap each downbeat (first beat of each measure) while they sing.

3. Talk briefly with the students about instruments associated with the Spanish people. (Their responses frequently will be "tambourines, castanets, and maracas.")

4. Ask them to describe the sound of castanets. (Sharp clicking.) Encourage them to think of some action they could do that would sound like castanets. (Some may begin "clucking" their tongues while others snap their fingers.) Decide with the class which might be the more appropriate action. (The snapping of fingers is usually chosen because its tone is sharper, more nearly resembling the castanets; frequently the Spanish people use clapping and snapping of fingers as the only rhythmic accompaniment to their songs and dances.)

5. Sing the song again while the students play their "castanets" on each downbeat. (Perhaps someone could bring real castanets to class.)

6. Since the song centers around the guitar as an instrument, suggest that the boys play "guitars" while the girls play "castanets." (As the boys "strum" point out that the downbeats should perhaps have a stronger, longer motion than the inner beats.) At this point ask the class to find out how many beats there are in a measure. (The top number of the time signature (3) indicates the number of beats or counts in each measure.)

7. Play the song on the piano or play a recording, and ask the students to count "ONE, TWO, THREE," to the music as they play their "instruments."

8. Reverse sides so that both boys and girls will have an opportunity to feel the downbeat with all kinds of "instruments" as well as the three counts to each measure.

Of course, there could be many variations to this procedure. Other instruments could be used, half the class could sing while the other group played "instruments" and counted the meter, or real instruments could be used to give greater authenticity and pleasure. At the conclusion a dance could be created, accompanied by the pretended or real instruments.

MAKING A PERCUSSION SCORE

Children on these levels can profitably spend some time in making up a percussion score (notation for rhythm instruments). This score should be constructed from the simple rhythm patterns that the class already knows, and is valuable in *relating the symbols* of the note values *to the sound* of the rhythm. Let's take, for example, the song "Home on the Range": [10]

1. Before attempting to make a percussion score, be sure that the class knows the song and enjoys singing

[10] Found in Book 3 of *Discovering Music Together* Revised Series, published by Follett Publishing Co.; Book 3 of *This Is Music for Today* Series, published by Allyn and Bacon, Inc., and in Book 6 of *The Spectrum of Music* Series, published by Macmillan Publishing Co., Inc.

it. If not, select some other song. The same rhythmic principles will apply.

2. The class can discover that this music is built rhythmically on a beat that sounds: STRONG, weak, weak (measure bar); STRONG, weak, weak (measure bar); over and over, to the end of the song. (This we can *see* by looking at the upper number of the time signature $\frac{3}{4}$. We can also feel, hear, and move to this three-beat meter.

3. Let half the class clap together on the STRONG beat while the other half sings the song. Alternate. Sometimes the pupils are taught to say "ONE" as they clap the STRONG beat, and to whisper "two, three" on the weak beats.

4. The class will soon realize that this song does *not* begin on the "ONE" (the strong beat, or the downbeat). We don't sing "*OH* give me a home," but "Oh *GIVE* me a home." The word "*GIVE*" is on the STRONG beat—the first beat of the first full measure. The class can be led to discover that the STRONG beat in this song always comes on the *first note or rest* immediately following the measure bar. This song begins on the upbeat, or "pick-up."

SCORING THE STRONG BEAT.   Let us now choose some instrument to play only the STRONG beat (or the "ONE") in each measure. Children often choose the drum to play the STRONG beats, because it has a loud "boom" that seems suitable. (If some other instrument is selected, try it to see if the class finds it appropriate.)

When the instrument has been selected, we can draw a score that tells exactly when it is to be played.

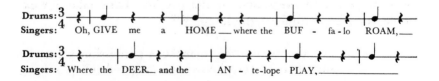

The class can (and should) notice that a percussion score for rhythm instruments of this kind needs *only one line*—not the full five lines and four spaces of the ordinary staff. Your children may be able to explain that these instruments are playing *only the rhythm, not the tune.* When a tune (melody) is played we need the full five lines and four spaces of the staff to show how high or how low the tune goes (melodic direction), a concept involving pitch.

This may be as far as you will care to go in the initial presentation. The class will notice that the first and second phrases both begin on the upbeat ("pick-up"). They can also find that at the end of the second phrase the word "play" is held for five beats, and that the drum plays on the STRONG beat of the fourth measure (second phrase) even though the voices hold the same note.

So far we have shown the class just the first two phrases played by one instrument that plays only on the STRONG beat (the downbeat, or the "ONE").

Some of the children will probably be able to tell you which phrases are exactly alike, and which ones are nearly alike. They can be helped to realize that:

1. Phrases 1, 3, and 7 are alike.
2. Phrases 4 and 8 are often alike (or nearly alike) rhythmically, depending on the part of the West where the song was sung. (There are several versions of this song, each slightly different from the others. It will be best to use it exactly as written in your music book because we are trying to develop reading skills. If this song is too confusing to the class, use another song.)
3. Phrases 2 and 6 are nearly alike rhythmically. The differences (if any) may occur in the *first full measure* of each phrase: "deer and the" in the second phrase, and "deer and the" in the sixth phrase.

In making these comparisons you may need to remind the class that we are concerned only with the *note values.* For example, the tune is usually not quite the same in phrases 2 and 6, but remember—the percussion score *does not show melody.* Melody is shown on the full staff. This score is for *rhythm* only.

Because your class will probably want to write out the percussion score for the entire song on large pieces of paper or tag board, it is a good thing to know *which phrases are alike.* Often, in initial experiences we use the *same instruments in the same way* on the

phrases that are alike. This will *emphasize the same ideas* that the
music is trying to bring out, and can help the children understand
form in music.

SCORING THE WEAK BEATS.   You might now call attention briefly
to the drum part: it emphasized the STRONG beat, or the
"ONE," of every measure, so a quarter note appears on each
downbeat. On the weak beats when this instrument does not play,
quarter rests appear on the score.

Now let us choose an instrument to play all three times each
measure, *exactly on the beats.* Your class might choose the
rhythm sticks for this part. If so, the score for the sticks will look
like this:

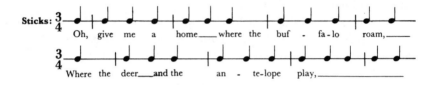

When the drum and the rhythm sticks play together the two parts
will look like this:

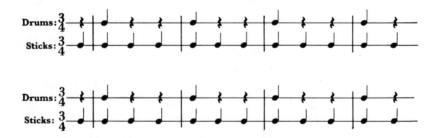

This time the words have been left out of the score in order to
make the note values of the rhythm pattern stand out in each part.
The class will be able to observe that the drum is playing only on
the "ONE," or the downbeat, of each measure (the strong beat),
and that the sticks are playing on all three beats in the measure.
Since this music begins on the upbeat, the sticks start to play (on
the upbeat, or third beat) *before* the drum comes in on the downbeat (or first beat of the measure).

Vertical Reading Experiences

When writing a percussion score (or any score) we must be careful to write the parts directly underneath each other. For example, the sticks have a quarter note on the pick-up (upbeat: in this case, the third beat of the measure), and *directly above* this quarter note is the quarter rest for the drum. After the measure bar, the drum has a quarter note to play on the downbeat (or the "ONE") and so do the sticks. The quarter note part for the sticks is shown *directly below* the corresponding quarter note in the drum part. This same careful notation is used throughout in order that we can see exactly which parts are played together. In music we not only read from left to right, but often vertically at the same time.

ADDING THE FIRST RHYTHM
PATTERN $\frac{3}{4}$ (♩. ♪ ♩)

So far, our percussion score shows *the basic, steady beat* of the music. The meter is very important, but its steady repetition makes a monotonous sound unless we add some *variety of note values* to make an interesting *rhythm pattern*.

If we will observe each phrase carefully in the book, we will find an interesting *one-measure rhythm pattern* that appears in the first, second, third, fourth, seventh, and eighth phrases: $\frac{3}{4}$ (♩. ♪ ♩). If the class is inexperienced, you may need to:

1. Help the children locate this rhythm pattern in the book, and see how many times it appears in the song.
2. Teach the children how it sounds, by having them clap or tap the pattern after you have established a steady, audible beat.
3. Select an appropriate instrument to play this pattern in the percussion score.

Because this pattern may sound a little like horses' hooves when it is played over and over, sometimes children like to score it for castanets or for cocoanut shells.

Also, because our purpose is to *provide some variety* at this point, we may want to use this rhythm pattern only on the phrases where it is *not found in the melody:* the fifth and sixth phrases.[11] The castanets or cocoanut shells will give a slow, galloping kind of effect that will look like this when scored:

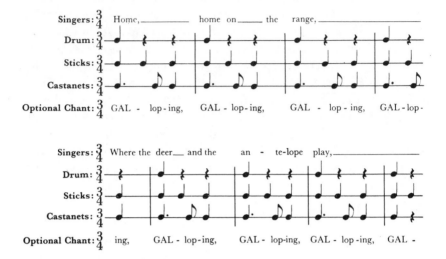

The optional chant has been added with the first rhythm pattern $\frac{3}{4}$ (♩.♪♩) to help the inexperienced children, but your class may not need it. Its use only emphasizes the fact that the first syllable, "GAL," is heard exactly on the first beat with the drum and the sticks. The third syllable, "ING," is heard exactly on the third beat with the sticks. The second syllable, "LOP," however, is heard all by itself on the *second half of the second beat*. This is what makes the castanet part interesting.

The proper notation of this rhythm pattern in the percussion score *shows exactly when the eighth note is played* by the castanets. The children will probably need some experience in pointing to the dotted quarter note over the syllable "GAL." It is found *directly below the quarter note* on the first beat of the parts for the drum and the sticks. The quarter note over the syllable "ING" is found *directly below the quarter note* on the third beat of the part played by the sticks.

The eighth note over the syllable "LOP," however, comes halfway between the second and third beats shown in the two parts

[11] In some versions of this song, this rhythm pattern is found in the sixth phrase, over the word "an-te-lope." It is best to use the song exactly as it appears in your music book, of course.

written above. Sometimes this visual spacing helps the children tremendously, because it gives a clear picture of how *the second beat is divided into two equal parts.* On the other hand, understanding this visual spacing requires that a child not only read the note values from left to right, but that he also observe the score vertically. This, of course, is not easy for all students to do. Those who cannot master the visual aspects should be helped to perform the rhythm pattern *by ear* without feeling undue pressure *to see it as well.*

ADDING A SECOND RHYTHM PATTERN (♩ ♫)

Because the first rhythm pattern contained a sound (eighth note) on *the second half of the second beat,* we should try to find a rhythm pattern that has a sound on the second half of either the first or the third beat. We find such a pattern (♩ ♫) in the first, third, and seventh phrases of the song, and sometimes in the second phrase ("deer and the") in some editions.

Since this pattern is made up of a half note on the first two beats, we can chant: "ho-me," followed by a quick "where the." This chanting may help inexperienced pupils to hear and perform the rhythm pattern accurately, but you can accomplish the same thing by other methods. The important thing is for the children to *hear and perform the correct sound of the rhythm* whenever they see the pattern of the note values.

This rhythm pattern can be added to the percussion score in the same manner as the first one.

1. Help the class clap or tap the pattern accurately after you have established a steady, audible beat.

2. Explore the possibilities of the available rhythm instruments, and select one to play the second rhythm pattern. Remember, the ♩ gets two beats and we will need an instrument that can play a *long tone* (like the shake of the tambourine or the trill of the triangle).

3. Select a few phrases of the song where this pattern will show to the best advantage (such as the fourth and eighth phrases, where it does not appear).

4. Score the pattern for the selected instrument:

Fourth Phrase:

The class should discover that the eighth phrase can be scored like the fourth phrase, except for the last measure of the eighth phrase (which is the end of the song). When your class experiments with sounds, they may want to score the ending of the song something like this:

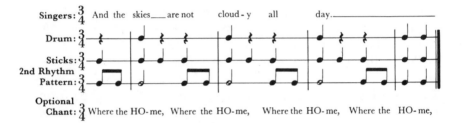

Be sure the notation of this rhythm pattern is carefully spaced in relation to the parts above it. The children should notice that the first of the two eighth notes (the one directly above the word "where") is played *exactly on the third beat* of the measure, and therefore is written *directly below:*

1. the quarter rest on the third beat of the drum part, and

2. the quarter note on the third beat of the part played by the sticks.

The second eighth note (the one directly above the word "the") is shown halfway between the third beat and the measure bar, because it is properly played on the second half of the third beat.

1. In this rhythm pattern, the two eighth notes together show clearly how *the third beat is divided equally into two parts.*

2. The half note shows clearly how *one single sound can be sustained for two full beats.*

CREATING A THIRD
RHYTHM PATTERN

By studying our percussion score, we can see that so far we have:

1. The drum playing on the *strong beat* of each measure.
2. The sticks playing on the *strong beat* and also on the *two weak beats* of each measure.
3. The castanets, or cocoanut shells, playing a rhythm pattern containing a dotted quarter note on the first beat and the first half of the second beat. *An eighth note is on the second half of the second beat.*
4. Some suitable instrument of our choice playing a rhythm pattern in which there are two eighth notes *on the third beat,* and *a half note that is heard for the first two beats of the measure.*

The drum and the sticks provide the basic beat that we cannot do without, while the castanets and selected instrument each play a different rhythm pattern that adds variety to the steady beat. These two rhythm patterns were taken directly from the song.

Can your pupils find which beat in our score *is not evenly divided into two equal parts?* Those children who understand the notation of the first and second rhythm patterns will look for the beat in which there are no eighth notes, and they will find, of course, that the first beat in each measure has not been divided.

Because we always seek variety in rhythm patterns, the third one that we are making up could simply show two eighth notes on the first beat. It would look like this:

Some children like to add a half note instead of the two rests, which is an interesting kind of reversal of the second rhythm pattern. It would look like this:

Whether or not the half note is used instead of the two quarter rests, the unique part of the third rhythm pattern is that it has two eighth notes on the first beat. This division of the first beat into two equal sounds is not found in any other part.

This pattern should be added in the same manner as the preceding ones: 1) by clapping, 2) by selecting a suitable instrument, 3) by selecting the phrases of the song where the pattern will sound the most effective, and 4) by adding the pattern to the score.

THE TOTAL SCORE

When completed, the entire score will look like this (allowing for the variation in creating the third rhythm pattern):

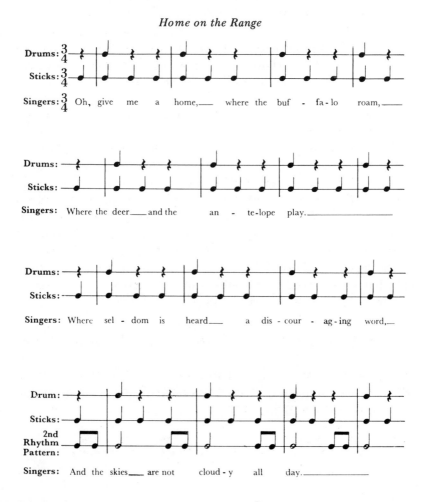

Home on the Range

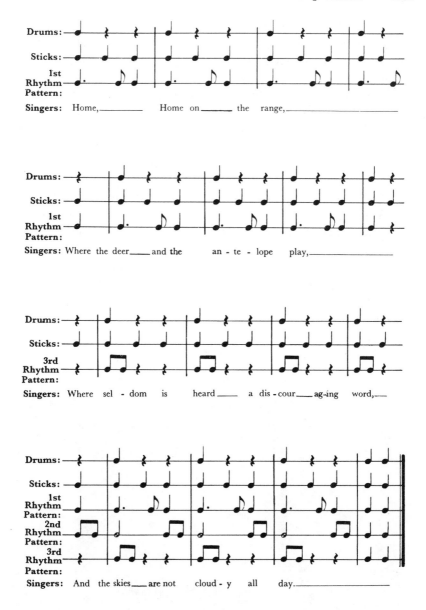

Theory Game

MUSICAL ROBOT

The robot shown in the picture is a successful teaching aid, and holds a great deal of fascination for the children. The music teacher finds a variety of uses for the mechanical man, but originally the robot was the outgrowth of class work on a unit of Electronic Music. The robot's voice comes from prerecorded tapes made by fifth and sixth graders.

The tapes give a variety of musical directions for the class to follow. Electronic synthesizers or synthesizer boxes were used to record rhythm patterns, and the "beep" was used to represent the quarter note. White sound was chosen by the class to represent rests. The robot is equipped with dry cell batteries that activate lights. The individual child inside the robot presses the lights so that they will blink in rhythm with the sounds on the tape.

Although the robot has been used at all age levels, the fifth and sixth graders at this particular school have learned to take dictation—both rhythmic and melodic. This skill greatly enhances their ability to read music, and the tapes used are directly related to the specific learnings planned for the unit of study.

For additional suggestions about music reading, see Chapter 6, "Instruments." For easy reference, page numbers are given here

Mrs. Lorna Dee Mistele and her pupils use this "Robot Game" to help them remember facts about music theory and history (photo, courtesy of The Birmingham (Mich.) Eccentric).

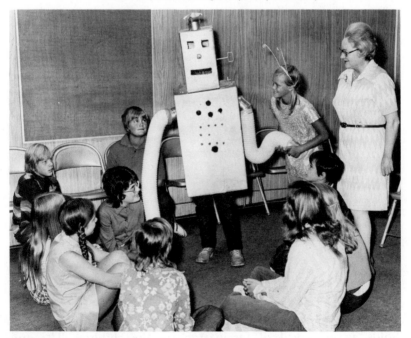

for some of the more common problems associated with reading:

> Dynamics 234, 273
> Form 234, 235, 243, 275
> Harmony 251-254, 262-271
> Key Signatures 261, 267-268, 271
> Meter Signatures 235, 242, 243, 261, 265
> Note Values 243, 260
> Pitch Concepts 234, 247-249, 276-278
> Pitch Names 249-254, 259-260, 277
> Tempo 234

SUGGESTED INDIVIDUAL
AND SMALL GROUP PROJECTS
FOR METHODS COURSES

Early Childhood (Levels 1 and 2)

1. Make a list of suitable records and well-known songs to use for *phrasing* with balloons. Toss large balloons back and forth gently to the phrases of the music. (The class will not be ready for this activity, of course, until the children have had success in discovering where phrases begin and end.) Emphasize the *floating* quality of the music, and remember that the purpose of the activity is to help develop phrase feeling. Be sure the balloons move *in time with the music.*

2. Make a list of all the songs you can find appropriate for these levels in which the first and third phrases are *exactly alike.* Make another list in which the second and fourth phrases are exactly alike; another, in which the first and second phrases are exactly alike, and another, in which the third and fourth phrases are exactly alike. Use these lists to develop a repertory of songs that can be taught by rote and then used for playing "phrase games."

3. Prepare a flannelgraph for use in the reading readiness program. Make notes, treble clef, and bars of felt. Indicate the difference in note value by color (*e.g.,* half—blue; quarter—brown; eighth—red). When

the flannelgraph is not in actual use during the class period, permit a student or committee to prepare it as a bulletin board emphasizing the problem that is being considered for the week (*e.g.,* direction of the melody, tonal patterns, or note values).

4. From the text for these levels of one of the current series, list all of the songs that would be suitable for: the study of phrases; tonal patterns; rhythm instrument accompaniment.

5. Try playing the melodies of the following songs on the piano or tone bells, using *only the black* keys:

> Peter, Peter, Pumpkin Eater
> Band of Angels (see page 84)
> Cindy
> All Night, All Day
> Lonesome Valley
> Sourwood Mountain
> Swing Low, Sweet Chariot
> This Train
> America the Beautiful

6. List any of the above songs that cannot be played (using the *black keys only*). They are not in the pentatonic scale. Discover which tones of the major scale are in the pentatonic scale, then write a sample of each scale, beginning on the same note.

7. Keep a list of pentatonic songs (including any of those above) that can be played on melody instruments and the piano—*using only the black keys.* Select your favorites, and again, using only the black keys (or pentatonic Orff instruments), create an ostinato to go with the music.

Middle Childhood (Levels 3 and 4)

1. Select one of the music texts for these levels and make a list of all the songs with four phrases that have:

   a. identical first and third phrases

   b. identical second and fourth phrases

   Learn to play a "phrase game" in which four children hold up a colored card in turn as each phrase is sung. Cards of the same color are held up for identical phrases, cards of contrasting colors for those phrases that are not identical.

2. Think of two other ways in which identical phrases and contrasting phrases can be shown through visual aids similar to the cards mentioned in number 1 above. Devise a simple game using these visual aids to give the class an opportunity to gain experience in musical form (design).

3. Select one of the series books for these levels and make a list of all the songs that do not begin on "ONE" (the downbeat; the first beat of the measure).

4. Select one of the series music books for these levels and make a list of all the songs that are *not* written in the major mode.

5. Make a list of recordings in which tonal and rhythm

The music theory game "Quizmo" is adapted for individualized instruction in a learning center (photo by Patrick Burke).

patterns are simple enough for these students to identify easily.

6. Create a theory game that will provide interesting drill on the music symbols these students should know.

Later Childhood (Levels 5 and 6)

1. Prepare a flannelgraph or some large oak tag charts featuring the symbols of notation to be studied on these levels.

2. Make a comparison of the syllable system of reading with the number system. Point out the strong and weak points of each.

3. Make a list of songs that have:

    similar and identical phrases;
    dotted rhythm patterns (particularly the dotted quarter followed by the eighth);
    harmony in thirds.

4. Choose ten Latin-American songs from the basic series and write a percussion score for each.

5. Suggest actions or dramatizations for several songs that would emphasize response to meter.

4

Rhythm

MOVING TO MUSIC

Even before he begins to crawl, the normal child expresses himself rhythmically. He waves his hands, kicks his feet, pushes, and pulls. From those earliest moments he has been moving actively. His body and mind are "tuned" for this.

FUNDAMENTAL MOVEMENT
TO RHYTHM

Early Childhood (Levels 1 and 2)

By the time he arrives at school the child will have experimented with every type of *fundamental movement to rhythm* with which he is concerned—running, walking, skipping, hopping, leaping, sliding, galloping, swinging, and many others. He will have been a train sweeping down the track, an airplane zooming in the sky, a pony racing across the plains. As a teacher of young children you will want to encourage this uninhibited activity, attempting, at the same time, to help each child relate his movement to the music he hears. You may find that playing these *fundamental rhythms* (running, skipping, etc.) on a wood block or drum *in the tempo of the child's own motion* will help him to become aware of the rhythm. He can concentrate on the rhythm alone, without having a tune to distract him. Many teachers like to ask a child to run on tiptoe and then "match the child's feet" with the beat of the tom-tom, some other drum, or wood block. This is an ideal approach because it emphasizes the necessity of *keeping in time with the beat.* Not all small children are able to do this, so the use of the tom-tom ensures that the beat will be in time with the child. Tell the child to keep a steady pace, however, so that *the beat is a steady recurring sound.*

As soon as you have "matched the child's feet" with the steady beat of the drum, choose other children to join in *rhythmically* without stopping the beat. When all these children are running in rhythm *exactly with the rhythm,* change the speed to a slow walk, or to a skipping rhythm (a jerky "long-short, long-short"). The rest of the class should also be involved in this activity, and may use their hands as "feet" to move *in time to the beat.* The purpose of the activity is to do what the tom-tom *tells the feet to do.* The teacher can also "match the child's feet" through the use of the Autoharp, which is very useful in providing a simple accompaniment for specific responses to rhythm.

USING THE AUTOHARP
FOR RHYTHMIC MOVEMENT

With the left hand, play the chord "buttons" of the Autoharp. With the right hand, strum running, skipping, galloping, or marching rhythms as follows:

> Running—even short strokes in rapid succession
>
> Skipping—long-short, long-short
>
> Marching—even short strokes in march tempo
>
> Walking—even long strokes in walking tempo of students.

Some good chord series to play with the left hand (play each chord four times, then repeat the pattern) are:

G	C	D_7	G
C	F	G_7	C
F	B♭	C_7	F

Sometimes pupils find it easier to respond to such an accompaniment, because the chords are satisfying and simple and there is no melody to prevent the children from hearing the rhythm easily.

These experiences with the tom-tom and Autoharp will be a good readiness activity for the addition of a musical accompaniment later. When you do add music you may want to use the piano. If you play, you can choose instrumental selections from your music books for rhythms; at times, you may want to play rhythmic variations using a simple song. You can adapt the melody to suit the rhythm. Just play the notes of the melody in the rhythm pattern you desire. For example:

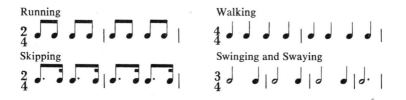

If you do not play the piano you will find appropriate records helpful.

SUGGESTED RECORDINGS FOR RHYTHMIC MOVEMENT

"Ballet" (Gluck)	RCA Basic R. I	(run)
"Barcarolle" (Rubinstein)	RCA Basic R. I	(skip, gallop)
"Basic Rhythms for Classroom Use"	Rhythm Record RRC-103	(directions on record)
"Childhood Rhythms, Album I"	Ruth Evans Records	(directions in album)
"Children's Rhythms in Symphony" (Wood)	Bowmar 027	(directions in album)
"Clowns" (Mendelssohn)	RCA Basic R. I	(run, skip, leap)
"Czardas" (Allegro) from *Coppélia* (Delibes)	RCA VIC-1130/ VICS-1130	(leap, jump, hop)
"Dance of the Little Swans" (Tchaikovsky)	RCA Adventures I	(run)
"Fairies" (Schubert)	RCA Basic R. I	(sway)
"Galloping Horses" (Anderson)	RCA Basic R. I	(gallop)
"Gigue" (Corelli)	RCA Basic R. I	(skip, gallop)
"Gnomes" (Reinhold)	RCA Basic R. I	(tiptoe)
"High Stepping Horses" (Anderson)	RCA Basic R. I	(giant steps)

"Indoors When It Rains"	C.R. Guild 1021	(directions on record)
"March" (Rossini-Britten)	RCA Adventures I	(march)
"March" from *Summer Day Suite* (Prokofiev)	RCA Adventures I	(march)
"March in F" (Anderson)	RCA Basic R. I	(march)
"Military March" (Anderson)	RCA Basic R. I	(march)
"My Playful Scarf"	C. R. Guild 1019	(directions on record)
"Nothing to Do"	C. R. Guild 1012	(directions on record)
"Out of Doors"	Young People's R. 724	(directions on record)
"Promenade" from *Pictures at an Exhibition* (Moussorgsky)	RCA VIC-1273	(march or walk)
"Rhythmic Activities Album" (Bassett & Chestnut), Vol. 1	Children's Music Center	(directions in album)
"Rhythms" (Album)	ABC AS-22	(directions in album)
"Sousa Marches"	Bowmar 127	(six marches, plus the "Star Spangled Banner")
"Sparks" (Moszkowski)	RCA Basic R. I	(run, hop)
"Sunday in the Park"	C. R. Guild 1010	(directions on record)
"Theme for Skipping" (Anderson)	RCA Basic R. I	(skip)
"Valsette" (Borowski)	RCA Basic R. I	(sway)
"Visit to My Little Friend"	C. R. Guild 1017	(directions on record)
"Walking Song" (Thomson)	RCA Adventures I	(walk)

When using records for any kind of rhythmic response, be sure the children *listen carefully* to the music at least once all the way through. Some teachers like to have their students close their eyes while they listen and *think* of what their feet will do. A second listening is often provided, so that the class can show with their hands *how their feet will match the rhythm* of the music.

These *fundamental* rhythms—skipping, galloping, running, marching, walking, swaying, jumping, hopping, tiptoeing, taking "giant steps," and other movements descriptive of animals, trees, and water—are all *specific* ways in which children respond naturally to rhythm. Try to include some *specific rhythmic movement* every day. These activities are easy to present, and they are important to the child's total growth and development. Musically they are very important because they *emphasize moving in time with the rhythm.* Sensing the beat is one of the early *music-reading-readiness* experiences that can enable the child to understand and interpret the printed page as he matures musically. Of course, you will be eager to help the child "tune his ear" to the music and give an accurate physical response; however, if the emphasis on refinement of skills overshadows the pleasure of the moment, the child may withdraw emotionally. When used effectively, good music has just the opposite effect—it draws out the shy and diffident. One technique that sometimes helps is the use of paper bag masks. When a shy child puts on a pony mask he frequently is freed from himself and gallops with gay abandon. A rabbit mask for hopping, a mouse or cat for running, will add a dramatic spark to these basic movements. Maintain a happy atmosphere.

You will want to use as much space as you have available for these rhythmic experiences. Some buildings have an all-purpose room that is excellent for activities involving rhythmic movement. As much as possible, provide the opportunity for free use of the body's large muscles. If you don't have access to an all-purpose room, you should probably have only a few children participate at the same time. This type of activity requires ample space for free movement.

Middle and Later Childhood
(Levels 3, 4, 5, and 6)

Although the students on these levels may not want to express themselves in exactly the same manner as those on the first and second levels, they will still be interested in giving specific and creative responses to music.

Earlier the students had many opportunities to develop their skills in such fundamental rhythms as skipping, walking, and marching. There is a need to continue this activity, although the approach should be changed. It is hoped, by this time, that these basic skills will have become so refined that they can now become incorporated in singing games and folk dances. This means that the students will still be running, walking, and skipping to the beat of the music, but as a part of a more complex activity than on the earlier levels. A more complete discussion of singing games and folk dances will appear under that category later in the chapter (see pp. 138–146).

MARCHING FORMATIONS

Unlike the fundamental rhythms of skipping and running that are frequently incorporated in singing games and dances, marching is not commonly used in these activities. Therefore you should give special attention to this rhythm. Children delight in "drills"— different figures and patterns that give a special "flavor" to marching. Criss-cross weaving, pivoting in groups, and the "grand march" exemplify some of the techniques that are so appealing to this age child.

ACTING OUT ROUNDS

Another popular activity on these levels that incorporates one of the fundamental rhythms (walking to music) is that of acting out rounds. (This might be particularly successful on levels 5 and 6.)

Keeping lines straight is a challenge in this "wheel" marching drill (photo by Patrick Burke).

The singing of rounds is often most enjoyable to children. When the class has become adept at this skill they may try "acting them out." This provides additional experience in moving to the beat of the music and in feeling the phrase. For example, let's consider the old favorite "Three Blind Mice."[1]

Actions:

Three blind mice	3 steps forward, knee-bend
Three blind mice	3 steps backward, turn left
See how they run	3 steps left, knee-bend
See how they run	3 steps backward, face center
They all ran after the farmer's wife	3 steps forward, knee-bend
She cut off their tails with a carving knife	3 steps backward (clap hands cymbal-fashion on the word "cut"), 1 step in place
Did you ever see such a sight in your life	with right hand over eyes, turn in place
As three blind mice?	3 stamps in place

Directions:

Form a square with four lines of children. Any number of children may be used in each line but it is usually best not to have less than five or six or more than eight or nine. Work out the actions first, with one line at a time. When the children in all four lines have mastered the directions well enough to be secure in what they are doing, then you might try just two lines first as a round.

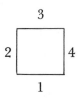

Suggest that line 1 begin. The children move toward line 3, singing and doing the actions for the first two phrases—"three blind mice, three blind mice." When they have returned to their original position they turn to the left, beginning the next phrase—"see how they run." As they do this line 3 begins with "three blind mice." Proceed with the rest of the song (one time through only). While lines 1 and 3 rest, ask lines 2 and 4 to practice this. Line 2 might begin, followed by 4. In each case the first line sings "three blind mice, three blind mice." Then the second line begins.

[1] The directions for this round are so universal that the original source is unknown to the authors.

If this "trial run" has gone well, try all four lines now. Begin with line 1, followed by 2, 3, and 4. Sing the song through only once. If this is successful, try doing the actions while singing the song through three times. This is the last step. When all four lines can sing the song through three times, always keeping their proper places, the round has been mastered!

You will notice that at the beginning of each phrase there is a change of direction. Such acting out of rounds can be most helpful in giving additional experience in the feeling for phrase.

IDENTIFYING FUNDAMENTAL
RHYTHMS AS EVEN
OR UNEVEN

Still another approach to fundamental rhythms on these levels is identifying them as even or uneven (jerky) rhythms. Play on a wood block or drum one of the basic rhythms, e.g., running (short, short, short, short, etc.) and ask one of the students first to identify the *specific* rhythm (running), then to state whether it was even or uneven (in this case, even). Repeat this procedure with other rhythms, giving the students opportunity at times to be the "teacher." After successful experiences using the wood block or drum, you might want to play excerpts from rhythm records to test the children's aural perception.

Running (short, short, short, short)	Even
Skipping (long-short, long-short)	Uneven or jerky
Walking (moderately slow beats)	Even
Marching (sharp, staccato beats)	Even
Galloping (short-long, short-long)	Uneven or jerky

CREATIVE (INTERPRETIVE) MOVEMENT

Early Childhood (Levels 1 and 2)

A child is normally creative. He can be anything he wishes—a person, an animal, a machine, or whatever. He can change swiftly from a cowboy to a policeman, from a pony to an elephant, or from an airplane to a fire engine. With this creative background of role playing, small children can have significant experiences in *interpretive* responses to music. With your guidance they can become quite discriminating about the mood of music.

When the music sounds heavy and lumbering, and when it sounds light and delicate, children can and will respond with appropriate movements. Many pupils are able to discuss what the music makes them feel like being and doing. All children should be given opportunity and encouragement to do this, because basic concepts about tempo, dynamics, pitch, texture, and timbre can be developed from experiences of this kind.

In interpretive movement motivation may come from the music itself, from a unit of study, from a known song, from a favorite game, or from a story.

Creative responses are easily motivated through any of the day-by-day events: the rain, the falling leaves, the wind, the snow, the story of a favorite animal, a visitor, the music of a favorite record, or any of the topics used in the regular units of study. A helpful sequence for presenting this kind of activity is:

1. Motivation—stimulating, but not too specific.
2. Opportunity to listen attentively.
3. Opportunity to exercise visual imagination.
4. Opportunity to "act out" the music.

In order to help the class listen attentively and purposefully, some teachers suggest that the children tune in imaginary television sets. Then they close their eyes, and as they listen they imagine what the music makes them *feel like doing.*

After opportunity is provided to act out these feelings expressively, a brief discussion may follow concerning the mood of the music: "How did the music make you feel?" "Was the music fast, slow?" "Light, heavy?" "Smooth, jerky?" etc. Much of the value of this activity results from the child's opportunity to respond from the totality of his experience to all aspects of the music. For this reason, it is a creative response to mood, melody, harmony, tempo, and dynamics, as much as to the rhythm of the music.

A child will feel free to *be himself* if he discovers that:

1. Uniformity is not the goal of this activity.
2. His individuality is prized.
3. Adult standards of performance are not imposed.

Sometimes it is difficult to find enough room so that the children can use large, free motions. However, if suitable space is not available, you can figure out ways to call on a few children at a time, while the others "pretend" until their turn comes. The use of scarves, balloons, and crepe paper streamers (cowboys' lariats) assist in this experience and are inexpensive.

ACTING OUT CREATIVE RHYTHMIC STORIES

If your students have had repeated successful opportunities to move to the rhythm of the music, they will enjoy making up little stories and acting them out.

The following is an example of the type of make-believe story that many classes have enjoyed:

A Visit to the Park for a Picnic

Each student takes a partner and walks in a happy, orderly manner out to the bus that is parked outside the school. (Record: "Air de Ballet"—Jadassohn—RCA Basic R. II.) They sing a song about the bus[2] as they ride through the streets, looking happily out the windows. As the bus approaches the park, the children hear the merry-go-'round. (Record: "Happy and Light of Heart"—Balfe—RCA Basic R. II.)

Happily the children climb out of the bus and rush to the swings and teeter-totters. (Record: "Walzer"—Gurlitt—RCA Basic R. II.) Some of the boys and girls play tag, while others have fun skipping and galloping. (Record: "Les Pifferari"—Gounod—RCA Basic R. II.)

After a good lunch, they pick up all the papers and clean up the picnic area. Suddenly a big thunderstorm comes up and everyone hurries to the bus. (Record: "Tarantelle"—Mendelssohn—RCA Basic R. II.) On the way home, everyone is tired. Some yawn, nod, and fall asleep on the bus. (Record: "Boating on the Lake"—Kullak—RCA Basic R. II.)

These records were selected from Volume II of the Rhythm Program of the RCA Victor Basic Record Library for Elementary Schools because they create definite moods and are not very long.

[2] From Books 1 and 2 of *The Magic of Music* Series, published by Ginn and Company.

Your children can choose other favorites and make up stories to go with them.

Additional records for rhythmic activities include:

SUGGESTED RECORDS FOR MOVING RHYTHMICALLY TO MUSIC

"Boating on the Lake" (Kullak)— Swinging and swaying rhythms	RCA Basic R. II
"Do This, Do That"—Free imitation of animals	C. R. Guild 1040
"Estamae's Toy Shop," Album 1— Directions on record	Estamae Records
"Halloween Rhythms" (Phoebe James)—Directions in album	P. J. Recordings, Box 286, Verdugo City, Calif. 91046
"Horses," *The Rhythms Hour* (White)—Sung directions	Rhythms Prod. CC-615
"How I Walk," *The Rhythms Hour* (White)—Sung directions	Rhythms Prod. CC-615
"Interpretive Rhythms"	Rhythm Record RRC-103
"Jumping" (Gurlitt)—Free response, or dramatization	RCA Basic R. II
"La Bergeranette"—Hopping or similar specific response	RCA Basic R. II
"March" (Gurlitt)—Good steady two-beat meter	RCA Basic R. II
"Polka" from the ballet *The Age of Gold* (Shostakovich)—Interpretive rhythms	RCA VIC-1184/VICS-1184
"Rhythms"—Directions with album	Audio-Ed. (ABC) AS-22
"Running Game" (Gurlitt)—Good two-beat meter	RCA Basic R. II
"Skating"—Well accented for specific response	RCA Basic R. II
"Tame Bear" and "Wild Bears" from *The Wand of Youth,* Suite No. 2 (Elgar)	Mus. Sound Books 78149
"Tarantelle" (Saint-Saëns)—Tiptoe or creative dramatization	RCA Basic R. II
"The Circus" from *Play Time Rhythms* (White)—Directions on record	Rhythms Prod. CC—618-1
"The Handsome Scarecrow"— Directions on record	*Listen and Do,* Vol. II Audio-Ed. (ABC) 2

"The Little Clown"—Directions on record	*Listen and Do,* Vol. II Audio-Ed. (ABC) 2
"The Toy Shop" from *Play Time Rhythms* (White)—Directions on record	Rhythms Prod. CC—618-3
"The Waltzing Elephant" (North-Graham)—Response to three-beat meter	CRG
"Two Hands" from *The Rhythms Hour* (White)—Sung directions	Rhythms Prod. CC-615
"Waltz" from *Les Patineurs* (Meyerbeer)—Good three-beat meter	RCA Adventures II
"Waltz on the Ice" from *Winter Holiday* (Prokofiev)—Response to three-beat meter	Westminster Records; RCA Adventures 3, Vol. II
"Walzer" (Gurlitt)—Good three-beat meter	RCA Basic R. II
"Wild Horseman" (Schumann)—Gallop	RCA Basic R. II

Middle and Later Childhood (Levels 3, 4, 5, and 6)

Although children on levels 1 and 2 often have opportunities for creative self-expression through movement to music, these experiences sometimes are neglected on the upper levels. This is regrettable. Not only do these children need such opportunities as a part of their total growth, they also need them as a part of their musical development.

USING RECORDINGS FOR CREATIVE AND SPECIFIC RESPONSES

One meaningful activity that can be continued for a time on these levels (particularly level 3) is the use of recordings for both creative and specific responses. Recordings that have directions for rhythmic activities as an integral part of the story and music can be very effective. In using this type of record, the following suggestions may prove helpful:

> 1. Be sure the class has the opportunity to listen to the entire record at least once before they attempt to act it out.

2. Before each repeated listening, give the class *something new to listen for.* These types of records usually have several distinct sections with great variety and contrast, and it is best to plan specific questions that will highlight some aspect for the class to listen for.

3. Act out only one section of the record at a time. Where lack of space prevents the entire class from participating at the same time, those who wait their turn can learn a great deal from *active observation.* Have the class suggest *appropriate things to watch for.* Brief discussions can help the students develop critical powers of discrimination.

Suggested titles of records are listed below:

SUGGESTED RECORDS FOR MOVING TO RHYTHMS

"Action Songs and Rounds" (Ed Durlacher)	Educational Activities L.P. #508
"Animal Rhythms" (Phoebe James)	AED-3
"Building a City"	Young People's Records 711
"Circus Fun and Ball Bouncing," Album 4	Estamae
"Dance Record" (without partners)	Rhythm Records RRC-1303
"Holiday Rhythms" (album)	Bowmar 025
"Let's Have Fun," Album 3 (Tyrolienne waltz good for ball bouncing)	Estamae
"Play Time—A Festival of Rhythmic Dramatizations"	Rhythms Pro. Album CC 618
"This Is Rhythm"	Scholastic Records

On these levels one of the most effective creative experiences in interpretive movement is making up actions or dance steps to songs that may be appropriate for this activity. The texts of some songs seem to suggest what to do. As an example, in the song "Come Rowing with Me"[3] the activity is obvious—rowing a boat. (You might find it helpful in this song to "pull" on the first beat

---

[3] From Books 2 and 3 of *Discovering Music Together* (revised), by Follett Educational Corporation; also appears in Book 3 of *Exploring Music* Series, published by Holt, Rinehart and Winston, Inc. (appears as "Come Boating with Me"—in key of D).

of *alternate* measures to ensure time for a rhythmic, even "rowing.")

In other songs the students may need to examine the music carefully as well as the text to determine by the mood, tempo, and phrasing what actions would be natural. Obviously not all songs lend themselves to accompanying actions. This creative, rhythmic experience, then, can also be an effective aid in the development of musical discrimination.

For detailed help in creating dance steps for a song, see page 145.

SINGING GAMES AND FOLK DANCES

Early Childhood (Levels 1 and 2)

ACTION SONGS

Each of the books of the basic series (see Appendix A) has excellent action songs at every level of difficulty. This kind of singing activity is very important for small children. It provides movement involving both the large muscles and the finer muscle coordination of the fingers. Often these activities make it possible for some children to participate who might not otherwise.

Here are some records of song stories and short action songs which students find appealing:

"Activity Songs" (9 songs)	Rhythms Productions B204
"Genie, the Magic Record" (song story)	Decca 1-108
"Jocko, the Dancing Monkey" (action song story)	Audio-Ed. ABC 3
"John, John, Johnny"	RCA Basic Primary Songs
"Kitty White" (action song story)	Bowmar 1513 B
"Manners Can Be Fun" (song story)	Decca VL 3683/VL 73683
"Our Exercises" (action song story)	Bowmar 1512 A
"Panda Balloon" (action song story)	Audio-Ed. ABC 3
"Songs of Safety"	Decca VL 3683/VL 73683
"Story of Robin Hood" (Walt Disney)	Capitol EAXF 3138

"The Sleeping Princess" (song story)	Bowmar 1514 B
"The Small Singer" #1 (25 short songs)	Bowmar 021
"The Small Singer" #2 (25 short songs)	Bowmar 022
"What Are Stars?" (song story)	Decca 4073

SINGING GAMES

These activities are most appealing to children. On stormy days, when you stay indoors during recess and lunch periods, you and your students will especially enjoy musical games. In fine weather, you may wish to play them outdoors. Your music book will probably contain some of these songs.

Be sure the children *know the song well* before they attempt the game that goes with it. Divide your class into two groups: let one group sing (perhaps also using simple instruments for color), and let the other group do the actions. Alternate. Be sure you select some good singers for each group, so your pupils will be making *music* as well as motion. Too often, the singing suffers when children try to play games and sing at the same time. It is important, also, to have as much room as possible for rhythmic activities. If your school provides an all-purpose room or gymnasium, the children can be unrestricted in their movements. Many teachers are able to arrange the regular classroom to provide as much space as possible.

SUGGESTED RECORDS AND AIDS
FOR SINGING GAMES AND RHYTHMS

"Did You Ever See a Lassie?"	Bowmar 1511 A
"Drummer Boy"	CRG 1015
"Farmer in the Dell"	Bowmar 1511 B
"First Folk Dances" (Album)	RCA LPM-1625/EPA-4144
"I Am a Circus"	CRG 1028
"Little Indian Drum"	YPR 619
"Little Polly Flinders"	Bowmar 1512 A
"Looby Loo"	Bowmar 1514 A
"Men Who Come to Our House"	YPR 737
"Mulberry Bush"	Bowmar 1513 B
"Nursery Rhymes & Singing Games," Album 7	Ruth Evans
"Oats, Peas, and Beans"	Bowmar 1512 B

Primary Musical Games (Ed Durlacher), Album 23	Educational Activities
"Pussy Cat"	Bowmar 1514 A
"Rainy Day"	YPR 712
"Rainy Day Record, The"	Bowmar 1514 A

Rhythmic Activities (Series I), by Frances R. Stuart and John S. Ludlam. Musical Arrangements by Earl Juhas, Burgess Publishing Co., 426 South Sixth St., Minneapolis, Minn. (This is a "kit" of singing games and folk dances written on file cards for easy access and storage. The music is on one card, the directions on another.)

Rhythms Today (Book and Record), by Edna Doll and Mary Jarman Nelson, published by Silver Burdett Company, Morristown, N.J. 07960

"Round and Round the Village"	Bowmar 1512 B

Sing and Dance (Book of folk songs and dances), by Hunt and Wilson, published by Schmitt, Hall & McCreary Co., 527 Park Ave., Minneapolis, Minn.

Singing Action Games (Ed Durlacher) (Album)	Educational Activities L.P. #508
Singing Games, Album 1	Bowmar
Singing Games, Album 2	Bowmar
Singing Games from Many Lands (Album)	Rhythms Productions CC 606
"Skittery Skattery"	CRG 1005
"Traditional Singing Games"	ABC AS-23
"Traditional Singing Games"	Audio-Ed. ABC AS 23
"When I Was a Shoemaker"	Bowmar 1513 A

Middle Childhood (Levels 3 and 4)

USING FOLK DANCES

There are many helpful books[4] and records that give specific directions for musical games and folk dances. In some schools these activities are conducted by the physical education staff, but many classroom and music teachers use them, especially in inclement weather. Here are some suggestions for your use:

1. A few comments about the kind of folk dance to be presented will help to interest the class and prepare them for the activity.

[4] See Appendix B for a list of excellent references about moving to the rhythm of music.

2. Play the music while the class listens quietly and attentively.

3. Select a few pupils to work out the steps with you while the rest of the class watches closely.

4. Step the first pattern out with the small group while you say the directions. Sometimes it is a good idea to work the patterns out in line formation first.

5. When the class has a clear idea of what to do, chant the directions as they go through the formations together.

6. Add the music.

7. Work out one short section at a time, before proceeding to a new part.

It is very important that the pupils learn to *get their "directions" from the music itself.* It may be necessary to raise some questions in order to get the class to discover that the patterns of the game change as the phrases change: that changes of direction are directly related to the music itself.

You may want to use one of your tone bells as a signal for the pupils to stop everything and give their attention to the directions. Without being prepared *to listen quietly on signal,* an activity of this kind can become so disorganized that only confusion results. It is always important for children to remember that *they must listen attentively* during all kinds of music experiences, and folk dances are no exception.

One teacher[5] worked out an easy system for teaching the "Grand Left and Right," as follows:

1. Choose twelve pupils: six "marchers" and six to form a line.

2. Have the six form the line, one behind the other, with enough space between so that others can move easily "in and out the windows."

3. Then select one of the six "marchers" to go around and behind the first child in the line, around and behind the second child in the line, and so on, passing "in and out the windows" in this fashion:

[5] Lila Lyle, a former teacher at the McCoy Elementary School in Independence, Mo., has used this method with repeated success.

$$O \swarrow X \searrow X \swarrow X \searrow X \swarrow X \searrow X \swarrow O$$

4. Select a second "marcher" to follow the first, and then a third, until all six "marchers" are going "in and out the windows" as the music is playing. Any good march will do. It's usually a good idea to have the six "marchers" keep time in place before they begin to go "in and out the windows."

5. Now the first pupil standing in the line offers his hand to the first "marcher" (either hand will do, so long as he offers the opposite hand to the second "marcher").

6. In this manner, those standing in line offer their hands alternately to each "marcher" and each "marcher" will be accepting naturally with alternating hands.

From this easy beginning experience, pupils gain confidence and are able to succeed in doing the standard "Grand Left and Right" pattern when needed.

SUGGESTED RECORDS FOR FOLK GAMES

"All-Purpose Folk Dances"	RCA LPM-1623
"First Folk Dances"	RCA LPM-1625
"Folk Dances for Fun"	RCA LPM-1624
"Folk Songs for Singing and Dancing"	Young People's Records 8005
"Honor Your Partner," Album 1 (Ed Durlacher)	Educational Activities
"Let's All Join In" (album)	Childcraft Records
"Let's Dance"	C. R. Guild 5021
"Let's Have Fun Dancing," Album 2	Estamae
"Let's Play a Musical Game"	Columbia HL-9522
"Let's Square Dance," Album No. 1	RCA LE-3000
"North American Indian Dances"	Folkways FD 6510
"Play Party Games #1"	Bowmar
"Play Party Games," Album 10 (Ed Durlacher)	Educational Activities

"Grand Left and Right" is easy when it is first learned in line formation (photo by Patrick Burke).

"Singing Games and Folk Dances," Album 3	Bowmar 112
"Square Dances"	Audio Ed. (ABC) SD-1

Just as in earlier years, these students need and enjoy many experiences with singing games and action songs. A well-balanced curriculum will include these activities.

In the later period of these levels, the children are capable of a more prolonged interest and can be attentive for a longer span. This is also the time when the "gang" influence is strongly felt, with boys "against" girls. Because of this, folk dancing under the careful direction of an understanding teacher can be a strategically helpful social factor.

The selection of the "right" records is important.

SUGGESTED RECORDS FOR FOLK DANCES

"Dance Steps"	Folkraft Album 21
"Festival Folk Dances"	RCA LPM-1621
"Folk Dances," Album II	Ruth Evans
"Folk Dances, Album IV	Bowmar 113
"Folk Dances for All Ages"	RCA LPM-1622
"Folk Dances From Round the World," Album 2	Rhythms Productions CC 602
"Fundamental Steps and Rhythms"	Folkraft Album 20
"Honor Your Partner," Album 2 (Ed Durlacher)	Educational Activities
"Let's Square Dance," Album I (Ages 8 to 10; Middle childhood)	RCA LE-3000
"Modified, Western Type Dances," Album 18 (Ed Durlacher)	Educational Activities
"Play Party Games #2"	Bowmar 175
"Rounds and Mixers Old and New," Album 1	Bowmar 119
"Singing Square Dances," Album 1	Bowmar 232

(Song plays, American play-party games, square dances, folk dances, and mixers for middle childhood can also be obtained on single records from Folkraft Records, 1159 Broad St., Newark, N.J. 07114)

Later Childhood (Levels 5 and 6)

SINGING GAMES

Usually the best source for singing games is the pupil's song book. Most of the current basic series include a number of these—often with accompanying instructions in the teacher's manual. Children have a great interest in this type of activity and should be given frequent opportunities to enjoy it. Many other excellent sources are listed in Appendix C.

Many times a new dimension can be added to the singing game experience. This can occur when the students create their own dance to a song that seems suitable. No rigid procedure can be suggested for this, since the dance or game will evolve in a spontaneous manner as a result of many sharing in the experience.

However, here are a few helpful ideas:

1. Select a song that you feel will be appropriate for this creative effort. Have the students learn it.

2. After the students know the song, suggest that they clap the correct meter and rhythm (whatever they feel) to the music. Follow this by encouraging them to clap their own rhythm.

3. Pass out rhythm instruments for the students to use in place of clapping. Try to "match" the instrument with the style of their rhythmic pattern.

4. After the class has had some experience in feeling the pulse and rhythm of the song, discuss its content with them, trying to determine what type of dance would be appropriate. (If it is a folk song from a foreign land talk about the native customs, manner of dress, and style of dancing.)

5. Proceed with the development of the dance steps, encouraging the students to express their ideas freely. (At this point it would be helpful if the class could use the gymnasium or all-purpose room, where they would have room to experiment.) Try to give guidance by pointing out any accents in the song (which might call for a stamp), rapid eighth notes (which might suggest light running), or slow passages (which might suggest a more deliberate type of action).

6. After the dance is completed and learned, discuss the possibility of using rhythm instruments to add color. Suggest that the students select those that are appropriate and encourage them to create a percussion accompaniment.

FOLK DANCES

Dances of other lands, as well as those of America, can be used very effectively on these levels. The simplified polka and schottische and various versions of the American square dance are especially popular. Rhythm experiences can also be particularly well-integrated with social studies and other subjects. Many texts base their studies on world cultures, with specific emphasis on the Latin-American countries. This provides an excellent incentive for learning folk dances of other lands. Often a fine climax to this study is a folk dance festival held in the spring—either on the playground or in the all-purpose room. A touch of costume (hats or aprons) will help identify the country and add color. With your assistance some students might write an appealing script or commentary. (The performance should be a natural outgrowth of stimulating classroom study, rather than "artificial fare" for audience approval. Most parents prefer this type of program and express genuine appreciation of it.)

Records for folk dances can be secured from several excellent sources.[6] At times you may want to select a dance record without specific instructions, in order to give your students an opportunity for creative expression. The same basic principles that apply to making up steps or actions to accompany a song can be used with dances or other music. In guided discussion establish with your students the mood and style of the composition, as well as the basic beat.

DEVELOPING AWARENESS OF METER AND RHYTHM PATTERNS

Opportunities to *hear and respond to the beat and the meter* of music should be provided children at all levels of learning. The beat is so basic to our natural enjoyment that sometimes we are not aware that we need to make it an area of study. Naturally, some children will be more skillful than others in sensing the meter and expressing it. This skill can vary from person to person according to native ability and past experience. However, this important skill *can* be developed and improved with opportunity and encouragement.

Early Childhood (Levels 1 and 2)

This subject was discussed in some detail in chapter 3, "Music Reading and Readiness" (see pages 69–79).

[6] Some of the available sources of folk dance records are: Bowmar, *Folk Dances, Album 6;* Folkraft Records; *Let's Square Dance,* Album 2, RCA Victor; *Ruth Evans Folk Dance Records, Vol. 2;* and *The World of Folk Dances* (selected albums), RCA Victor.

Middle Childhood (Levels 3 and 4)

Some of the children (and some adults, too) may not be able to "hear the strong beat" very well at all. The "strong beat" is sometimes referred to as the "accent." Although we may think of the strong beat (the first beat in the measure) as the accented beat, the term "accent" can be confusing. An accent can occur on any beat of the measure; when it occurs on a weak beat or on the second half of a beat, it is known as *syncopation,* a common rhythmic device. People who have difficulty in feeling the strong beat (whether it is accented or not) can profit from additional experience in meter sensing.

Let your class listen carefully at least once through before they try to move to the beat. The response can take any one of a wide variety of forms. You'll find some of these practical:

1. Swaying in time with the strong beat;
2. Clapping or tapping on the strong beat;
3. Bending in time with the strong beat;
4. Bouncing an imaginary ball (or a real one) on the strong beat;
5. Moving one step forward on the strong beat, standing still on the weak beats;
6. Swinging the arms (while seated or standing) on the strong beat, remaining still on the weak beats.

The children in your class can think of many other ways to respond to the strong beat. Any free movement using the large muscles is best. On the weak beats it's best to remain motionless (or nearly so), in order for the vigorous motion to be associated with the pulsation of the strong beat. Some teachers like to use a form of "patschen" for meter sensing. The children all clap their hands sharply on "ONE" (the strong beat), and then raising both hands, they pat their shoulders gently but briskly on the weak beats. Precision is emphasized. This is a practical way to help students develop a clear concept of meter; and it is also relatively easy for the teacher to see if the entire class is moving in time with the music.

In the following list of recordings a notation beside the title indicates the beats in each measure (for example: "S, W, W" indicates three beats—STRONG, weak, weak). Be sure the response is *exactly in time with the beat,* otherwise the entire activity is meaningless.

SUGGESTED RECORDS FOR DEVELOPING AWARENESS OF METER

"Come Lasses and Lads" (Folk)	S, W	RCA Basic R. III
"Country Gardens" (Folk)	S, W, W, W	Mus. Sound Books JT 11
"Dagger Dance" from *Natoma* (Herbert)	S, W, W, W	RCA Adventures III, Vol. 1
"Dance of the Moorish Slaves" from *Aida* (Verdi)	S, W	RCA Basic R. III
"Hornpipe" from *Water Music* (Handel)	S, W, W	Mus. Sound Books 78001
"Lavender's Blue" (Folk)	S, W, W	RCA Basic R. III
"March of the Toys" from *Babes in Toyland* (Herbert)	S, W, W, W	RCA LM-2229/LSC-2229
"Menuetto" from *Royal Fireworks Music* (Handel)	S, W, W	RCA Adventures III, Vol. 2
"Papillons" (Schumann)	S, W, W	RCA Basic R. III
"Polly Put the Kettle On" (Folk)	S, W	RCA Basic R. III
"Silhouette" (Reinhold)	S, W	RCA Basic R. III
"Skaters' Waltz" (Waldteufel)	S, W, W	RCA Basic R. IV
"Stars and Stripes Forever, The" (Sousa)	S, W	RCA LPM-1175
"The Beautiful Blue Danube" (Strauss)	S, W, W	Mus. Sound Books 33100 A
"Waltz in E Major" (Brahms)	S, W, W	Mus. Sound Books JT 8

This type of activity can obviously be useful any time during the school day when the children need a change of pace from quiet work, or it can be included in your regular music class.

CONDUCTING THE "DOWNBEAT"

Another "fun" activity that can help strengthen the feeling for the strong beat and increase the awareness of meter is "conducting." Your students may enjoy being "directors" of the chorus (the class). As you sing familiar songs encourage the boys and girls to bring their hands straight down whenever they hear the downbeat (the first beat of the measure). As the children are sitting at their desks they can all "direct" together. Then select several individuals, one at a time, to come up and direct the group. When the feeling for the downbeat is well established you may want to help your students develop the "feel" of the other beats in the measure. A procedure like this might help, using a familiar song like "Yankee Doodle":

1. Sing the song with words.
2. Discuss the top number of the time signature $\frac{2}{4}$. Talk about the number of beats in each measure. Then have the class sing the entire song with only two numbers—1, 2; 1, 2; 1, 2, etc.
3. Sing the song again with the two numbers. This time clap the beats as you sing. Accent the first beat strongly, giving a lighter motion to the second.
4. Sing other songs with words and numbers, clapping the first beat heavily and giving lighter claps to the remaining beats of the measure.

RHYTHM GAMES

Games with a specific musical purpose can be very valuable rhythmic experiences. Only two are given here as illustrative examples.

1. QUESTION AND ANSWER

This is a creative experience intended to develop a student's ability to perceive the rhythm pattern that he hears accurately and to respond with one of his own in the same meter.

A possible approach might include these steps:

a. Tell the students that you are going to clap (play on the drum, wood block, etc.) a short rhythm pattern in $\frac{4}{4}$ ($\frac{3}{4}$, $\frac{2}{4}$, $\frac{6}{8}$) meter. You want them to listen closely, then be prepared to clap exactly what they hear. (It is usually wise to make the first step an "echo" response until they feel at home with the technique.)

b. Inform the students that you will clap two full measures of four beats each ($\frac{4}{4}$ meter) before you clap the pattern they are to repeat. This is necessary to establish the basic framework, tempo, etc. After you have clapped the rhythm pattern, ask one student to repeat it. Continue this for a time, using different rhythm patterns, until many students have had this experience.

c. When the steps up to this point have been success-fully experienced, explain to your class that you are now going to alter the procedure. When you clap a pattern, they are to "answer" with one of their own. Theirs must have the same number of measures and the same number of beats in each measure as yours, but the pattern must be different. You will call your rhythm pattern the "question," theirs the "answer." It would be helpful if you did one or two examples, playing both the question and answer (identifying each) by way of demonstration.

d. At first your patterns should be kept quite simple and short. The students' responses will usually be uncomplicated. Frequently the first attempts are something like this:

D staff
Question

Answer

e. As soon as you feel it is wise, add variety and in-terest to your rhythm patterns. This will stimulate answers of similar quality.

f. Extra dimensions can be added to this game such as:

1) Having studens notate on the chalkboard the questions they hear—or their answers. They might use "stick" or "stem" notation, e.g.,

2) Encouraging individual students to ask the "questions" for other students to "answer."

2. CHANGING RHYTHM PATTERNS

This game tests the skill of the student to hear accurately just one change in a rhythm pattern.

a.   Place a short pattern on the chalkboard. Explain to
the class that you will play this on the wood block
(drum, rhythm sticks, etc.). They are to follow the
pattern on the board visually as you play. Then you
will repeat it with one rhythmic change. Following
that, you will choose someone to go to the board
and make the correction.

For example:

Rhythm pattern on the board as it is played the first time.

Rhythm pattern as it is played the second time.

b.   To give variety to this game you might create a
simple melody for the rhythm patterns and play
them on the bells or piano. The techniques of the
game will be the same.

c.   As the students become more skilled some of them
might be selected to clap the original rhythm pattern and the correction.

Later Childhood (Levels 5 and 6)

On earlier levels the students had frequent opportunities to become aware of meter and rhythm patterns.

CLAPPING RHYTHM PATTERNS

Students enjoy clapping the rhythm patterns of songs. Perhaps the
first thing the teacher needs to do is to help the class understand
what the words "rhythm pattern" really mean. Demonstrate by
clapping the tune of familiar songs such as "America," "Skip to
My Lou," and "Yankee Doodle." Do not sing as you clap. Help
the boys and girls to understand that you are clapping the rhythm
pattern of the words of the song.

Follow this introduction by having the students clap or tap the
rhythm pattern of many familiar songs as they sing the words.
Then suggest that they can be an "orchestra" and clap the rhythm
pattern without singing or saying the words. When they do this it
might be well to play the piano with them or use a recording to
maintain a steady rhythm.

Children frequently enjoy a good game based on this skill. One student is "It" and begins clapping the rhythm pattern of a familiar song. As soon as someone can correctly guess what it is, he becomes "It" and continues the game in the same manner.

CLAPPING METER

Clapping the meter actually means clapping the number of beats in each measure. For some, the words "keeping time with the music" may be more familiar and meaningful. Many lively songs can be enhanced with a clapping accompaniment. More significantly, clapping can help develop a strong feeling for beat. Frequently, with such songs as "Oh! Susanna,"[7] have the students clap as they sing. At times it would be helpful to have them clap and count the beats aloud while you play the song on the piano or use a recording. In "Oh! Susanna" the children would say, "ONE," "TWO," "ONE," "TWO," as they clap. (Since the song begins on the last half of the second beat, they should clap and count two or three measures before the music begins.)

*CLAPPING RHYTHM PATTERN
AND METER*

After the students have had experience with clapping the rhythm pattern and the meter separately, they are then ready to clap both of them at once. Divide the class into two groups. Choose a song such as "Oh! Susanna," and ask one group to clap the rhythm pattern while the other claps the meter. (It is usually best to use a recording with this or have someone play the piece on the piano.) Then reverse the two groups for experience and interest. This activity is usually very popular with the students, and helps them to clarify concepts about beat, meter, and rhythm pattern.

*CLAPPING AND PLAYING
ROUNDS*

For variation the students might chant a round in rhythm rather than sing it. After they have done this successfully, they might substitute clapping for the chanting. (They may still need to whisper the words for a time in order to keep their place.) After

---

[7] From Book 5 of *Growing with Music* Series, published by Prentice-Hall, Inc.; Book 5 of *This Is Music for Today* Series, published by Allyn and Bacon, Inc.; and Book 4 of *Discovering Music Together* Revised Series, published by Follett Publishing Co.

some experience with clapping, the children might enjoy using rhythm instruments.

RHYTHM ROUNDS

Boys and girls of this age are particularly interested in rhythm rounds. They are unusually responsive to the rhythmic element of music and enjoy experiences that feature this.

The presentation of a rhythm round might include these procedures:

1. Select a poem or jingle (rhymed or free verse) that has both repetition and variety of rhythm. Scan the poem rhythmically and notate it.

   You may find it easier and more satisfying to write your own chant. Then you can specifically relate it to some phase of study in your classroom.

   For example, suppose you composed a chant about the first space flight of the astronauts to the moon. The first verse might go something like this:

   I watched the moon flight
   Just before Christmas.
   Astronauts were soaring
   Into outer space.

   The next step would be to notate the verse:

   It is immediately apparent that this rhythm pattern is in $\frac{4}{4}$ meter. Additional verses would need to be written within the same framework.

2. Having selected or created your chant for this rhythmic experience, put it on the chalkboard or on a large chart that all students can see.

3. Explain to the class that one of the activities for this day will be to *chant* a round in rhythm rather than to *sing* it as they have been accustomed to doing up to this time. As preparation, have them sing a famil-

iar round in unison (one time through), clapping the rhythm pattern of the words as they sing. Then ask them to chant rather than sing the words as they clap.

4. They are now ready to chant in unison the words of the rhythm round. It might be well at first to have them just chant without clapping. Then, when they have the feel of it, add the clapping.

5. When this part of the experience has been successful, try dividing the class into groups and doing it as a round. (You may want to use only the first verse for a time until the students become familiar with the idea. If so, divide the class into four groups, beginning each new group as the one preceding it finishes the first line.)

6. To enrich the experience, rhythm instruments can be substituted for the clapping. For a time the pupils will need to say the words as they make this substitution. Then let them try whispering the words very softly as they play.

Encourage students to write their own chants (centering around current events in the world, important happenings at school, etc.) and bring them to class. As a group activity, let the students enjoy creating tunes for the rhythm rounds they use.

Using a chant having at least three verses with varied rhythm patterns will add dimension and interest to this experience. An example is given here to demonstrate the procedure for this.[8]

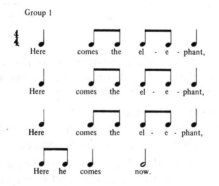

[8] From Book 6, "Music for Young Americans," the *ABC Series,* published by American Book Company.

Group 2 (start on Group 1 chant when Group 1 completes its
first four lines)

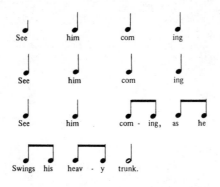

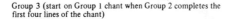

Group 3 (start on Group 1 chant when Group 2 completes the
first four lines of the chant)

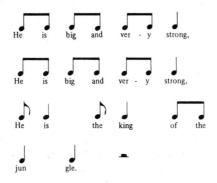

LUMMI STICKS[9]

An interesting type of activity involving rhythm sticks in a game
of coordination and skill has become very popular in some
schools. An album of records accompanies a kit of twenty-four
sticks, accommodating twelve players. The students (seated on the
floor) face each other in a double line. At various points in the
game they toss the sticks to their partners (in time with the
music). Drills such as this help to refine rhythmic skill and develop
a feeling for the beat. One of the greatest values of this game is the
desire it often develops in the students to attempt their own "rou-
tines" with familiar songs from their books.

[9] Lummi sticks can be purchased from Twinson Company, 433 LaPrenda Rd., Los Altos,
Calif. 94022 (see Appendix L).

Students enjoy using Lummi sticks to help them develop rhythmic skills (photo by Ken Raveill).

SUGGESTED INDIVIDUAL AND SMALL GROUP PROJECTS FOR METHODS COURSES

Early Childhood (Levels 1 and 2)

1. Develop a list of appropriate records that can be used for *meter sensing*. (The class will not be ready for this activity until the children have had success in finding and moving to the *strong beat*.) Pupils can bounce a large playground ball in time with the beat of the music, or pretend to do so. Be sure the ball actually hits the floor (or pretend that it does) *exactly on the strong beat.*

2. Select appropriate piano pieces and records that are suitable for *creative rhythmic response.* Provide paper streamers, scarves, or kerchiefs to be used by the children to show *contrasts* in the music. Note specifically where the changes take place in the com-

positions you have selected, and whether the contrasts are due to changes in tempo, dynamics, melody, or rhythm.

3. Write a creative rhythmic story, selecting appropriate records to describe each activity. As you use this with your class make sure that the *children identify the activity* they hear in the music. Encourage them to create their own stories.

4. As an individualized activity, have the pupils listen to the records at school and find one that makes them feel like:

a big bear,
a bunny,
a butterfly, or
an astronaut

5. After they have found just the record they want, ask them to play it for the class and tell the other students why it made them feel like that.

6. Use the record for a class activity in interpretive rhythms.

Middle Childhood (Levels 3 and 4)

1. Create steps for a familiar round, so that it can be acted out by students on these levels. Plan the rhythmic activity in such a way that the phrases are clearly observed.

2. Work out a marching drill that will be appealing to students of this age.

3. Write a series of rhythm patterns to be practiced by a class on these levels.

4. Take a rhythm pattern from one of the students' favorite songs and help them learn to clap it *exactly right* while you play a steady beat. When they can do it perfectly, see if some of the class can write it down accurately. Help those who are having trouble.

5. Make a list of songs you know that have distinctive rhythm patterns. Write each of the patterns on a separate card and give them to your students to practice as an individualized activity. Then have each student play the pattern he has learned on a rhythm instrument while the class sings the song.

Later Childhood (Levels 5 and 6)

1. Create a dance to go with a folk song.

2. Write a variety of rhythm patterns that students on these levels might clap, tap, or play on rhythm instruments.

3. Without placing them on the staff, make a chart showing the meter signature and the distinctive rhythm pattern for each of the following:

   Tango
   March
   Minuet
   Polka
   Polonaise
   Rumba
   Your favorite dance

4. Make a set of cards containing rhythm patterns that students on these levels can play. Make up a game using these cards. You could number the cards, then play each pattern on the wood block, piano, or bells and see if the class can correctly identify it.

5

Listening

Because it involves the whole person—intellectually and emotionally—listening to music is a highly personal experience. Even for a large audience who share simultaneously in a concert the experience is individual and unique. This awareness needs to guide the teacher constantly in planning such activities for children. A well-balanced listening program that includes music of many styles is essential.[1]

With music of all types being heard in many public places—the supermarket, the drive-in, the drug store, the doctor's office, the restaurant, and other places of business—the teacher has the added responsibility and opportunity of aiding students in their understanding and enjoyment of music, and in developing discrimination. The listening program is probably one of the most vital parts of the total music program, since most of the children will be listening to music (of one type or another) all of their lives, while few of them will become concert performers. Right from early childhood, then, we should give careful attention to listening experiences.

---

[1] For this reason the record lists that appear in the text are intended as resource aids from which the teacher CHOOSES. No one is expected to use every record suggested. Hopefully, enough selections are given to provide freedom of choice.

EARLY AND MIDDLE CHILDHOOD

Early Childhood (Levels 1 and 2)

One of the most important habits for young children to develop is *the ability to listen.* How many times parents and teachers have said to children, "But you didn't listen to what I told you!" Good listening habits *can be developed,* and can contribute to success both inside and outside school.

All music activities tend to develop careful listening habits. In fact, *the ability to hear* takes precedence in all music education. The first grade pupil who sings well has already learned to distinguish the differences between *high and low tones.* The child who responds rhythmically to the music—either through expressive movement or by using a simple instrument—does so because he can *hear the beat.* Some authorities believe the greatest single index of talent in music is the ease with which a person sings or plays "by ear." The pleasures of music come to us through our ears, and the good teacher remembers to *emphasize the importance of careful listening.*

LISTENING FOR MOOD

INDIVIDUALIZED ACTIVITY. With adequate equipment, the presentation of listening experiences is quite simple. Children naturally respond to the *mood* of the music with little direction from the teacher. Try to find time each day for some *quiet listening.* Many teachers feel that listening to music helps to create an atmosphere conducive to art activities or other individual work. This kind of passive listening provides opportunities for introducing music of high quality. Many children will also learn to recognize the titles and the names of the composers.

The following records are recommended for *quiet listening for mood.* You and your pupils can find others to add to this list.

SUGGESTED RECORDS FOR INDIVIDUALIZED QUIET LISTENING

"Badinage" (Herbert)	RCA Basic L. I
"Ballet of the Sylphs" (Berlioz)	RCA Adventures I
"Beautiful Blue Danube" (Strauss)	Mus. Sound Books 78021

"Berceuse" (Stravinsky)	RCA Adventures I
"By the Fireside" (Schumann)	Mus. Sound Books 78006
"Children's Prayer" from *Hansel and Gretel* (Humperdinck)	Mus. Sound Books 78303
"Cradle Song" (Schubert)	RCA Basic L. I
"Cradle Song" from *Children's Games* (Bizet)	RCA Adventures I
"Halloween" (Ives)	Vanguard Records C-10032/4
"Hickory Dickory Dock" from *Mother Goose Suite* (Guion)	Mus. Sound Books MSB 78301
"Hobby Horse" (Pinto)	RCA Basic L. I
"Holidays for U.S." (Frank Luther)	Ed. Record Service
"Humoresque" (Dvorak)	RCA Basic L. I
"Lullaby" from Ballet *Gayne* (Khachaturian)	RCA LM-2267/LSC-2267
"Mazurka of the Mice" (Voormolen)	Mus. Sound Books 78302
"Nocturne" from *A Midsummer Night's Dream* (Mendelssohn)	London 6186
"Pines of the Villa Borghese" from the Suite *Pines of Rome* (Respighi)	RCA VIC-1244
"Pussy Is Ill" (Gretchaninov)	MSB 22
"Sunbeam Play" (Toch)	Mus. Sound Books 23
"The Little White Donkey" (Ibert)	MSB 78310
"The Paper Doll" from *The Baby's Family* (Villa-Lobos)	Mus. Sound Books 78310
"The Rag Doll" from *The Baby's Family*	Mus. Sound Books 78310
"The Rain Song" (Reinecke)	Mus. Sound Books 78319
"The Snail in the Rain" (Voormolen)	MSB 78302
"To a Wild Rose" (MacDowell)	Mus. Sound Books 5a and b
"Valse Serenade" (Poldini)	RCA Basic R. I

Although listening for mood in music is a basic response to its expressive elements, children also need to develop the ability to listen *actively*. Four kinds of *active listening* are recommended:

1. Listening for tempo (the fast and slow of music)
2. Listening for dynamics (the loud and soft of music)
3. Listening for descriptive or story elements of music
4. Listening for orchestral instruments

LISTENING FOR TEMPO

One of the basic concepts to be developed at this age is the understanding of *tempo,* or *the fast and slow of music.* This type of activity is not difficult, but it should not be neglected. True, some children are aware of this element of music before they ever come to school. Others have developed an understanding of it through effective activities in the classroom. However, it should not be taken for granted that all young children can hear and recognize *tempo* in music. You will want to make sure all your pupils have this opportunity.

An understanding of tempo can come from many kinds of music experiences: from listening, from singing, from rhythmic movement, and from the use of simple instruments in the classroom. One of the easiest listening activities is the simple presentation of two short recorded pieces—one fast, the other slow.

The teacher will not want to say too much by way of introduction. Simply give the class *something to listen for:* "Which one is faster? Which one is slower?" Remind the class to wait until both records have stopped playing before anyone gives an answer. Emphasize the necessity to *listen actively* and *quietly* while the music is playing, just as at a real concert.

LISTENING FOR DYNAMICS

Along with recognizing the fast and slow of music, we hope that the student can also distinguish *the loud and the soft,* or the *dynamics.* Many pupils have already had opportunities to experience this element in music and to verbalize it. The creative teacher can provide many opportunities for children to recognize the dynamics and to respond to them through rhythmic movement, singing, playing simple instruments, and listening attentively to records.

Children will discover that just as tempo can change in a single piece of music, so also can the dynamics. Some music even goes from soft to loud and back to soft again right away, as in the well-known "Andante" movement from the *Surprise Symphony* by Haydn.[2] Other music may sound soft (or loud) all the way to the end.

---

[2] You may need to remind the class that famous composers like Haydn and Mozart are properly called by their last names alone. Point out that this is not discourteous, but traditional (as with poets, artists, actors, etc.). We never say, "Mr. Haydn," or "Mr. Mozart"—even though it is polite and proper to call our principal "Mr. Jones."

SUGGESTED RECORDS FOR TEMPO AND DYNAMIC CONTRASTS

"Air Gai" (Gluck)	RCA Adventures I (loud and soft contrasts)
"Berceuse" from *Dolly* (Fauré)	RCA Adventures II (gradually slower, soft and loud)
"Bydlo" from *Pictures at an Exhibition* (Moussorgsky)	RCA VIC-1273, RCA Adventures II (soft and loud contrasts)
"Cats and Rats"	Bowmar 1511 A (Slow and fast contrasts)
"Charlie Over the Water"	Bowmar 1512 A (Slow and fast contrasts)
"Gavotte" (Pepper)	RCA Basic L. I (fast)
"Gigue" (Grétry)	RCA Adventures I (loud and soft contrasts)
"Hens and Cocks" from *Carnival of the Animals* (Saint-Saëns)	Columbia MS-6368 (fast and slow contrasts)
"Impromptu: The Top" (Bizet)	RCA Basic L. I (fast, then slower)
"Leap Frog" (Bizet)	RCA Adventures I (loud and soft contrasts)
"Legend of the Bells" (Planquette)	RCA Basic L. I (fast, high bells and slow, low chimes)
"March" from *Soirées Musicales* (Rossini-Britten)	RCA Adventures I (soft and loud contrasts)
"Parade" from *Divertissement* (Ibert)	RCA Adventures I (soft and loud contrasts)
"Soft and Loud" (Album)	ABC AS-20
"The Ball" from *Children's Games* (Bizet)	RCA Adventures I (soft and loud contrasts)
"The Storm" from *William Tell* Overture (Rossini)	Columbia MS-6701 (soft and loud contrasts)

Of course, you will not expect children at this age to listen attentively for any great length of time. At first, two or three minutes of active listening for tempo, or for dynamics, is enough. It is much better to *listen often,* for short periods, in this type of activity.

When the students have begun to evidence some understanding of tempo (fast-slow) and dynamics (loud-soft), you may want to introduce the concept of range (high-low). Fast-slow and loud-soft are not as difficult to isolate sometimes as high-low.[3] The latter is really an artificiality in the literal sense of the words, but we have

[3] See pages 47–48 for suggested activities of this type.

to have some label for these sounds, so traditionally we have used these terms.

No matter what the activity, attention can be given to determine if the class can distinguish between fast-slow, loud-soft, and high-low.[4] Any song will have these characteristics, and careful questioning will help to point them out to the class.

PROGRAM MUSIC

Some of the most delightful musical experiences for children are in the form of descriptive or story music. This is the kind of music in which *the composer deliberately describes things or tells a story*. This is called *program music*. One favorite piece of this type is the "March of the Little Lead Soldiers" by Pierné.[5]

Of course, there are many ways to present this kind of music, but here are some suggestions:

1. Without telling the class the name of the record, encourage them to listen quietly and attentively for "clues." Tell them that if they will use their ears well, they may be able to detect what this music is about!

2. Play the record while the children listen quietly. Don't allow the discussion to begin until the music has stopped.

3. You may need to help the class describe the music by asking questions such as: "What do you think was going on?" Typical responses are: "I heard marching," "I heard a band," "There was a parade," etc.

4. Be sure the discussion moves rapidly. If one child has mentioned any of the above responses, try to avoid repetition. Ask for those who heard anything different, but limit the discussion. The point to be discovered is that *someone was marching,* and many good ears will hear that. If not, play the music again, after you have asked an easier question such as: "What do you suppose these people were doing: skipping, swaying, or marching?"

---

[4] Through the study of simple acoustics, we realize that "high" tones are those which vibrate at a greater rate per second than "low" tones.

[5] From the RCA Victor Basic Record Library for Elementary Schools, Vol. I, *Listening Activities.* See also Book 1, *Discovering Music Together* Series, Follett Publishing Co.

5. Play the music a second time, after telling the class to listen for some "clues" about *who* is marching.

6. After the music is played, you may want to ask those whose response was "soldiers" why they thought so. There are many musical reasons why, but keep the discussion as brief as possible.

7. Now ask the class to listen again, to see if anyone can tell *what kind of soldiers* the composer had in mind when he wrote the music. Usually the children will notice that the music is not about grown-up soldiers, but about *toys*. However, if they are unable to do so, you may need to ask questions like these: "Does this sound like a march for real soldiers, or for play soldiers?" "Does this band sound like a big military band, or a toy band?"

8. Each time the class hears the record, suggest definite things to listen for in the music. Play the record as many times as there are new things to hear. Have as much music and as little talk as possible. Conclude by giving the title of the composition and the name of the composer.

The children will enjoy a follow-up lesson, in which the music is played and identified by the class and then acted out *in time with the music*. Sometimes the students will be interested to learn that although some toy soldiers are made of tin, in many foreign countries they are made of lead. Pierné may have played with lead soldiers as a boy. He was born over 100 years ago (1863–1937) and lived much of his life in France.

Because of the nature of the music there may be times when you will want to give the students some "clues" BEFORE they hear the music. "Of a Tailor and a Bear," by MacDowell,[6] is an example of this.

1. Without telling the name of the record, say that an animal will "speak" in the music. Suggest that the boys and girls listen for his voice and try to decide what animal it is.

2. Play the record. Encourage an alert, quiet attitude.

[6] From the RCA Victor Basic Record Library for Elementary Schools, Vol. II, *Listening Activities*.

3. After the children have heard the music, encourage them to discuss briefly some questions such as: "Did the music sound like a big animal, or a little animal?"

4. Tell the class the story the composer had in mind when he wrote the music.

5. Write the title and the composer's name on the chalkboard, then play the record again so that all may hear the story the music tells.

6. Follow this with an opportunity for the children to dramatize the story.

You may want to use this composition later as the basis for a lesson in creative rhythmic movement. Having become familiar with the music in the manner just described, the children should be ready for this type of expression.

SUGGESTED RECORDS FOR DESCRIPTIVE OR STORY ELEMENTS

"Beauty and the Beast" from the *Mother Goose Suite* (Ravel)	Mus. Sound Books 78014
"Dance of the Mosquito" (Liadov)	Mus. Sound Books 78016
"Dwarfs" (Reinhold)	RCA Basic R. I
"Little Gray Ponies"	Young People's R. 735
"Little Sandman" (Brahms)	RCA Basic L. I
"Little Windmills in the Breeze" (Couperin)	Mus. Sound Books 26a
"Lonesome House"	C. R. Guild 5013
"March of the Little Lead Soldiers" (Pierné)	RCA Basic L. I
"Pavane of the Sleeping Beauty" (Ravel)	Mus. Sound Books 78013
"Sleeping Time" (Pinto)	RCA Basic L. I
"Syncopated Clock" (Anderson)	RCA LM-2638/LSC-2638
"The Canary" (Mozart)	Mus. Sound Books 78140
"The North Wind Doth Blow" (Guion)	Mus. Sound Books 78301
"The Organ Grinder" (Mozart)	Mus. Sound Books 78140
"The Sleighride" (Mozart)	Mus. Sound Books 78140
"Waltz of the Doll" (Delibes)	RCA Adventures I

This kind of activity has great appeal. It also helps to develop the ability to *listen actively* because it gives the class something specific to *listen for*.

Middle Childhood (Levels 3 and 4)

Although on these levels you will want to place an increasing emphasis upon *absolute music* (music that is not intended to tell a story or describe anything), you will still need to continue listening experiences with program music (narrative or descriptive).[7] One technique that you might find helpful is to play two or three short compositions, then have your class compare these in terms of mood. For example, you might choose "Bear Dance," by Bartók, "The Swan" from *Carnival of the Animals,* by Saint-Saëns, and "In the Hall of the Mountain King" from *Peer Gynt* Suite No. 1, by Grieg.[8] You might want to use a presentation similar to this for your lesson (or lessons, if this is too long for one session):

1. Announce to the class that there will be three short compositions on today's "program." Instead of giving the titles of each, you will identify them only by a number. (Write the numbers 1, 2, 3 on the chalkboard, spacing them well apart.) Warn any child who may recognize the music to keep the title a secret for the time being.

2. Suggest to your students that you would like them to be especially attentive to mood as they listen. At the conclusion of each selection, ask them to give you words that they feel best describe the mood. Then write these words under the identifying number on the board.

3. Play the first composition, "Bear Dance," and *briefly* discuss the mood. Write the descriptive words on the board. Proceed in the same manner for the next two compositions, "The Swan" and "In the Hall of the Mountain King."

4. When these steps have been completed, write the title of each composition next to its identifying number. (You may need to give a short explanation of the third selection to establish the children's understanding of this composition.)

5. Add the composer's name to the list on the board, and lead the children to discover that the composer, in each case, deliberately planned his music to de-

---

[7] RCA *Adventures in Music* for Grades III and IV, and *Musical Sound Books* (The Sound Book Press Society, Inc.) are excellent sources of material for both absolute and program music.

[8] From RCA *Adventures in Music,* Grade 3, Vol. 2.

scribe some object (bear or swan) or some story-
telling situation (trolls and imps battling Peer, "In
the Hall of the Mountain King").

6. Contrast the characteristics of the bear and the
   swan. Examine the descriptive words on the board
   to see if they seem to "match" the characteristics
   just given. In this discussion show why Bartók wrote
   music that was heavy, vicious, excited, and "jumpy"
   for "Bear Dance," while Saint-Saëns created a beautiful, smooth-flowing melody to suggest the quiet,
   calm serenity of the swan. Compare the similarity of
   mood between the "Bear Dance" and "In the Hall
   of the Mountain King."

If you find you need to divide this presentation into two sessions
because of time, you might want to use steps 1 through 4 the first
day, concluding after a brief review with steps 5 and 6 in a follow-
up lesson. Throughout the year the children may enjoy hearing
these compositions played again individually.

*ABSOLUTE MUSIC: EARLY
CHILDHOOD (LEVELS 1 AND 2)*

Much of the joy of listening comes to us individually and vividly
through music that is not intended to tell a story or describe
anything. Children enjoy the opportunity to listen to recorded
music for its own sake, and can give sensitive reactions to such
questions as:

1. Was the music gay?
2. Was it sad?
3. How did the music make you feel?

SUGGESTED RECORDS ILLUSTRATING ABSOLUTE MUSIC

"Badinerie" from *Suite No. 2 in B Minor* (Bach)	RCA Adventures III, Vol. 1
"Barcarolle" from *The Tales of Hoffmann* (Offenbach)	RCA Adventures III, Vol. 1
"Berceuse" (Ilyinsky)	RCA Basic L. III
"Gigue" from *Suite for String Orchestra* (Corelli-Pinelli)	Columbia MS-6095
"Liebeslieder" Waltz No. 4 (Brahms)	Mus. Sound Books 78308

"March" (Bach)	RCA Basic R. III
"Menuetto" from *Royal Fireworks Music* (Handel)	RCA Adventures III, Vol. 2
"Minuet" from *Don Giovanni* (Mozart)	Mus. Sound Books 78003
"Northern Song" (Schumann)	RCA Basic R. III
"Polka" from *Schwanda* (Weinberger)	Westminster-18690/14030 (S)
"Polka" from *Slavonic Dance No. 3* (Dvorak)	RCA VIC-1054/VICS-1054
"Rondo for Bassoon and Orchestra" (Weber)	Young People's R. 1009
"Rondo" on *Folk Tunes*, No. 31 (Bartók)	Vox SVBX-5426
"Scherzo in B-flat" (Schubert)	Mus. Sound Books 78308
"Siciliana" from *L'Allegro* (Handel)	RCA Basic R. III
"Spring Song" (Mendelssohn)	Mus. Sound Books 78309
"The Fairy Garden" from *Mother Goose Suite* (Ravel)	Mus. Sound Books 78014
"Theme" from *Sonata in A* (Mozart)	Mus. Sound Books 78307
"Waltz," Op. 9a, No. 3 (Schubert)	RCA Basic R. III

ABSOLUTE MUSIC: MIDDLE
CHILDHOOD (LEVELS 3 AND 4)

During the third and fourth levels increasing use can be made of absolute music. Give the students frequent opportunities to become acquainted with the gavotte, the minuet, and other dance forms. Listening lessons centered around these dances can emphasize rhythm, design, and interesting information about the composer and his era.

THE GAVOTTE: TRADITIONAL DANCE FORM. There are a number of ways to present lessons on absolute music. Many times you may want to make a detailed analysis of what is heard. For example, let's consider the record "Gavotte" by Gossec.[9] The steps in such a procedure might be:

1. Ask the students to determine, from listening to the recording, what type of music it is—march, lullaby, dance, hymn, etc.

[9] From the RCA Victor Basic Record Library for Elementary Schools, Vol. IV, *Listening Activities.*

2. The less experience your class has had in the past, the more "clues" you will have to offer them, of course, but they should be able to recognize that this music is a dance. In a *brief* discussion they should discover that it is an "old-fashioned" dance.

3. Give the title of the composition and the origin of the gavotte, naming some of its peculiar characteristics. (See program notes in Vol. IV, *Listening Activities,* RCA Victor Basic Record Library.)

4. Ask the students to listen again to the recording. This time encourage them to be aware of the mood. At the conclusion discuss this briefly and ask about any solo instruments that they may have heard.

5. Play the recording again. Suggest that the class be alert to the rhythm of the composition.

6. Play the first four phrases of the recording again and ask the class to clap the rhythm lightly.

7. Suggest that the students listen as you clap the first phrase (without the music). Ask them to identify the note values that you clapped—quarter, eighth, etc.

8. Ask the students to clap the first phrase with you while they chant the rhythm syllables. (♩= tah, ♪ = tee)

9. Invite a student to place the rhythm pattern on the board.

10. To increase skills in performing note values divide the class into two groups. Have one group clap the quarter notes, the other the eighth notes. On the quarter rests the class should make some quiet motion with their hands to indicate the beats are *felt* but not *heard.*

11. The use of rhythm instruments can enhance this experience. Ask the class to suggest some instruments that might sound like eighth notes; for example:

Castanets
Jingle clogs
Bells
Tambourines
Maracas or rattles

And quarter notes; for example:

Rhythm sticks
Tone block
Drum
Triangle

12. Exchange instruments between the two groups so that each student has an opportunity to experience both quarter and eighth notes.

Obviously, this presentation may be too long for one lesson. It might be wise to do activities 1 through 8 the first day, and 9 through 12 another day. You can adapt this method in any manner that will best suit your purposes.

SUGGESTED RECORDS FOR ANALYSIS OF ABSOLUTE MUSIC

"Air for the G String" from *Suite No. 3 in D Major* (Bach)	Mus. Sound Books 78040
Allegro in G from *Christmas Pieces* (Mendelssohn)	RCA Rhythmic Activities, Vol. 4
"Andalucia" from *Suite Andalucia* (Lecuona)	RCA Adventures in Music, Grade 4, Vol. 1
Andante from *Symphony No. 94 in G Major,* "Surprise Symphony" (Haydn)	RCA Listening Activities, Vol. 4
Bourree from *Water Music* (Handel)	Mus. Sound Books 78002
"Canzonetta" from *Quartet No. 1,* Op. 12 (Mendelssohn)	Decca DL-9751
Largo from *Xerxes* (Handel)	Mus. Sound Books 78001
Minuetto from *L'Arlesienne Suite No. 1* (Bizet)	RCA Adventures in Music, Grade 4, Vol. 2
Passepied (Delibes)	RCA Rhythmic Activities, Vol. 4
"Rondo" from *Eine kleine Nachtmusik* (Mozart)	Vanguard SRV 162
Slavonic Dance in C Minor, Op. 46, No. 7 (Dvorak)	RCA Adventures IV
String Quartet in C Major ("The Emperor's Hymn") (Haydn)	Deutsche Grammophon Gesellschaft LPM 138886

"The Cat's Fugue" (Scarlatti)   Mus. Sound Books 78039

"Three Pieces for Piano," Op. 198   Mus. Sound Books 78210
(Gretchaninov)—Lament; Mazurka;
Romance.

"Traumerei" from *Scenes from*   RCA Adventures in Music, Grade 4,
Childhood (Schumann)   Vol. 2

CONTEMPORARY STYLES:
EARLY CHILDHOOD
(LEVELS 1 AND 2)

Just as children need a well-balanced, nutritional diet for their
physical growth, they also need a well-balanced listening program
to assist in developing their musical growth. It is well for them to
hear works of composers of the past, but they need also to enjoy
contemporary music. One such composition that would be useful
in stressing tempo, dynamics, and descriptive elements, is "Pizzicato Polka" from *Ballet Suite No. 1* by Shostakovich.[10] Using the
procedural steps just outlined, you will want to help the children
discover:

1. The air of subdued mystery in the opening section,
    contrasting with the wild excitement of the middle
    section, and finally returning to the mood of the
    first section—since the composer intended no struc-
    tured story, guard against the creation of one by the
    children. Encourage them instead to express their
    feelings about the mood. Until they have had suffi-
    cient experiences in listening to do this by the use of
    such words as "mysterious," "playful," etc., they
    will probably respond in terms of association. Ex-
    pressing their feelings about the first section, a
    number may say that someone was tiptoeing. Others
    may think a game was being played in which the
    object was to "sneak up" on someone and frighten
    him. By careful questioning, help the children to
    discover what it was in the music that made them
    think of tiptoeing (the pizzicato of the strings) or
    the attempt to frighten another (the air of mystery
    produced by the minor mode). Although you will
    not want to discuss the minor mode in detail, you
    can lead the children to discover that it sounds dif-
    ferent. You may want to repeat short excerpts of

[10] From RCA *Adventures in Music*, Grade 1.

the minor and major sections to show this contrast. Remember always to keep the discussion brief, while at the same time pursuing it long enough to establish your point clearly.

2. The contrast in dynamics—here is a good opportunity for the children to become aware of dynamics as they hear the music gradually growing louder and louder until it reaches its intensity in the middle section, then recedes again in the closing part. Just a few well-pointed questions such as, "Was the music soft/loud all the way through or did it change?" will direct the attention of the students to this contrast.

3. The contrast in tempo—this awareness can be developed in much the same fashion as that described for the contrast in dynamics. Help the children to perceive how these changes in tempo and dynamics alter the mood of the music. As it grows faster and louder it increases in excitement.

4. The design or form of the composition—this understanding should be the natural result of the total listening experience. After the children have discovered the contrasts in the music: soft-loud-soft, not too fast—fast—not too fast, they should be helped to realize that the first and third parts are alike, and that the second part is different.

CONTEMPORARY STYLES:
MIDDLE CHILDHOOD
(LEVELS 3 AND 4)

CONTEMPORARY BALLET.   Be sure to include contemporary music that has an unusual appeal for children this age. One composition that youngsters expecially enjoy is "Hoe-Down" from *Rodeo,* a ballet suite by Copland.[11] Although there are many ways of introducing this music, you might want to proceed in this manner:

1. Point out to the class that the music they will hear today was written by an American composer, Aaron Copland, who is still living. (Relate the word "contemporary" to this.)

[11] From RCA *Adventures in Music,* Grade 5, Vol. 2.

2. Explain that you will not give the title of the selection. Instead, you want them to listen attentively to determine what kind of music it is.

3. After playing the record, invite the students' response. Most of them will immediately identify it as some type of square dance. At this point ask what they heard in the music that revealed this. Many of them will have heard the "fiddlers"[12] tuning their instruments. Others will suggest that the rhythm of the composition sounds like the square dance.

4. Discuss the tempo and mood. (Extremely fast throughout with only one or two departures from this pattern and a mood of hilarity and gaiety.)

5. Give a brief sketch of the story of the ballet, then listen again. Ask the students to identify solo instruments and families of instruments assuming solo roles on themes.

6. As a follow-up teach your class a simple square dance.

ORCHESTRAL INSTRUMENTS:
EARLY CHILDHOOD
(LEVELS 1 AND 2)

Young children are naturally interested in instruments of all kinds. Many pupils have had the opportunity in the preschool years to become familiar with formal instruments of the band and orchestra (such as the violin, the trumpet, and the flute) because of the activities of their older brothers and sisters or their parents. Television programs also afford a look at many instruments.

In the early school years, children also become familiar with some of the *informal instruments* (rhythm sticks, tone bells, jingle clogs, the Autoharp, and others) that *require no formal training* to learn to play.

Other familiar instruments such as tone flutes, Flutophones, recorders, harmonicas, ukuleles, guitars, banjos, and accordions are not legitimate instruments of the band or the symphony or-

[12] Sometimes today's boys and girls are not aware that a "fiddle" is really a violin (often—but not necessarily—of a somewhat less expensive model) and that square dance "fiddlers" use a different and somewhat primitive technique in playing the instrument. Fortunately, many Western programs on television show how the "fiddler" holds the instrument rather low on his shoulder, and often bows on the open strings with remarkably little manipulation of the finger board.

chestra. Even the piano is not a regular part of the symphony orchestra, although it does appear as a guest member when a composer wishes to use it in his composition.

Children cannot be expected to understand all this at first, but study about orchestral instruments can be begun early. A simple beginning can be made by presenting some of the following records:

SUGGESTED RECORDS FOR LISTENING FOR INSTRUMENTS

"A Child's Introduction to the Orchestra and All Its Instruments"—Golden Records	GLP: 1
"Aragonaise" (Massenet)—tambourine	RCA Adventures I
"Drummer Boy"	C.R. Guild 1015
"Impromptu, The Top" (Bizet)—flute	RCA Basic L. I
"Legend of the Bells (Planquette)—high bells above lower chimes	RCA Basic L. I
"March" (Bizet)—trumpet and snare drum	RCA Basic L. I
"March, Little Soldier" (Pinto)—trumpet, snare drum, and bass drum	RCA Basic L. I
"Military March" (Anderson)—"bugle call" at beginning played by the trumpet	RCA Basic R. I
"Mr. Grump and the Dingle School Band"	C. R. Guild 5007
"Pantomime" from The Comedians (Kabalevsky) —snare drum, cymbals, bass drum	RCA Adventures I
"Pizzicato Polka" (Shostakovich)—violin strings are plucked (that is, played "pizzicato") rather than bowed	RCA Adventures I
"Ring Around the Rosy" (Pinto)—xylophone	RCA Basic L. I
"Skipping Theme" (Anderson)—good example of snare drum	RCA Basic R. I
"Spotlight on Percussion"	VOX
"The Wonderful Violin"	YPR 311
"Valsette" (Borowski)—violin plays melody	RCA Basic R. I
"Waltz of the Doll" from Coppélia (Delibes)– violins and flutes	RCA Adventures I

It is certainly not necessary to present a long record entirely at one time. You can make an effective "continued story" of it. The presentation can be greatly enhanced by pictures of the instruments.

Whenever possible, try to use actual instruments. Children should be taught that these instruments are not toys; that they can easily be broken, and that they cost a great deal of money. If they are handled at all by the pupils, the owner's permission should be secured first.

Through many different types of pleasurable experiences with orchestral instruments, children can discover that:

1. Some are played by *blowing* (horns, clarinets, flutes, etc.)
2. Some are played by *striking* (drums, gongs, triangles, etc.)
3. Some are played by *bowing* (violins, violas, etc.)
4. Some are played by *plucking* (harp, and sometimes violin, viola, cello, and string bass)

Later on, in other levels, they will learn the names of the "families" (or choirs) of the symphony orchestra, and the names of all the instruments in each "family."

After the children have had sufficient time to become reasonably well acquainted with some orchestral instruments, you might try this activity:

1. Ask the children to name all the instruments they can think of.
2. As they name them, make two lists on the board: one, those instruments that play in the symphony orchestra (see pages 180–181 for a checklist), and the other, those that do not.
3. Now have the boys and girls name the instruments of the symphony orchestra that they listed on the board.
4. Tell the class that they are going to hear a recording of one of the instruments they have just told you about. You are going to see if they can guess which one it is.
5. Play one of the recordings listed below that is particularly good for this experience. Begin with a familiar instrument. If the children have mentioned violin, trumpet, or flute, it might be well to start with one of these.
6. See if the class can recognize the instrument by its sound. If not, show them the picture of the instru-

ment, and ask if they can identify it. If they still do not know what it is, give them the name and have them pronounce it with you.

7. Proceed in a similar manner to acquaint them with these instruments:

Violin	Snare drum
Trumpet	Cymbals
Flute	Triangle
Piccolo	Harp
Clarinet	Piano (if the composer wants it)
Bass drum	

You may wish to add other instruments to this list. It is not necessary to have the children learn "families" of instruments. Just help them to discover whether the instrument is played by *blowing* it, *bowing* (and plucking) it, or *striking* it.

Some of the recordings listed below are musical stories designed to introduce orchestral instruments to children. You need not attempt to play the entire recording at one "sitting." Try to make it a "continued story."

SUGGESTED RECORDS ILLUSTRATING ORCHESTRAL INSTRUMENTS

"April-Snowdrop" from *The Seasons* (Tchaikovsky)—Violin and viola	Columbia CML-4487
"Brother John and the Village Orchestra" (Jurey)—Musical story introducing brass and percussion instruments	Bowmar 299
Carnival of the Animals (Saint-Saëns) The Elephant—double bass The Swan—cello	Columbia MS-6368
"Dance of the Sugar Plum Fairy" from *The Nutcracker* Suite (Tchaikovsky)—Celesta	RCA VIC-1263
"Departure" (Prokofiev)—Good example of French horn at the beginning; triangle near the middle, and xylophone toward the end	RCA Adventures II
"Evening Bells" (Kullak)—Orchestra bells and celesta (pronounced:	RCA Basic L. II

chay-lest-ah), with strings helping;
celesta looks like small organ,
sounds like chimes or bells

"Fairy Pipers" (Elgar)—Clarinets and bells	RCA Basic L. II
"Greensleeves" (English folk tune) —Violin	Mus. Sound Books 78311
"Jack in the Box" from *Mikrokosmos Suite No. 2* (Bartók)—Sleigh bells, tambourines, xylophone, wood block, snare drum, timpani, and cymbals	RCA Adventures II
"March of the Toys" from *Babes in Toyland* (Herbert)—Muted trumpets and snare drum at the beginning, followed by flutes in opening *Fanfare;* repeated at end as music fades away	RCA Adventures II
"Serenata" (Moszkowski)—Violin sings melody; listen for tinkling of small bells	RCA Basic L. II
"Tacky O'Rick and the Licorice Stick"—Musical story of the clarinet	Audio-Ed (ABC) AS-29
"The Golden Goose"—Well-known fairy tale introduces sounds of orchestral instruments	C. R. Guild 5002
"The Little Shepherd" from *Children's Corner Suite* (Debussy)— Flute	Columbia MS-6567

ORCHESTRAL INSTRUMENTS:
MIDDLE CHILDHOOD
(LEVELS 3 AND 4)

On these levels you might introduce the study of orchestral instruments in this manner:

1. Ask the class to name all of the orchestral instruments that they know.
2. List these on the board.
3. Have the students give the proper method of playing (blowing, bowing, etc.) for each instrument on the board.
4. Make a new list, grouping all of the instruments

under the appropriate method of playing. The list might look something like this:

Bowing

Violin	Cello
Viola	String bass

Blowing

Flute	Oboe
Trumpet	Tuba
Trombone	French horn
Clarinet	Bass clarinet
Piccolo	Bassoon

Striking

Snare drum	Triangle
Bass drum	Castanets
Cymbals	Gong

Plucking

Harp	Bowing instruments (sometimes)

(As you can see, this list is not complete. The students may be able to name more under each category—or they may not know this many.)

FAMILIES, OR CHOIRS.   The next step is to assist the class in placing the instruments in families (choirs). To begin you might explain that those instruments that seem to be "related" in some manner belong to the same family. To illustrate, it might be best to begin with the "bowing" division. Suggest that your students name something on the violin that can be found on all of the other three instruments listed in that group. When the correct answer is given (strings) it should be easy to lead the class to the conclusion that this is the string family. Call attention to another instrument that belongs in this family but appears under another category on the board (harp, under "plucking"). The class can discover the difference between plucking the harp and bowing the violin. Be sure to emphasize that, at times, the violin, viola, cello, and string bass are also plucked (pizzicato).

When the "striking" group is discussed you may need to help your students discover that the characteristic that "relates" these instruments is the manner in which they are played. That is why this family is called the percussion group. If possible show the class pictures of these instruments (or perhaps a student can bring an actual instrument in) and discuss with them the way they are played.

The "blowing" group is actually made up of two families—the woodwinds and the brasses. The woodwinds have a key system and reeds. (When you attempt to explain reeds to your class (both single and double reeds), it would be a good plan to have some to pass around for the students to see and feel. The word "reed" means little to them unless they have some visual experience with it. Secure some reeds made from different materials in order to give the class the opportunity to make comparisons between modern materials such as plastic and those used originally.) The brasses have valves (with the exception of the slide trombone). Perhaps one of the easiest ways for the children to distinguish between the woodwind and brass families is to discuss the materials from which the instruments are made. (Care has to be exercised here, of course, because today various new materials are often used for their manufacture.) It might be easier to select the brasses first: trumpet, trombone, French horn, and tuba. Explain that because these instruments are played by blowing they were placed in that category on the board. However, because they are made of brass they belong to the brass family.

Analyze the word "woodwind" for the class. Explain that it takes "wind" to blow an instrument. Since most of the members of this family were originally made of wood, the name "woodwind" was given to this group. The flute, piccolo, clarinet, bass clarinet, oboe, English horn, bassoon, and contrabassoon make up the woodwind family.

Some of the students will inquire about the saxophone and its family status. It is really a "hybrid" instrument—because it has a key system and a reed it is related to the woodwinds; because it is made of brass it is related to that family. Some educators place this instrument in the woodwind group, others in the brass, and still others in no family at all.

When the families are finally decided the list should look something like this:

String

Violin	String bass
Viola	Harp
Cello	

Woodwind

Flute	Oboe
Piccolo	English horn
Clarinet	Bassoon
Bass clarinet	Contrabassoon

Brass

Trumpet	French horn
Trombone	Tuba

Percussion

Snare drum	Cymbals
Bass drum	Castanets
Timpani	Triangle
Gong	Chimes
Tambourine	Xylophone or Marimba
Bells	Celesta

There are many good books about orchestral instruments available today. Some are written to help the teacher; others are designed to be read by the children. Specific titles, authors, and publishers are shown in Appendix H. Large charts, pilot lessons, overhead projection cells, and other instructional aids (and their sources) are listed in Appendix L.

Listening to recordings planned to highlight certain instruments is important in this study. As the students give careful attention they can develop discrimination of *tone quality* (or *timbre*). Many classes often learn to identify each instrument by its characteristic sound.

SUGGESTED RECORDS FOR LISTENING TO INSTRUMENTS

"Brother John"[13] (brass and percussion)	Bowmar
"The Hen, the Ass, and the Cuckoo" (Hugenin)	Mus. Sound Books 78318
"Instruments of the Orchestra" (Charles Walton)	RCA LE-6000

[13] *Brother John and the Village Orchestra, The Old King and His Fiddlers Four,* and *Tom the Piper* (Bowmar) are also excellent recordings for teaching form and style in music, rhythm, and creative movement, as well as recognition of the instruments of the orchestra. Teaching suggestions are presented in a sequence of difficulty: simple directions and learning for the lower levels, and more complex directions for the upper. The music was arranged, composed, and conducted by Edward B. Jurey; the stories are by Inez Schubert and Lucille Wood, with narration by Hal Smith.

"Licorice Stick"	Young People's Records 420
"The Little Shepherd of Bibleland"	YPR 3404
"Meet the Instruments of the Band and the Symphony Orchestra" (two filmstrips with album)	Bowmar
"The Old King and His Fiddlers Four" (string quartet and full string orchestra)	Bowmar
Toccata for Percussion, 3rd movement (Chavez)	Columbia CMS-6447
"Tom the Piper" (woodwinds)	Bowmar
Young Person's Guide to the Orchestra (Britten)	Columbia MS-6368

While the study of instruments is in progress you could add emphasis by displaying a different family on the bulletin board each week for a month. You may prefer to let the students choose from published pictures of excellent quality, or to let them draw their own pictures of the instruments and arrange the bulletin board themselves. Your class might also enjoy making miniature instruments using pipe stem cleaners, clay, or other materials. If they want to make larger-scale models they could select some members of the percussion or string family.

In addition a new type of game can be both informative and enjoyable—such as a musical *"Bingo"* based on instruments. Each child could make one card. You should assign the instruments to be drawn in the squares. (This would, of course, avoid repetition and would ensure all instruments of the orchestra being included.) Then type or write on separate slips of paper the names of the instruments—one name on each slip. When you are ready to play, a student could draw one of these from a box or other container, read, and the game would be on. This game can be most helpful on snowy or rainy days, and it is surprising how much information the students can acquire.

DEVELOPING DISCRIMINATION:
MIDDLE CHILDHOOD
(LEVELS 3 AND 4)

PREPARATORY WORK. In earlier listening experiences, children normally have had the opportunity to:

1. Explore and describe the many *moods* of music,
2. Identify the *descriptive elements* in music,
3. Identify *tempo* in music through an understanding of faster and slower *speeds,*
4. Identify *dynamics* in music through an understanding of louder and softer sounds,
5. Identify *range* through an understanding of higher and lower pitches, and
6. Identify many *instruments* of the symphony orchestra and the band as distinguished from informal classroom instruments.

If these preparatory listening opportunities have been rich ones, your students have probably developed the ability to *listen purposefully and intelligently* at their own maturation level.

In the suggested list of recordings that follows, you will notice that some of the elements of the music have been abbreviated as follows:

1. "M"—to indicate mood
2. "DES"—to indicate descriptive elements
3. "T"—to indicate tempo
4. "DYN"—to indicate dynamics
5. "RA"—to indicate range

The predominant *instrument* and the "family" to which it belongs in the band or orchestra are written out when they are easy to distinguish in the recorded example.

RECORDINGS ILLUSTRATING SOME OF THE ELEMENTS OF MUSIC

"Aviary" from *Carnival of the Animals* (Saint-Saëns) (DES).	Columbia MS-6368
"Bear Dance" from *Hungarian Sketches* (Bartók)—(M) wild, exciting; (DES); (T) quick, but not steady; (DYN) loud throughout, but softer at end; (RA) low bassoons, high flutes.	RCA Adventures III, Vol. 2[14]

[14] *Adventures in Music*, RCA Victor's graded record library for elementary schools, has Teaching Guides prepared by Gladys Tipton and Eleanor Tipton; musical selections are performed by the National Symphony Orchestra, Howard Mitchell conducting.

"Changing of the Guard" from *Carmen* Suite No. 1 (Bizet)—(DES); (T) steady; (DYN) begins softly, increases in volume, ends softly. *Trumpet* (brass family) at the beginning.

RCA Adventures III, Vol. 2

"Departure" from *Winter Holiday Suite* (Prokofiev) (DES).

RCA Adventures II

"Funeral March of a Marionette" (Gounod)—(M) begins solemnly but basic mood is humorous.

Mus. Sound Books 78021/78119

"Garden of Live Flowers" from *Through the Looking Glass Suite* (Taylor)—(M) contrast in middle section; (DES); (T) quick, slow, then quick; (RA) begins and ends high; middle, low.

RCA Adventures III, Vol. 2

"In the Hall of the Mountain King" from *Peer Gynt Suite No. 1* (Grieg) —(M) mysterious, exciting; (DES); (T) increasingly faster; (DYN) increasingly louder; (RA) increasingly higher.

RCA Adventures III, Vol. 2

"Little Train of the Caipura" from *Bachianas Brasileiras No. 2* (Villa-Lobos)—(DES); (T) starts slowly, picks up speed.

RCA Adventures III, Vol. 1

"March" and "Gallop" from *The Comedians* (Kabalevsky)—(DES); (T) March: steady, moderate; Gallop: very fast; (RA) March: drops rapidly from high to low; Gallop: high notes on xylophone in second theme.

RCA Adventures III, Vol. 1

"March of the Dwarfs" (Grieg)—(M) Mood changes with themes; 1 and 2 excited; 3 calm.

RCA Basic L. III

"Overture" to *The Flying Dutchman* (Wagner)—(T) fast; (DYN) growing louder.

Mus. Sound Books 78147

"Polka" from *Age of Gold* ballet (Shostakovich)—(M) jesting.

RCA VIC-1184/VICS-1184

"Saturday Night" from *Ozark Set* (Siegmeister)—(M) Typical hoedown.

Mus. Sound Books 78130

"Semper Fidelis" (Sousa)—(M) exciting, vigorous; (DYN) loud, with

RCA Adventures III, Vol. 2

few soft contrasts. *Snare drum* (percussion family).

"Snow Is Dancing" from *Children's Corner Suite* (Debussy)—(M) quiet, vague; (DES); (T) little change; (DYN) soft, with few contrasts.	RCA Adventures III, Vol. 1
"The Swan" from *Carnival of the Animals* (Saint-Saëns)—(M) quiet; (DES); (T) gracefully slow throughout; (DYN) soft throughout. *Harp and cello* (string family).	RCA Adventures III, Vol. 2
"Tambousin" from *Céphale et Procris* (Gretry)—(M) contrasting sections; (DYN) loud to soft.	RCA Adventures II
"Tarantella" from *The Fantastic Toyshop* (Rossini-Respighi)—(M) exciting; (T) fast throughout; (DYN) sudden changes; (RA) some very high tones. *Tambourine* (percussion family).	RCA Adventures III, Vol. 2

At first you may want to select and emphasize a single element of the music each time the record is played. With experience, the children are able to distinguish several of the elements in a composition, and discover them for themselves. In this way, *musical discrimination* can be fostered.

MUSICAL FORM—A BLUEPRINT:
MIDDLE CHILDHOOD
(LEVELS 3 AND 4)

The attempts to assist your students to develop an understanding of form (the design of music) should be kept very simple. Extending and expanding the experiences of the earlier levels in this (see pages 85-89 and 234-236) should probably be the guidelines for you. Perhaps discussing a presentation here would be helpful. For specific illustration let's consider the third movement of *The Children's Symphony,* by Harl McDonald:[15]

1. Tell the children that today they will hear one part of a symphony. Explain simply that a *symphony* is a very long composition divided into parts. Each part is called a *movement*. Today they will hear the third movement from *The Children's Symphony,* by

[15] From the RCA *Adventures in Music* Series, Grade 2.

McDonald. This music is made up mostly of two songs that they know very well. After they have heard the music *all the way through,* you will ask them to tell you what these two songs are.

2. Play the record. Have the children identify the tunes.

3. With the suggestion that the children might like to sing along with the music, play the record again. Ask them which of the two songs ("The Farmer in the Dell," "Jingle Bells") appeared first in the music. Which was last? Since "The Farmer in the Dell" is heard both first and last, it is obvious to the children that "Jingle Bells" is in the middle.

4. Write the names of the songs in vertical order on the chalkboard:

   "The Farmer in the Dell"

   "Jingle Bells"

   "The Farmer in the Dell"

5. Explain to the boys and girls that people have to decide how their house is going to be built before they can live in it. Composers are "builders" too, and decide the design of their music before they write it. Call attention to the song titles on the board. Suggest that, since "The Farmer in the Dell" is the first song in the music, we give it the first letter in the alphabet—A. Then proceed with such questions as: "What shall we call 'Jingle Bells'? Since the next song ("The Farmer in the Dell") is exactly the same as the first, what shall we call it?"

6. Conclude simply with the statement that the composer's "blueprint" for the design of the music was ABA. (At this point some teachers have found success with still another comparison: with the "design" of a sandwich. The bread on the top is A; the meat, cheese, or peanut butter-jelly, etc., is B, and the bread on the bottom is A.)

To reinforce this basic presentation of *form* in music, there are other characteristics of this composition that can be explored and related to its *form*. For example, you might want the children to sing the two songs (without the recording), clapping the rhythm as they sing. They will discover the *galloping* movement of "The

Farmer in the Dell" and the *trotting* movement of "Jingle Bells."
The form can then be recognized also through the rhythm:
galloping-trotting-galloping.

DANCE FORMS

The study of such dance forms as the allemande, bourrée, cour-
ante, gigue, sarabande, and others might be included in your
plans—especially in their relationship to the 18th century *suite*.
However, they should not be presented in depth if there is no time
to include some of the Latin-American dance forms in use today
and the better-known traditional ones. Can your class identify
most of these traditional dance forms when they hear them?

As each type discussed here is heard and studied you should
make sure that a few important facts are clearly understood by the
class. Long, detailed explanations only prove confusing and tiring.
However, some basic information is essential.

1. *Waltz*—a popular dance written in $\frac{3}{4}$ meter, with
   "swinging and swaying" rhythm. The waltz is
   thought by some music historians to be of Bohe-
   mian origin.
2. *Minuet*—a French dance originating probably in the
   17th century as a rustic, round dance. Later adopted
   into the court of King Louis XIV, it is characterized
   by slow, measured steps, pointing of toes, and deep
   bows and curtsies. This dance is in $\frac{3}{4}$ meter.
3. *Gavotte*—a gay, French dance originating with the
   peasant class. When it was later adopted into the
   court of King Louis XIV it became more sedate and
   polite. However, it retained its sparkling manner.
   This dance is in $\frac{4}{4}$ meter.
4. *Polka*—a vigorous round dance in fast $\frac{2}{4}$ meter originating in Bohemia in the early 1800s, and still popular in certain sections of the U.S.A. and Scandinavian countries.
5. *Mazurka*—a Polish national dance written in triple
   time (usually $\frac{3}{4}$). The strong accent frequently falls
   on the second or third beat of the measure. The
   mazurka is somewhat slower than the polka.
6. *Polonaise*—one of the oldest dances of Poland. Although in triple meter, it was originally used as a
   "Grand March" by the nobility and other dignitaries

on state occasions. It is still popular today because of the many well-known piano compositions written by Chopin in this form. The characteristic rhythm is:

Many of the Latin-American dances that we hear today have Spanish and French names, but their origin are found in the music of the African Negro, the Moor, and the Indian of Central and South America. The intriguing and energetic rhythms have become very popular throughout the world, and are often performed in North America and Europe. Some of the best-known are:

1. *Bolero*—a national dance of Spain in triple meter, with a lively tempo. One of the well-known accompanying rhythm patterns is:

2. *Tango*—said to have originated in Africa in the 16th century, it has been very popular in Spain since the time of the Moorish migration there. It is a slow dance in duple meter with these characteristic rhythms:

3. *Jarabe*—popular Mexican dance with alternating duple and triple meter. Some forms are danced with a large sombrero.

4. *Habanera*—national dance of Cuba, named for the city of Havana. It is similar to the tango, but contains more syncopated rhythms.

5. *Conga*—another Cuban dance, popular in many countries. Dancers form a winding line. The music is in a fast $\frac{4}{4}$ meter, highly accented on the fourth beat.

6. *Rumba* (or *Rhumba*)—popular dance originating with the Cuban Negro. It is in a fast duple meter.

7. *Samba*—generally believed to have Brazilian origins. It is in duple meter.

8. *Beguine*—has a French name, but its origins are in Africa.

9. *Malagueña*—named for the Spanish province of Malaga, this is a dance similar to the fandango. In triple meter, it has a characteristic rhythmic accompaniment:

Many upper-level children enjoy listening to these dance forms and are often willing to practice the intricate rhythms using castanets, guiros, maracas, and claves.

There is, of course, no "one way" to present any music lesson. Each teacher is an individual, and should experiment with a suggested approach and then make plans of her own. From year to year the personalities of the students will also be different, so the presentation of the music experience must be adapted to suit the needs of the time, the place, and the learner.

As is apparent, some of the information given in these brief definitions must either be presented by you to the class, or the students must find it in an encyclopedia or music dictionary. However, some essentials (such as the meter) can be discovered by the boys and girls themselves as they listen to the composition. For example, let's consider some plans for a possible music lesson centering around three dances: "The Skaters Waltz" (Waldteufel),[16] "Gavotte" (Grétry), and "Minuet" from *Don Giovanni* (Mozart).[17]

An approach similar to this could be used:

1. Explain to the class that you will play three selections on the record player. Ask them to listen carefully and decide what type of music each is. (Review with them the kinds they have become acquainted with in earlier experiences—marches, lullabies, dances, hymns, etc.)

2. Play one of the three dances and ask the class to identify the type. Proceed with the other two in the same manner.

[16] From RCA Victor Basic Record Library for Elementary Schools, Vol. IV, *Rhythmic Activities.*

[17] From same source as above, but in Vol V.

3. After it has been established that all three compositions are dances, ask the class to listen to one of
them again—for example, the minuet. Following the
first three or four phrases suggest to the students
that they find the heavy beat in each measure.(This
could be done by clapping, bringing the right hand
straight down on the first beat, tapping a finger on
the desk, or any other method that seems natural
and wise.) After a few moments ask the students to
say "one" softly as they clap or tap.

4. Once the students have felt the strong pulse or
heavy beat, ask them to find the "in-between"
beats. (If they are clapping the "one" beat, they
could tap "two" and "three" on their desks or in
the palms of their hands. If they are swinging their
arms on the downbeat, they might swing out and up
for the other two counts. The method is not important. The essential thing is that they *feel* the meter:
strong, weak, weak; *one,* two, three. It would be
well for them to count aloud, softly, all three beats.)

5. Proceed in a similar manner with the other two
selections. With the waltz the students might enjoy a
variation, by having half the class snap their fingers
on the "one" beat while the other half taps "two"
and "three" on their desks. Then reverse sides to
increase interest. (Swinging the hands gently while
snapping the fingers would emphasize the swaying
rhythm.)

6. At the close of the lesson, ask the class to sum up
what has been learned:

a. A waltz is a dance in $\frac{3}{4}$ meter. It has a swinging,
swaying rhythm.

b. A minuet is an "old-fashioned" dance in $\frac{3}{4}$.

c. A gavotte is a dance in $\frac{4}{4}$ meter.

In addition to the discovery of meter there should be some discussion about the mood and personal characteristics of each dance.
For example, the students should be aware of a sharp contrast
between the style of the waltz and that of the minuet. Although
each is in $\frac{3}{4}$ time, they do not resemble each other in any way. The
class members should be able to point out that the waltz has a
gliding, sliding motion, while the minuet is unique in its "de-
tached" action—so suited to the delicate dance steps.

It is amusing to discover that when the lively dances of the 17th and 18th centuries were adopted by the nobility and other gentry (including George Washington and his contemporaries), the vigorous movements became "stately" by necessity. How else could the gentlemen manage to move around in their tight knee-length breeches, long silk hose, high-heeled satin slippers, and heavy powdered wigs! The elaborate garments the ladies wore in those days were equally fragile, and probably more cumbersome than the gentlemen's, and were suitable only for dainty dancing.

To vary this lesson just one dance might be used, with two selections of other types to emphasize the difference in design and purpose. For instance, "Come, Let Us to the Bagpipe's Sound" from *Peasants' Cantata* (Bach),[18] "March of the Priests" from *The Magic Flute* (Mozart),[19] and one of the dances just mentioned might be correlated.

Integration of Listening with Classroom Subjects: Early and Middle Childhood (Levels 1, 2, 3, and 4)

Many units in social studies and reading could be enhanced by the use of recordings. When a class is learning about some specific country their study could be enriched by hearing folk songs, art songs, and instrumental selections that would reveal even further the culture and customs of the people. Here would also be a good time to do some folk dances of the country in question. Such a close blending of music with other classroom subjects can make learning much more meaningful and pleasant.

LATER CHILDHOOD (LEVELS 5 AND 6)

With TV and radio an absolute "must" in every home today, the listening habits of children have taken almost a 180-degree turn. Especially is this true for the older children on the fifth and sixth levels of learning. An examination of the types of music they are hearing reveals that they are very knowledgeable about the current

[18] *Ibid.*, Vol. V, *Listening Activities.*
[19] *Ibid.*, Vol. V, *Rhythmic Activities.*

"Top 10"—even the "Top 40"—but they are almost illiterate about other contemporary or traditional music. This forces the teacher to make a difficult decision—whether to introduce music that may be distasteful to them and risk persistent antagonism, or yield to their demands for Pop music.

Many teachers have found a happy answer in materials prepared by Michael D. Bennett, Associate Professor at Memphis State University.[20] Paralleling the concept of the Record of the Month Club, Mr. Bennett has prepared *Pop Hit Listening Guides* for a nine-month period—September through May. Each lesson features one current Pop tune (sometimes a little in advance of its peak popularity) with a simple yet detailed analysis of the music. A student worksheet and teacher's supplement are included with one stereo 45-rpm record. Two selections are on the record, but the lesson concentrates on only one. This leaves the teacher free either to develop a guide for the other selection or to encourage the class to create one. The second selection is usually by the same composer or performer, or from the same musical show.

In addition to the enriching experience of better understanding Pop music, this approach is a perfect "launching pad" for introducing traditional music that shares common elements with the Pop music being studied. Many teachers have reported that not only have the children been quite willing to listen to the traditional music, but they have been able to understand its structure much better after having "worked through" one of the Pop tunes.

Perhaps Mr. Bennett's own words can best describe his objectives in the *Pop Hit Listening Guides—A Contemporary Listening Program:*

> Each month a "Top 40" tune is selected for listening guide development because of its inherent musical interest and clear demonstration of common principles of music—logical form, melodic-rhythmic variation, unique orchestration, apt social commentary, expressive variety, etc. The three to five worksheets comprising each lesson are semiprogrammed to encourage students to base musical discriminations on what they hear as they hear it. Each listening guide is divided into several segments—easy to difficult. Young or inexperienced students may be given only the first portions of a lesson,

---

[20] Write to *Pop Hit Listening Guides,* 3149 Southern Ave., Memphis, Tenn. 38111.

while older or experienced students can complete the entire lesson. Teachers are given copyright permission to make unlimited copies of *PHLG*s for use within the purchasing school.

To make this discussion more meaningful, three lessons are reproduced here in their entirety with a possible follow-up suggestion for each. (The authors recognize that no Pop tune presented here could reasonably be expected to still be "popular" when you study this text but the principles remain constant.)

POP MUSIC

POP HIT LISTENING GUIDE   NAME_____
VOL. II, NO. 1

"DELTA DAWN" (HELEN REDDY)

No, this is not a test! But let's face it; you are in school to learn things that you probably wouldn't pick up out of school. You also know that there are "bad" and bad ways to do this. Pop Hit Listening Guides give you a chance to hear music you like. They also make it easy for you to learn things about music as you listen. (Your teacher likes this!) So, if everybody likes the listening guides they've got to be really "bad." Read on; important words will be italicized.

Music, like nearly everything else, is made up of sections or parts. If you can learn to identify the parts, learn how they are made up, and learn how they fit together you will have learned how music "does its thing."

Many popular songs have two different kinds of section, *chorus sections* and *verse sections*. A chorus section uses the same tune or *melody* and the same words or *lyrics* each time it is repeated. Chorus lyrics usually give the central thought of the song. A verse section uses melody and lyrics different from those of the chorus. When a verse section is repeated, it, like the chorus, uses its same melody, but the lyrics are different each time. Verse lyrics tell the story or give the details of what the song is about.

Got it? Let's find out. (Try to remember the answers without looking back.)

1. Another name for a song's tune is its_____ .

2. Another name for the words of a song is its
    _____ .

3. _____ sections repeat the same lyrics each time.

4. The lyrics of the_____tell the story of a song.

ANSWER CHECK

(When you see this phrase please wait until your teacher asks for your answers. Others may not be done yet, so keep calm.)

Enough heavy stuff; let's listen to the song. "Delta Dawn" has seven complete sections and one incomplete section, each one either a chorus or a verse. As you listen to the song complete Chart 1 by writing either "chorus" or "verse" on each of the blank lines. We have made it easy by telling you what the first section is. Your teacher will help you keep track of the sections. Ask questions now if you're not sure what to do. Once the music starts, no talking.

CHART 1

Section Identification

First section	___chorus___
Second section	_____
Third section	_____
Fourth section	_____
Fifth section	_____
Sixth section	_____
Seventh section	_____
Eighth section	_____

5. Easy, wasn't it? Which of the two kinds of sections was emphasized most?_____Give as many reasons as possible for your choice. _____
    _____
    _____

ANSWER CHECK

You now have some understanding of "Delta Dawn" 's *musical design*—the way the sections are arranged. Chart 2 contains three important design concepts—*repetition, contrast,* and *repetition with variation.* Decide which of these concepts best fits each of the statements in Chart 2.

CHART 2

Design Concepts

	CHOICES
The first section is a chorus and the second section is a verse. This is an example of _____ .	
	repetition
There is a total of six chorus sections, each one using the same words and the same melody, but with differing accompaniments. This is an example of _____ _____ .	contrast
	repetition with variation
The melody and the lyrics of each chorus section stay the same. This is an example of _____ .	

ANSWER CHECK

6. Still pretty easy? OK, we'll make it a little tougher—discovering the different things composers and arrangers do to achieve repetition, contrast, and _____ _____ .

7. Let's compare the opening chorus and the first verse sections to find some specific contrasts. You already know two things that are different between the chorus and the verse; the _____ and the _____ .

Chart 3 describes some of the sounds from the first two sections—mixed up, of course. (There may even be some things listed that are not heard at all!) As your teacher plays the first two sections of the song check the correct column for each statement.

CHART 3

Contrasts between Chorus 1 and Verse 1

Chorus 1	Verse 1	
		Helen is the only singer.
		A group of men and women sing back-up harmony.
		Drums, cymbal, bass guitar, organ, and piano play.
		Drums, cymbal, bass guitar, and piano play.
		No instruments play.

So, in addition to having different melodies (the biggest contrast) and different lyrics, we also discovered that these two sections have different *vocal* and *instrumental accompaniments*.

8. By the way, when singers sing in harmony with no instrumental accompaniment, as they did in the first _____ section, we say that they are singing in *a cappella* style. The term is Italian, meaning "like in the chapel," since in the 1400s singing in the European bishops' and kings' chapels was usually done in harmony without accompaniment. Today_____ means any harmonized, unaccompanied singing.

OK, now let's take a closer look at the two verse sections. Listen to determine if there is any variation, other than different lyrics, between the verses. (We're still looking for vocal or instrumental accompaniment differences.) Chart 4 lists some possible differences—check those that you actually hear.

CHART 4

Vocal or Instrumental Accompaniment
Differences between Verses 1 and 2

_____	Verse 2 is sung in a higher key.*
_____	Violins are added in verse 2.
_____	Singers are added singing "oo" in verse 2.
_____	Singers are added singing the lyrics with Helen in verse 2.
	The cymbals are played more often during verse 2.

*When music is sung in a higher key all the pitches are sung higher. (A higher pitch becomes DO.) When this happens we say that the music has *modulated*—it has changed _____ .

9. The overall effect of the added instruments and voices in verse 2 is to_____ increase_____ decrease the excitement and intensity of the music.

ANSWER CHECK

10. The rest of the song is all repeats of the chorus section, so we know there won't be any contrasts between sections in terms of the melody or the _____ . How then does the song continue to hold our interest? Check all the statements in Chart 5 that are true about these repeated chorus sections as you listen and find out.

CHART 5

Variation between Chorus Sections

_____ The song modulates upward two times.

_____ The song modulates upward once.

_____ During one of the chorus sections all the singers except Helen drop out completely, creating a big contrast.

_____ During one of the chorus sections the piano and strings drop out completely, creating a big contrast.

_____ During the quieter section we hear a new instrument, the maracas.

_____ Brasses are heard toward the end, increasing the complexity and excitement of the song.

ANSWER CHECK

Most of you already knew how to listen to the lyrics of a song and understand what is being sung about, but just to test you, how about a couple of questions on the lyrics:

11. In general, what is Delta Dawn's problem?_____
_____ .

12. By the end of the song has Delta Dawn resolved her problem?_____What clue did the music give to help you answer this question? _____

13. Everything considered, does the music make you feel optimistic or pessimistic (positive or negative) about Delta Dawn's problem?_____
Why?_____

IMPORTANT TERMS TO REVIEW: chorus section, verse section, melody, lyrics, musical design, repetition, contrast, repetition with variation, vocal and instrumental accompaniment, *a cappella* style, modulate

POP HIT LISTENING GUIDE   TEACHER'S SUPPLEMENT
VOL. II, NO. 1

"DELTA DAWN" (HELEN REDDY)
Capitol Records 3645, 45 rpm

OBJECTIVES: By completing this listening guide students will be able to:

A. Identify chorus and verse sections of the song.

B. Distinguish three design concepts between sections of the song through perception of the vocal and instrumental accompaniment—contrast, repetition, and repetition with variation.

C. Define verbally and distinguish aurally *a cappella* style and modulation.

D. Recognize that modulation and increased accompaniment activity are two techniques used to increase the intensity and excitement of music.

QUESTIONS 1-4, PRESENTATION SUGGESTIONS:

Each student should have a copy of the listening guide. You could make overhead projection transparencies and have students answer on separate answer sheets. Either way, give students time to read the questions before calling for their answers. For variety you can ask individual students to read narrative sections aloud. Stress individual decisions on the answers.

ANSWERS: 1. melody   2. lyrics   3. chorus
4. verse

CHART 1—QUESTION 5,
PRESENTATION SUGGESTIONS:

To assist the class in keeping track of the eight sections you could announce "1," "2," etc., at the beginning of each section or tap next to a list of numbers on the board. Keep your cueing as brief as possible. If students complain that they don't know what the verse or chorus section sounds like, ask them to reread page 1, then to transfer their ideas to their listening. Play the record once through.

ANSWERS: Chart 1: chorus, verse 1, verse 2, chorus, chorus, chorus, chorus, chorus.   5. Chorus. Perceptive students may give answers such as the following, but don't spend too much time digging at this point: a) it was done more often; b) the song begins and ends with choruses; c) most of the added voices and instruments happen during chorus sections; d) the modulations occur before chorus sections, making them more intense.

CHART 2, PRESENTATION SUGGESTIONS:

If the students are confused about the meaning of the three design concepts, initiate a class discussion on how our everyday lives demonstrate them. Chart 2 should be answered without additional listening.

ANSWERS: Chart 2: contrast, repetition with variation, repetition.

QUESTION 6–CHART 3,
PRESENTATION SUGGESTIONS:

Have the students answer questions 6 and 7 before you play the first two sections of the song. You will probably need to play these sections twice, with a few seconds of "think time" in-between.

ANSWERS: 6. repetition with variation   7. melody, lyrics

Chart 3

Chorus 1	Verse 1
	X
X	
	X
X	

QUESTIONS 8-9, PRESENTATION SUGGESTIONS:

Question 8 gives you an opportunity to introduce other *a cappella* music, perhaps even a fifteenth century motet? Again, you will probably need to play the two verses twice, with some time in-between.

ANSWERS: 8. chorus   Chart 4   *key

X
X
X

9. increase

QUESTION 10–CHART 5,
PRESENTATION SUGGESTIONS:

Same procedure, two playings. Be sure to start slightly ahead of the choruses so that the first modulation will be heard.

ANSWERS: 10. lyrics   Chart 5

X
X
X

QUESTIONS 11-13, PRESENTATION SUGGESTIONS:

These questions can probably be answered from memory, since most students are familiar with the song. However, it might be a good idea to play the song all the way through to get better quality answers on questions 12 and 13.

ANSWERS: 11. She was deserted by her man friend many years ago. He left town without fulfilling many of his promises. She still walks around waiting to be whisked away to her dream life. By now she may indeed be mentally defective.   12. No, the fade-out implies that she has not resolved anything.   13. Optimistic. The rather rapid tempo, the intensification of feeling caused by the two upward modulations, and the increased accompanimental complexity tend to give an uplifting feeling. (You might get valid differences of opinion here.)

IMPORTANT TERMS TO REVIEW:
Chorus section, verse section, melody, lyrics, musical design, repetition, contrast, repetition with variation, vocal and instrumental accompaniment, *a cappella* style, modulate

SUPPLEMENTARY ACTIVITY:

You can make some interesting comparisons between Helen Reddy's version and Bette Midler's version of "Delta Dawn." (Midler's is on the flip side of "Boogie Woogie Bugle Boy," Atlantic Records, 45-2964.) Midler's version is more in the plaintive ballad style at the beginning, going to a black gospel style at the end—lots of lead *ad. lib.*, repeated vocal ostinato, tambourine shaking, etc. (You have noticed, I'm sure, that Helen Reddy's version is in the white gospel and gospel rock style.) Bette does some nice rubato tempo and "bending" pitch treatments too. If you are in a school where you can do such things, you could try to develop the religious symbolism present in "Delta Dawn."

Do you have very sharp kids? If so, ask them to sing along on the root movement in the chorus sections, one chord every two beats—I, I, IV, I, etc. Ask them to identify the keys used—C, D, E$\flat$. Does the bass singer goof, or does he intentionally slide from B natural to B flat on the second phrase, second verse?

"Delta Dawn" effectively identifies chorus and verse sections of a song. In addition it introduces to the students the musical idea of contrast, repetition, and repetition with variation. At this point it is a simple matter to introduce a favorite spiritual, "Go Tell It on the Mountain."[21]

Go Tell It on the Mountain

After the class has learned the spiritual and you have discussed with them the origin of spirituals and the content of the song, proceed to an informal, brief analysis.

1. Identify the chorus and verse sections of the song. Which is repeated?

2. How do the chorus lyrics and verse lyrics differ?

3. What is the central thought of the song? Do you find it in the chorus lyrics or the verse lyrics?

4. What is the musical design of the song? (repetition-contrast-repetition)
   What do we call this design or form? (ABA)

[21] From Book 6 of *This Is Music for Today* Series, published by Allyn and Bacon, Inc.; also found in Book 6 of *Discovering Music Together* Revised Series, published by Follett Publishing Co.; Book 6 of *Exploring Music* Series, published by Holt, Rinehart and Winston, Inc.; and in "Experiencing Music" (Book 5), of *New Dimensions in Music* Series, published by American Book Co.

(Children should have been made aware of the elements of form throughout their primary and elementary years. They should have had much practice in discovering phrases that were alike. They also should have learned to distinguish between repetition and contrast and been introduced to the ABA or three-part song form. This idea, then, is not usually new to children on these levels.)

5. Name as many ways as you can think of in which "Delta Dawn" and "Go Tell It on the Mountain" are alike.

Without overdoing it you might introduce one or two other songs in this same manner.

After reviewing the simple ABA form by the "Pop" approach, you might want to use another such tune to introduce or review the rondo. Scott Joplin's "The Entertainer" (theme from *The Sting*) should be enjoyed in its own right, but its structure could easily be related to the rondo form of "Viennese Musical Clock" from the *Háry János* Suite by another twentieth century composer, the late Zoltán Kodály. Before presenting the student guide and teacher's supplement for "The Entertainer," a brief word of explanation about the rondo might be helpful.

THE RONDO

The rondo was originally a dance song but now it has become an established form in instrumental compositions where one principal theme alternates with contrasting themes. The concluding movement of traditional symphonies and concertos is frequently written in rondo form.

Throughout the plans for listening experiences at this level you may be concerned about helping your students recognize and identify themes in instrumental compositions. This skill will be unusually important in the study of the rondo. The principal theme, A, is called the *rondo theme*. Next comes a different or contrasting theme, B. This is followed by the return of the rondo theme, A. The rondo theme continues to alternate with other themes so that the form takes on the structure of ABACADA, etc.

The rondo form in "Viennese Musical Clock" is ABACADA with a brief coda. The principal theme is played by the woodwinds and French horns.

POP HIT LISTENING GUIDE   NAME_____
VOL. II, NO. 7

"THE ENTERTAINER," THEME FROM
THE STING (MARVIN HAMLISCH)

1. Hello again. Say, why didn't you write me for a free record last month? The question was too hard? You're right, so I'll give you another chance! Your teacher will play "The Entertainer" all the way through, one time. If you list every instrument heard on the record, verified by your teacher, I'll send you a free 45 record. Play fair, no helping each other. Just remember to listen carefully for instruments in the different families or groups. Ready?

ANSWER CHECK

2. In previous listening guides you have learned that the term *dynamics* or *dynamic level* means how_____ the music sounds.

   CHOICES

   high or low
   fast or slow
   loud or soft
   short or long
   up or down

3. You have also learned that the term *tempo* refers to how _____ the beat of the music moves.

Read Questions 4 and 5. Then you will hear the introduction and first main section of the song ("A" section) twice.

4. After the short introduction, which has a generally _____ melodic direction or *melodic*
   upward / downward
   contour, the pianist does something a little different with the tempo. Quietly tap the beat as he plays and in your own words describe what happens to the tempo during the first "A" section. _____
   _____

5. Also, check the block that best describes the dynamics used during the first "A" section._____ all loud _____
   alternating medium soft and loud _____ all soft_____
   gradually gets softer

ANSWER CHECK

6. When the tempo of a tune varies as it does in section "A," slightly faster, then slightly slower, we say that *rubato tempo* is being used. What English word, meaning stretchy, has the same first syllable as *rubato?* _____. So, whenever the tempo of a tune stretches a little faster, then is pulled back a little, we say that _____ tempo is being used.

7. When the dynamic level shifts suddenly from one level to another, that has a special name too—*terraced dynamics.* In this tune the dynamic level shifts from short sections of very loud to short sections of very soft, right? WRONG? (Better stay awake.) How did the_____ dynamics function in the first "A" section? From _____ to _____ .

ANSWER CHECK

8. Part of the fun in listening to music is being able to tell differences between sections. But in instrumental music where there are no lyrics to help out, how can you tell the sections apart? List all the ways you can think of._____

_____

ANSWER CHECK

9. I'm glad if many of you already knew that the direction of the tune or melody, its melodic_____ , is a very important factor in our being aware of different sections in music.

10. One more new idea, then we'll listen some more. If we listen carefully to a melody we usually find that the first short pattern of pitches and rhythm we hear is repeated several times in the section and tends to be what we recall if someone asks us to show them "how that section goes." We can keep sections straight by remembering that a *melodic motive,* a short pattern of _____ and _____ that is repeated several times during a section, is called the main melodic _____.

11. Chart 1 shows the main melodic motive from the introduction on a line graph and in musical notation. As your teacher plays the introduction follow the contour of the motive. How many times do you hear the motive?_____ Listen.

CHART 1

Melodic Motive from the
Introduction of "The Entertainer"

ANSWER CHECK

Good, you have the idea. Chart 2 shows the line graphs and musical notations of four melodic motives. Your job is to determine which of these motives is the main melodic motive of each section of the piece. First, your teacher will play or sing each motive and ask you to sing along to get an idea of how each one goes. Then you will hear the piece straight through. Your teacher may tell you when each of the seven sections starts, but it is your job to figure out which motive you hear being repeated several times in each section. Sections may be repeated and all choices might not be used! Write your choices in the blanks following question 12.

CHART 2

Melodic Motive Choices
from Sections of "The Entertainer"

12. The section design of "The Entertainer" is Intro. $\overline{\hspace{1em}}$ $\overline{\hspace{1em}}$
                                                        (1)   (2)

$\overline{(3)}$ $\overline{(4)}$ $\overline{(5)}$ $\overline{(6)}$ $\overline{(7)}$

13. Music in which at least two different sections alternate with a repeating section is in *rondo form* section design. Check the following section designs that are rondo forms:

___ ABACABA ___ ABCD ___ ABACA ___ ABA ___ AABB

14. Have you ever gone on a mystery clue hunt? You know, where you look for things right out in the open that can help you solve a puzzle or mystery. The trick is, you have to know the clues or you'll just pass right by the evidence. Well, sometimes it is fun to listen to music this way. Our clue will be the number three (3). (We got the clue from the introduction. Remember how the melodic motive was used three times?) Our task is to find all the musical things involved with the number three in the "A" section. Your teacher will play the two "A" sections at the beginning of the piece two times, then will ask for an open discussion. (Try to get as much as you can on your own.) LISTEN. _____

___

ANSWER CHECK

15. "The Entertainer" is a *"Ragtime"* composition. This is a musical style in which the bass rhythm moves along very evenly every half beat while the melody rhythm often is "ragged" or off the beat—*syncopated.* A rhythm part that does not match up with the beats is called a _____ rhythm.

16. OK, this last project will separate the fakers from the musicians! Your teacher will "drop the needle" somewhere on the record. Listen for the evenly moving bass rhythm and tap along with it with your left hand. When everyone "has it" your teacher will stop the record. (Please don't tap too loudly.) GO.

    Not too hard, eh? OK, this time when your teacher "drops the needle" tap along with the syncopated melody rhythm with your right hand. GO.

    Still no sweat? We'll see! This time tap the even bass rhythm with your left hand AND tap the syncopated melody rhythm with your right hand. GO.

IMPORTANT TERMS TO REVIEW: dynamic level, tempo, melodic contour, rubato tempo, terraced dynamics, melodic motive, rondo form, ragtime, syncopated rhythm

POP HIT LISTENING GUIDE   TEACHER'S SUPPLEMENT VOL. II, NO. 7

"THE ENTERTAINER," THEME FROM
THE STING *(MARVIN HAMLISCH)*
MCA Records 40174, 45 rpm

OBJECTIVES: By completing this listening guide students will:

A. Recognize the sounds of the instruments used in the arrangement.

B. Be led to discover the concepts of rubato tempo and terraced dynamics as used in the first "A" section of the arrangement.

C. Be able to identify, by ear and from notation, the main melodic motive of each section of the arrangement.

D. Discover the rondo section design of this arrangement.

E. Discover four levels of musical organization using the number three in the "A" section.

F. Be able to tap, at the same time, the even and the syncopated rhythms used in the composition.

If you care to delve further into the ragtime music of Scott Joplin, composer of "The Entertainer," read Roland Nadeau's excellent article in the April 1973 *Music Educators Journal.* Then, listen to some of Josh Rifkin's "researched" recordings (Nonesuch, H-71248 or H-71264).

QUESTION 1, PRESENTATION SUGGESTION:

The preparation for this question is spelled out on the student's page. If you have good reproduction equipment some of your students might get 100% this time, but there are some difficult perceptions to be made!

ANSWER: Any order—piano, tuba, trombone, trumpet, clarinet, piccolo, bass drum, snare drum

QUESTIONS 2-5, PRESENTATION SUGGESTIONS:

Make sure the students answer questions 2 and 3, then read through questions 4 and 5 before you play the intro. and first "A" section (45 seconds). Have the students start tapping the "A" section, not the intro. Even though the tempo/meter is a moderate two, it will be helpful to tap at a fast four to answer question 4. Repeat the music once if necessary.

ANSWERS: (*Note:* When you call for answers to these questions be careful not to give away the answers to questions 6 and 7 in your discussion.) 2. loud or soft 3. fast or slow   4. downward; the music speeds up and slows down a little every now and then (or some similar statement)   5. alternating medium soft and loud

QUESTIONS 6-7, PRESENTATION SUGGESTIONS:

As soon as you have completed the answer discussion from the previous question, have the students answer questions 6 and 7. Don't let students look back at question 5 for the answer to question 7.

ANSWERS: 6. rubbery; rubato   7. terraced; moderately soft, loud

QUESTION 8, PRESENTATION SUGGESTION:

You might want to have an open discussion on this question if you think your students do not have sufficient background to individually answer the question. In either case, make a list of things on the board at answer check time so that all students can share the ideas.

ANSWERS: Probable answers are: A. by the way the melody goes   B. through different instruments playing C. through the use of different dynamics   D. by the different number of things going on (texture)

QUESTIONS 9-11, PRESENTATION SUGGESTIONS:

Have students answer questions 9 and 10 first. After they have read through question 11, play the introduction no more than two times. Avoid answering any questions concerning questions 9 and 10 until you have completed question 11. Some problems will clarify themselves.

ANSWERS: 9. contour   10. pitches; rhythm (either order); motive   11. three

QUESTIONS 12-13, PRESENTATION SUGGESTIONS:

After the students have read the introductory paragraph, play each motive on the piano several times. If you have no piano you could tape the motives from the record. As a last resort you could sing each motive to the class. In any case, make sure the class sings each motive back to you as they tap the beat and follow either the line graph or musical notation. Play the tune just once through. If you do not expect your class to recognize the beginning of each new section, call out the number of each section as it begins. When the tune is over remind students to answer question 13 on page 4.

ANSWERS: 12. Intro AABACA   13. ABACABA and ABACA (*Note:* The original version of "The Entertainer," as written by Scott Joplin, had a "classical" piano rag form of Intro. AABBACCDD. Gunther Schuller, the arranger, changed the tune's design—even omitted one complete section. This was probably done to provide listeners with the expected "A" section at the end.)

QUESTION 14, PRESENTATION SUGGESTIONS:

This is a difficult question, but it might be fun to try anyway. If a couple of your students pick up two or three uses of the number three, you'll know you have some talent on your hands. The students' paragraph explains the question preparation.

ANSWERS: A. There are three complete statements of the motive   B. There are three repetitions of the two-note fragment in the motive   C. the motive uses three beats D. The new one-measure motive used in the last four measures of the section is heard three times

QUESTIONS 15-16, PRESENTATION SUGGESTIONS:

If you have done a little research in your April 1973 *Music Educators Journal* you can supplement this question with a great amount of historical and/or musical style information. The last three tasks in question 16 should be fun. If you detect one or two students who can just about "play" both rhythm parts, why not get them in front of the class to show off their abilities and to motivate the rest of the class.

ANSWERS: 15. syncopated

SUPPLEMENTAL ACTIVITY:

If members of your class are motivated to see the movie after "doing" the listening guide, ask them to compare the instrumental arrangement and the section design of "The Entertainer" as used in the opening of the movie with the arrangement on the record. There are quite a few differences.

You could "get into" classical rondo form very nicely from this lesson, should it be a matter of interest.

When the students have had sufficient experience with the general format and procedures of the *Pop Hit Listening Guides,* then they should take on the challenge of writing their own guide. This final presentation will reveal ways of accomplishing this.

POP HIT LISTENING GUIDE   STUDENT SUPPLEMENT
VOL. II, NO. 8

LAST TIME I SAW HIM (DIANA ROSS)

Hello, music lovers. (Likers?) (Tolerators?) Well anyway, here we are again, so let's do something. This time you are going to make the listening guide. That's right, YOU will write questions or charts based on things you hear going on in the song!

Here is some help. Column 1 lists musical ideas you have discovered in previous listening guides that might be present in this tune. Column 2 lists some of the ways questions have been written to guide your discovery. Your teacher will help you recall examples from previous listening guides.

You will hear the song four times with several minutes between each playing. Concentrate on just one musical idea during each playing (unless you're very swift) and listen to what happens—make notes on a piece of scratch paper. Then write one or more questions, statements, charts, etc., that would lead someone to discover the things you heard. Don't forget to give hints in your questions. Bring out only those things you think are important or interesting.

1.	*2.*
MUSICAL IDEAS	*QUESTION STYLES*
A. The meaning of the lyrics: What is the song about, what happens?	A. True/false:
	B. Fill in or completion:
	C. Matching:
B. The mood or feeling intensity of the song: Is it stable or changing? What causes us	D. Multiple choice (one or more than one correct answer):
	E. Chart (to show feel-

to feel the way we do?

C. The design or sections of the song: Verse/chorus, etc.? ABA, etc.?

D. The instrumentation: What instruments play? Where do they play?

E. Discover musical terms: Tempo, meter, rhythm, word painting, texture, etc.

ing intensity, section design, instrumentation, etc.):

F. Direct question (requiring a specific or a personal opinion answer):

LISTEN

Your teacher will play the song all the way through. Listen carefully to the lyrics so that you can answer questions 1-5 when the song is over. Read the questions now.

1. Why did the man say he had to leave? (What does "to set us up" mean?) _____
   _____

2. Do you believe what he told her?_____ . If not, why do you think he left? _____
   _____

3. Does Diana Ross believe what he said?_____. How can you tell?_____
   _____

4. Generally, this song is about some guy leaving his girl and how she misses him, right? So, why does the girl sound happier and happier as the song goes along?____
   _____

5. Do you think she will find him?_____. Make up a moral to the story. _____

ANSWER CHECK

Read questions 6-8. If you know any answers, complete the questions now. Otherwise, wait until you have heard the first part of the song to decide.

6. At the beginning of the song the quiet, even tapping of the high hat cymbal might be representing a _____. (Remember, she is waiting for him to return.)

7. When the music does something that matches a word or idea in the lyrics, we say that _____ (rubato tempo /

_____

terraced dynamics / word painting / melodic contour) has been used.

8. The high hat cymbal also shows us the speed of the song's beat. So, we know that the song has a _____ fast /

_____   _____ .

moderate / slow   tempo / meter / rhythm

ANSWER CHECK

Now read questions 9-12, concerning the end of the song. Again, if you know any answers, complete the questions now. Answer question 9 now, from memory. You can complete the rest of the questions after hearing the music. Your teacher will play a short section from the first part of the song before skipping to the end of the song.

9. By the end of the song the tempo is _____ slower /

_____ .

still the same / faster

10. The song ends with a gradual _____ rubato / interlude / coda /

_____ .

fade-out

11. Although this is a common technique in popular music, why is it a very good way to end this song? _____

_____

12. In this case it demonstrates another example of _____

_____ .

ANSWER CHECK

Chart 1 contains an outline of the song's sections. The numbers under each section tell how many beats are felt in each section. As you listen to the song, keep track of the beats by lightly tapping beneath the numbers. Be aware of the sections changing. Pay special attention to the following facts, because I will ask you questions about these things after you listen:

A. One verse is only half as long as the other verse.

B. There are four extra beats in one chorus section.

CHART 1

Section Outline of "Last Time I Saw Him"

Intro.	Verse 1		Verse 2		Chorus	Verse 3	
	pt. 1	pt. 2	pt. 1	pt. 2		pt. 1	pt. 2
8	16	16	16	16	28	16	16

Verse 4	Chorus 2	Chorus 3	Chorus 4
16	32	28	28

LISTEN

13. Even though verse 4 is only half as long as the other verses, I bet that most of you did not realize this when you first heard the song. What could be the possible reasons? What other musical things might have made up for length?_____

_____

14. Chorus 2 was four beats longer than the other chorus sections for a special reason. The four beat *extension* to the chorus was used to move the song to a higher key. The song _____

                        modulated / crescendoed / syncopated

    here.

ANSWER CHECK

Chart 2 is another outline of the song's sections. This time we will listen for changing *instrumentation*. I have listed the instruments playing during the introduction, then again during verse 3, part 1. Your job is to list the instruments ADDED in each section as the song goes along, choosing from the list in Chart 2. I have given you the correct number of blanks for new instruments in each section.

   To get you started, the instrument added in verse 1, part 1 is shown on the line. Your teacher will stop the record after verse 1, part 2 to make sure you are getting the idea. Then you will hear the entire song.

CHART 2

Instrumentation Outline
for "Last Time I Saw Him"

Section	Instrumentation	Choices
Introduction:	elec. guitar, bass guitar, cymbal	snare drum violins
Verse 1 Pt. 1:	elec. piano	bass drum banjo
Pt. 2:	_____	tambourine

Section	Instrumentation	Choices
Verse 2	Pt. 1:_____ _____ Pt. 2:_____ _____	trumpets trombones clarinet
Chorus 1:	none	
Verse 3:	Pt. 1: elec. guitar, bass guitar, cymbal, elec. piano, bass drum, violins Pt. 2:_____ _____	
Verse 4:	_____ _____	
Chorus 2:	none	
Chorus 3:	_____ _____	
Chorus 4:	none	

IMPORTANT TERMS TO REVIEW: word painting, tempo, fade-out, extension, modulated, key change, instrumentation

POP HIT LISTENING GUIDE   TEACHER'S SUPPLEMENT VOL. II, NO. 8

LAST TIME I SAW HIM (DIANA ROSS)
Motown Records M1278, 45 rpm

OBJECTIVES: By completing the student supplement students will be able to:

A. Critically listen to this song, without assistance, to recognize a few specific uses of musical concepts discovered in previous listening guides.

B. Formulate these recognitions into listening guide type questions.

OBJECTIVES: By completing the listening guide students will:

A. Be aware of the literal and the implied chain of events described in the songs' lyrics and write a potential moral.

B. Discover two examples of accompanimental word painting.

C.   Follow the section outline of the song by keeping track of the beats.

D.   Select instruments added in each section from a list of instruments.

STUDENT SUPPLEMENT,
PRESENTATION SUGGESTIONS:

One of the implicit goals of the listening guide program is for students to acquire self-activating habits of listening, similar to those used in the guides. When these listening skills become established with popular music the chances of their use in more sophisticated listening tasks is improved. The supplement gives you a chance to test the ability of your students to listen critically. Their proof of this will be their constructing listening questions.

If your room has some physical flexibility I strongly suggest that you assign students into heterogeneous ability groups of three to five to complete the supplement. Plan to take one period for this task. If you have additional time, collect the questions and put together a listening guide from the best efforts. If you have time, then have your class "do" the assembled guide. If you like, send me a copy of the guide and I will send the class a review letter.

The musical ideas and question formats suggested in the supplement have all been demonstrated in previous listening lessons. It would be a good idea for you to make transparencies of some examples to refresh memories.

QUESTIONS 1-5, PRESENTATION SUGGESTIONS:

After students have read the questions, play the song all the way through.

ANSWERS: 1. He had to leave to set them up, meaning to get a job, get some money, get a place to live, etc. 2. No; to spend her money, to find a new girl.   3. Yes; because she says she trusts him, she loves him, he must be in trouble, otherwise he would have returned.   4. She really believes that he loves her, so she is all excited getting ready to go look for him.   5. No. Girl who give love and money to man leaving on bus will end up "heartbroke." (Bad!)

QUESTIONS 6-8, PRESENTATION SUGGESTIONS:

Play the introduction and a few bars of the first verse two or three times. (The high hat cymbal is the small drum set pair of cymbals secured to a foot pedal rod. In this instance the closed cymbals are being tapped with a drum stick.)

ANSWERS: 6. clock   7. word painting   8. moderate tempo

QUESTIONS 9-12, PRESENTATION SUGGESTIONS:

Many students will recall the answers to questions 10-12, but play the intro. and a portion of the first verse before playing the final two chorus sections, to allow a careful check of their answers to question 9. One playing should be sufficient.

ANSWERS: 9. still the same. If several students thought the tempo got faster, try to find out why they thought so. The illusion may result from the increase in textural polyphony and dynamics plus her scat singing. All of these things tend to give us an increased emotional intensity, thus we register a faster pulse rate (perhaps imagined) and think the tempo has increased. My turntable registers 92 bpm at the beginning and end. (Ravel's *Bolero* tends to create a similar illusion.)   10. fade-out   11. The fade-out might represent her going off to find him.   12. word painting

CHART 1–QUESTION 14,
PRESENTATION SUGGESTIONS:

Before the music starts ask the students to locate, in the outline, the verse and chorus sections referenced in the two statements. Make sure the students can follow the steady beat of the music and not get mixed up with the rhythm of the tune. You show the speed of the beat with them for a few bars, then drop out. Ask the students to tap beneath the correct part of the outline as they listen to the song. You could put the outline on the board or on a transparency to help students keep their place if you think this is necessary. If you have a good stereo system and a quiet class, some students will hear the beginning of chorus 5 as the music fades out. I did not include this section on the chart, but kudos to those who hear it. Have the students answer questions 13 and 14 as soon as the song is over.

ANSWERS: 13. Possible answers are: A) We were led to expect the thirty-two beats because of the three previous verses– a habit or expectation was set up. B) The full instrumentation, high dynamic level, and rising emotional tension of the song may have substituted for length.   14. modulated

CHART 2, PRESENTATION SUGGESTIONS:

The essential presentation method is listed on the student's page. Ask the students to read the instructions aloud, explaining what they think the instructions mean. You can better determine what supplementary explanations are needed this way. After the test playing, through verse 1, play the entire song. Repeat the playing if quite a few students act "unfinished." You may need to assist very young or inexperienced groups by stopping the record briefly after each section.

ANSWERS: Verse 1, pt. 2: bass drum; Verse 2, pt. 1: violins and snare drum; Verse 2, pt. 2: banjo, trombones; Verse 3, pt. 2: banjo, trombones; Verse 4: trumpets; Chorus 3: clarinet, tambourine

SUPPLEMENTARY ACTIVITY:

If your students completed the "Delta Dawn" listening guide, you might draw parallels between the two female "tales of woe."

More advanced groups might enjoy a discussion of the style synthesis demonstrated in the tune. Beginning with a contemporary "cool" soul sound, the tune adds a country flavor, then a show tune sound, then a Dixieland vaudeville style. In other words, it seems to add on progressively older and older styles.

This particular lesson suggests a creative experience—writing a listening guide. This creative opportunity could be further enhanced by suggesting that the class compose a song of their own. They could decide upon a structure: verse, chorus, or perhaps as in this song under study, two verses and then a chorus, etc. They might write their own lyrics or adapt a poem of their choice. Perhaps some students play guitar or accordion and could accompany the group when the song is finished.

ETHNIC MUSIC

As an enhancement of a social studies unit—or as an enrichment experience in music—you may want to study in some depth the music of ethnic groups that perhaps have unusual meaning to you and your students. In the black culture you could do a period study of spirituals, the blues, ragtime, or jazz. In the American Indian heritage you could study the mood and style of some of the tribal music. The opportunities in the area of ethnic music are limitless.

(Appendix J is devoted entirely to sources of ethnic music suitable for use in the elementary school. This is not limited to ethnic communities in North America but includes suggestions about music from all over the world.)

TRADITIONAL MUSIC

There are some traditional forms that still seem to have an appeal for the boys and girls of today. Three of these are: the suite, the ballet, and the tone poem.

THE SUITE. A suite can be explained simply as an instrumental composition (usually for orchestra) in four, five, or more parts (called *movements*). Although the eighteenth century—or *classical* suite—is a prime example of absolute music, suites may also be narrative or descriptive.[22]

Following this definition the presentation of a suite could be done in any of several ways. Here is one approach:

1. Give the title of the music. Explain it if necessary.
2. Give the name of the composer and *briefly* discuss interesting facts concerning him—such as where and when he lived.
3. If the suite is based on a story, such as *The Nutcracker,* tell the story.
4. Play only two or three selections from the suite the first day, concluding with the atmosphere of "To be continued."

    (If possible, play other selections from the suite the next day.)

    To motivate listening and to improve musical discrimination you might let the class guess what part of the story each selection is portraying. This increases interest and encourages an alert, attentive attitude. For example, in *The Nutcracker* Suite, play one of the dances and see if the class can distinguish whether it is the "Dance of the Sugar Plum Fairy," the "Chinese Dance," or the "Waltz of the Flowers."
5. Through guided discussion draw from the students their response to the music in terms of mood, style, and instrumentation. Encourage them to show how

[22] For example, *Suite No. 3 in D Major,* by Johann Sebastian Bach, and countless similar works.

the use of a particular instrument or group of instruments was unusually effective in telling parts of the story or in establishing the mood or atmosphere.

There are many suites that are appealing to boys and girls of this age. From the following list you should find an adequate number to enjoy with your students during the year. Any of these selections can be found in a standard record catalog.

SUGGESTED RECORDED SUITES

Bachianas Brasileiras No. 2 (Villa-Lobos)

Death Valley Suite (Grofé)

English Folk Song Suite (Vaughan Williams)

Facade Suite (Walton)

Grand Canyon Suite (Grofé)

Háry János Suite (Kodály)

In the Bottoms (Dett)

Irish Suite (Anderson)

Karelia Suite (Sibelius)

Lieutenant Kijé Suite (Prokofiev)

London Suite (Coates)

Mississippi Suite (Grofé)

Mother Goose Suite (Ravel)

On the Waterfront (Bernstein)

Peer Gynt Suites Nos. 1 and 2 (Grieg)

Der Rosenkavalier Suite (Richard Strauss)

Santa Fe Trail Suite (McDonald)

Scheherazade (Rimsky-Korsakov)

Suite Andalucia (Lecuona)

Suite francaise (Milhaud)

Suite No. 3 in D Major (Bach)

Wand of Youth Suite No. 1 (Elgar)

BALLET. Most children on these levels already have some idea of what a ballet is. Some of the girls may be taking lessons. Nearly all of the class will have observed a ballet at some time on TV. Just a mention of the word will bring a knowing nod from most of the boys and girls. However, their understanding may be limited to a graceful dance done on the toes. They should also learn that a ballet frequently tells a story or, if it occurs in an opera, enhances the plot in some way. A reference to *The Nutcracker* Suite by Tchaikovsky will remind them of the narrative function of a ballet. If any of the children have seen a light opera or operetta they will be aware of the enrichment of the story by the dances. Frequent use of recordings in the classroom will provide much enjoyment for all.

SUGGESTED RECORDED BALLETS

Billy the Kid (Copland)

Cakewalk Ballet Suite
(Gottschalk-Kay)

Cinderella (Prokofiev)

El Amor Brujo (De Falla)

Fancy Free (Bernstein)

Fantastic Toyshop
(Rossini-Respighi)

Firebird Suite (Stravinsky)

Le Cid Ballet Suite (Massenet)

Nutcracker Suite (Tchaikovsky)

Perfect Fool (Holst)

Petrouchka (Stravinsky)

Pocahontas (Carter, Elliott)

Red Poppy (Glière)

Rite of Spring (Stravinsky)

Rodeo (Copland)

Sleeping Beauty (Tchaikovsky)

Swan Lake (Tchaikovsky)

Three-Cornered Hat (De Falla)

THE TONE POEM. The tone poem (often called "Symphonic Poem") is a large instrumental form in one movement that is usually very appealing to listeners because of its descriptive elements. The presentation of a specific tone poem, *The Moldau* (by Smetana), could be planned something like this:

1. Through the use of the simple definition above, try to lead the class to discover that the tone poem is called *programmatic,* or *program music,* because the composer INTENDED to describe something definite when he wrote the music.

2. This composition is the second of six such works that form a group called a *symphonic cycle.* Each tone poem has its own title (as the chapters in a book) and the entire cycle has its own title (as the

title of the book itself). This particular tone poem is called *The Moldau*. The name of the symphonic cycle from which it comes is called *My Country*.

3. Smetana's intense feeling of nationalism is evident in this symphonic cycle. The class should be reminded that the word "Moldau" is the name of a mighty river in Bohemia (now a part of Czechoslovakia). Smetana is describing musically the country through which the river flows. The composer really intended his music to be a personification of the river in such a way that the river actually seems to describe what it "sees" along its course. (A comparison could be made with the mighty Mississippi, which could "tell" of the many different scenes it would encounter as it cuts its way through the heart of the continental United States.)

4. Smetana meant for his music to describe definite sights, which can be shown on a list on the board or on a large chart. Begin the list with the origin of the river itself—two springs: one hot, the other cold, which merge to form the Moldau River.

   I. The Springs
   II. The River
   III. The Hunt
   IV. A Peasant Wedding
   V. The Moon Rises—Dance of the Nymphs
   VI. The Rapids of St. John
   VII. Vysehrad (legendary castle of the ancients)
   VIII. The River vanishes beyond the listener's "sight"
   IX. Coda (two loud chords)

5. In order to "sharpen" the listening experience and give it greater meaning these questions about what to expect in the music are suggested:

   a. The springs will be represented by a dialogue between two instruments of the same kind. At the close of the composition can you identify these? (flutes)

   b. What instruments would you expect to hear in a hunt? (French horns)

   c. How would you expect the music to sound at a peasant wedding?

   d. When the moon *rises* what do you think the

music will do there? What will be characteristic of the music in the Dance of the Nymphs?

e. What instruments will you anticipate hearing in The Rapids of St. John? (Children are usually very perceptive in their answers, especially if you phrase your questions in this manner—What will describe the boiling, thundering, churning water? (timpani) The water striking sharply against the rocks? (cymbals) What other family would you expect to hear that can describe this loud tumult? (brasses))

f. What will the music do when the river goes away? (become softer)

g. Explain the very quiet atmosphere established by the music with the departure of the river. Then tell them, after a brief pause, there is a coda (two chords) that concludes the composition. Later you are going to ask what their reaction was to these chords. (A number will say, after hearing the composition, that they seemed to say, "The End.")

As you examine these questions you may feel that there would be too much conversation before hearing the composition and that this would not be wise. Actually, this discussion takes only the *briefest* time and *should* not delay the listening experience, or its effect will be lost. Move very rapidly from one comment or question to the next, not encouraging intensive discussion at this point, but rather getting quick answers. This can serve as a guide in giving the class specific things for which to listen.

6. As the class becomes familiar with the composition they can indicate the beginning of each theme by: a) raising one finger for the first theme, two for the second, and so on, or b) writing the numbers of the themes on cards to be held up by seven different children as the themes are identified, or c) selecting a volunteer to write on the board as the music is played. The class will discover that number seven, the river theme, will return frequently.

7. Listen attentively to the composition, then have a brief follow-up discussion to decide which theme is

the most characteristic, and therefore the most helpful in learning to identify the composition.[23]

PREPARATION FOR CONCERTS

One of the most effective ways for students this age to hear both contemporary and traditional music is by attending concerts. It is indeed an enriching experience for pupils to attend a concert together. In many cities the local symphony orchestra cooperates with the schools in planning special children's concerts for those of elementary school age. Where no orchestra is available, students can often be transported to a nearby city for these events. For many of the children such a concert will be their very first. Because of this the music supervisor or consultant and the classroom teacher have a unique opportunity to help the students develop proper attitudes and achieve adequate understanding and appreciation. Many orchestras are willing to furnish program notes for children's concerts in advance. Whenever possible, the class should have many opportunities (spaced over a long period of time) to become familiar with the music they will hear at the concert. This is especially important in the case of the larger forms that require sustained attention.

YOUNG AUDIENCE CONCERTS.   In recent years another extraordinary concert opportunity has been made available to schools. The Young Audiences program literally brings the concert hall to the children. In an informal setting in the elementary building (such as an all-purpose room with the students sitting on the floor) a small group (string, brass, woodwind, jazz, opera, Baroque, or American ensemble) presents short compositions or brief excerpts from longer ones interspersed with interesting commentary. Using the vocabulary of the young audience (primary, levels 1-3 or intermediate, and levels 4-6), the members of the group give informative facts about their instruments or the music they perform. However, this is not "one-sided." The children are invited to ask questions or comment. Thus it is an exchange rather than a lecture-demonstration format.

In most areas where such concerts are available, the performing musicians are from the local symphony orchestra, the local

[23] Some of the themes for this composition can be found in Book 6 of *This Is Music for Today* Series, published by Allyn and Bacon, Inc.

opera theater, or are engaged in other activities as professional musicians. The concerts take place during school hours and are planned for a forty-five-minute period. The student audience is limited to 250 for levels 1-3, and 4-6. The smaller the group, the more effective the rapport.

Half the concert cost is paid by the school (this may be financed in a variety of ways; e.g., the Board of Education, the PTA, service clubs, individual patrons, fund-raising projects, etc.). The other half is matched by funds from the local Young Audience chapter, the musicians' union, trust funds, or other means.

The concerts have proved to be extremely popular with the students. (Interestingly enough, next to jazz presentations, opera has been an unusual favorite with many children on levels 4-6). Almost without exception, however, all of the groups have evoked an outstanding response from the students. Without question the Young Audience program is one of the finest available to school children today.

Young Audiences, Inc., is a national group with offices located at 115 East 92nd St., New York, N.Y. 10028. The local concerts are arranged and presented by urban city chapters or regional chapters.

LEARNING ABOUT THE ORGAN.   Another "live" performance that intrigues students on these levels is an organ demonstration. Although the organ is not a regular member of the "symphony family," as "king" of the instruments it is, of course, most intriguing to boys and girls. Most of them will have heard an organ in church or in a public auditorium. However, few if any will have had the opportunity to examine the instrument at close range and learn its intricacies. If possible, arrange a field trip with your class to visit the largest organ in your town or city, and ask the organist to tell your students about the pipes, stops, and manuals. Suggest that he demonstrate as he makes his explanations.

As a part of this study you might also have your students observe a very small organ—or a reed instrument. Plan this study so it will be fascinating and "alive" to your class.

(Following the field trip your students might be interested in lifting off the top of the piano in your classroom to study the hammer action of the keys and to observe other parts of the mechanism.)

Other field trips could include visits to:

1. Museums where ancient instruments are displayed
2. A rehearsal of the local high school choir or orchestra
3. A local music store, emphasizing that music is also a business

One "real life" situation can be enjoyed frequently in the classroom. Those who are members of the elementary orchestra or band should be invited at frequent intervals to put on concerts in the classroom, to provide firsthand acquaintance and to give the players an opportunity to perform for their own peer group.

However, all of these excellent opportunities just discussed can only be highlights of the year's experience—special treats—not the usual business of the day! For that reason, visual aids can bring a frequent spark to the day-by-day routine.

VISUAL AIDS

STUDYING ORCHESTRAL INSTRUMENTS. Specific facts about the instruments can be presented in a variety of ways. Pictures can be unusually helpful.

One of the most effective aids in presenting information about instruments is a series of colored filmstrips with accompanying records.[24] Each family is presented in a separate filmstrip, with an intriguing historical narrative giving the origins of the instruments. With the record this approximates a sound movie, which is appealing to the class. It is wise to have a follow-up discussion to help the children sum up the essential information and to correct any inaccurate impressions. If the students will be attending a concert as a group these filmstrips provide excellent preparatory material.

STUDYING COMPOSERS. In addition to the materials presented in the current basic series, portraits of the composers are also available.[25] Seeing the person makes his life and music more interesting

[24] These filmstrips and records are available from the Jam Handy Organization, 2821 E. Grand Blvd., Detroit, Mich. 48211, and Bowmar Records, 622 Rodier Drive, Glendale, Calif. 91201.

[25] The Willis Music Co. (Florence, Ky.) has charcoal and pastel drawings of most of the "traditional composers." Bowmar Records (Glendale, Calif.) has large reproductions of original paintings of composers (sets one and two—each contains twenty portraits), plus study prints for students.

to the students. Colored filmstrips and records of some of the composers' lives and music can also be used for further enrichment.[26]

ELECTRONIC MUSIC

Today's boys and girls respond with interest and enthusiasm to these innovations. If the teacher feels at a loss in planning this kind of experience there are some suggestions in the newer series of basic music books. In addition, the November 1968 issue of *The Music Educators' Journal* has an interesting article on electronic music. The January 25, 1969 issue of the *Saturday Review* contains a "Guide to Electronic Music Terminology." One of the most effective plans appears in the May 1967 issue of *Keyboard Junior*. Columbia recording MS-7194, "Switched-on Bach," is a fascinating performance "scored" by Walter Carlos and "played" on a MOOG SYNTHESIZER (an electronic device named for its inventor, Robert A. Moog (rhymes with "VOGUE")). There are also interesting recordings by RCA Victor of Dr. Vladimir Ussachevsky operating the console of the RCA Electronic Music Synthesizer. These effective materials have been used extensively and can be highly recommended.

Upper level students hear an explanation of the synthesizer constructed by their music teacher, Mr. Keith Schult (photo by Patrick Burke).

[26] The Jam Handy Organization (Detroit, Mich.) has filmstrips on the lives of Bach, Beethoven, Handel, Haydn, Mozart, and Schubert. Bowmar Records has produced an equally fine series on the lives of Beethoven, Haydn, Mozart, Puccini, Schubert, Verdi, and others. (See Appendix L.)

EVALUATING MUSIC HEARD
OUTSIDE THE CLASSROOM

In these times, when music seems to "assault" one from all sides, it is especially necessary that a *wise* evaluation be made of which music is to become a part of one's daily life. What children hear on TV, radio, at the theater and summer opera, in church and in the choir—all of these need to be considered and discussed. In this discussion the teacher must be unusually understanding, tactful, and cautious. A strong negative tone against music that is distasteful to *you* may bring a vigorous defense from your students and defeat the real purpose of the discussion. By all means, you should always have the situation "in hand" and give strong guidance, but this can best be accomplished only in a democratic exchange of ideas.

A strong encouragement (both in tone and words) of those music activities that seem most worthwhile will frequently be influential. It might be helpful to keep a bulletin board with interesting pictures of composers, instruments, new stories about some musician, announcements of concerts, TV, and radio programs, or other items that can point your students to the "better" opportunities. Try to keep your bulletin board up-to-date with current information that is at the "appeal" level of your class. Use every possible aid to guide your children to the more worthwhile things in life.

SUGGESTED INDIVIDUAL AND
SMALL GROUP PROJECTS
FOR METHODS COURSES

Levels 1 through 6

1. While listening to some music that you really like, paint a picture or make a design in color to show how the music makes you feel. Are your feelings related to the title of the composition? What do you know about how the composer felt and why he expressed himself with this music?

2. Choose your favorite Pop record and make a chart or diagram of the music. Do the tunes (themes) go up or down? Are they repeated? Extended? Who

performs each melody? Singers? Which instruments are heard with each melody? How does the composer achieve contrast in the tunes (themes)?

3. Compile a list of suitable children's stories that are related to listening activities for use in your class.

4. Write brief sketches of the lives of five famous composers in the language of your class.

5. Make a list of all available filmstrips that could be used in listening experiences. Decide at what learning level each filmstrip could most appropriately be used.

6. If possible, secure advance information about a particular musical program on TV or radio (such as symphony concerts or broadcasts of opera performances), then prepare program notes for your students to take home with them. Follow the broadcast with a period of classroom discussion.

7. Choose a recording of a musical composition with a distinctive rhythm and write a percussion score for it.

8. Prepare colored tagboard squares in as many different colors as there are themes in the favorite recording of your class. Number the squares and have some pupils hold them up when they hear the appropriate themes.

9. Mark separate squares "introduction" and "coda," then have the students find a recording that has both an introduction and a coda. As they listen, have them identify these segments.

6

Instruments

EXPLORING WITH INSTRUMENTS

Sounds fascinate children. They can discover music in the patter of rain on the roof, the "drip, drip" of a leaky faucet, or the humming of a motor. This perceptive quality is essential in the use of informal instruments.

RHYTHM INSTRUMENTS

Rhythm instruments are the most numerous and offer the greatest variety of types. This group of instruments is played by 1) *beating,* 2) *shaking,* or 3) *striking* in time with the *beat* and the note values of the *rhythm pattern* (rhythm of the melody).

Rhythm instruments usually include:

Drums and tom-toms	Castanets (mounted on a stick)
Rhythm sticks	Sand blocks
Triangles	Sleigh bells
Cymbals	Tambourines
Jingle clogs (jingle blocks)	Wood blocks

Early Childhood (Levels 1 and 2)

One of the ways in which rhythm instruments can be introduced effectively is through a *known song.* For purposes of illustration,

229

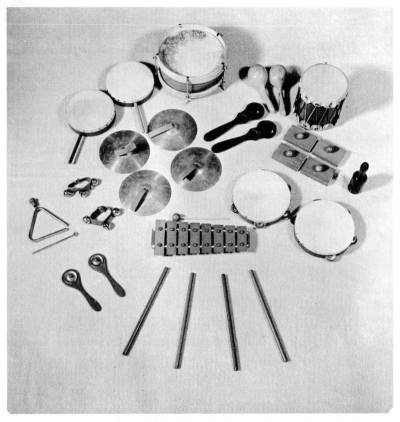

Commercial rhythm instruments that can be used in elementary school music programs (photo by Ken Raveill).

take the song "Hickory, Dickory, Dock."[1] Be sure the children can sing it all the way through, accurately and expressively, before you present the instruments.

Hickory, Dickory, Dock

Mother Goose   J. W. Elliott

Hick-o - ry, dick-o - ry, dock;   The mouse   ran up   the clock;   The

---

[1] Found in Kindergarten Book of *Exploring Music* Series, published by Holt, Rinehart and Winston, Inc.; "Music for Early Childhood," from *New Dimensions in Music* Series, published by American Book Co.; Kindergarten Book of *The Magic of Music* Series, published by Ginn and Co., and Kindergarten Book and Book 3, *The Spectrum of Music* Series, published by Macmillan Publishing Co., Inc.

clock struck One, The mouse   ran down; Hick-o - ry, dick- o - ry,   dock.

1. On the day you plan to introduce this activity, put a set of rhythm sticks and a triangle in the "music corner" where the children can experiment with them.

2. Choose part of the class to clap their hands exactly on "*one*" (when the "clock struck one"), while the rest of the class sings the song. Remind them to listen attentively.

3. Now hold up the set of rhythm sticks, strike them together, and ask the class to tell you the name of the instrument. Do the same with the triangle. (The children usually have become acquainted with these instruments in nursery or preschool.)

4. Ask the class which of the two instruments sounds more like "the clock struck one." Most children will think the triangle sounds more like the clock striking, but if someone chooses the sticks, try it out both ways and let the class decide.

5. Select one of the children who was able to clap in time with the music, and let him play the triangle while the others sing "the clock struck one." You may want to have others strike "make believe" triangles, also exactly in rhythm.

This may be as much as you can do the first time. If an uncertain singer can play the triangle at the right place, give him this opportunity to be successful in music.

A follow-up presentation (or a continuation of the same one) may be made in a number of ways. Here are some suggestions for the rhythm sticks:

1. Choose part of the class to stand and clap "hick-o-ry, dick-o-ry, dock," each time it comes in the song, while the rest of the class sings. Remind the clappers to *listen carefully* so that they clap exactly in time with the music.

2. Give out one pair of rhythm sticks to a child who you think will be able to play them with the music.

> Let him stand with a few selected singers. While they sing and he plays, the rest of the class plays imaginary sticks.
>
> 3. Now have several sets of rhythm sticks in the hands of the pupils, and at least one triangle to imitate the striking clock.

In these early experiences, make a careful selection of children who you feel reasonably confident can *play the instruments in time with the singing.* Later, all of the children should have an opportunity to play each of the rhythm instruments before the school year is over.

There are two purposes to keep in mind in using rhythm instruments. First, it is very important that this activity be *musical.* The singing should be accurate, expressive, and in a good, quick tempo. The instruments should be played, at first, only by those who can keep in time with the singing. Just as in other musical experiences, children need opportunities to hear presentations that have *musical worth.* There is nothing to be gained by having all the youngsters singing and banging away all during the song.

Secondly, it is important that the instruments be introduced a few at a time. Give the children a chance to experiment with the *sounds* they make, and to learn to make *discriminating choices* in the use of the instruments. The children will want to learn or review the names of these instruments and call them by name. Therefore, we should use them only a few at a time.

Here are some suggestions for another kind of follow-up presentation using "Hickory, Dickory, Dock":

> 1. Choose part of the class to whisper a steady "tick-tock" (on the first and fourth beat of each measure) while some of the capable singers sing. Let the rest of the class swing back and forth rhythmically, like the pendulum in an old-fashioned grandfather's clock. Be sure the "tick-tocks" and the pendulums keep exactly *in time* with the singing.
>
> 2. Choose someone who was able to whisper "tick-tock" successfully to play the same pattern on the wood block.
>
> 3. When each part is successful, combine all the instruments and singers. Those who are not singing or

playing should be swaying to the music. The first phrase will look something like this:

Singers and sticks:	*HICK*	*DICK*	*DOCK*	(rest)
Wood blocks:	(tick)	(tock)	(tick)	(tock)
"Pendulums":	(sway)	(sway)	(sway)	(sway)

The three other phrases are just like the first, except that, on the third phrase (when "the clock struck one") the triangle plays on "one." Notice that the steady beat of the wood block is heard all by itself at the end of the first, second, and fourth phrases (after the words "dock," "clock," and, again, "dock"). The sticks, however, play only on the first and fourth phrases. The triangle, of course, plays only once in this piece. Some teachers like to encourage the new players, by telling them when to play, or having them move their hands silently to the music as they play imaginary instruments, until they are sure of their part.

In many classrooms, the students enjoy playing games with these rhythm instruments. Here are two suggestions:

1. Place all of the rhythm instruments with which the class has had experience on a table. Let one child select an instrument to hold up for the class to see. He then chooses another child to tell the name of the instrument, and must decide if the name is correct.

2. Place all of the rhythm instruments with which the class has become familiar on a table. This time, let a child select one while all the other children cover their eyes. The child will play the instrument of his choice for the class to *hear but not look at*. The child who has played chooses another to name the instrument that was heard, and must decide if the name is correct.

After the children can recognize simple instruments by sight, sound, and name, they are ready to make creative and discriminating choices. The value of using rhythm instruments in the classroom should not be underestimated. The fact that they are simple sound-makers does not detract from the excellent help they can provide in *the development of musical discrimination*. You can help your pupils realize that each instrument makes a distinctive sound that can be described, in part, by answering some of the following kinds of questions:

1. Is the sound high or low? (to develop concepts about pitch)

2. Is the sound short, or can it be held for a long time—or both? (to develop concepts about duration)

3. Does the sound "ring" (as with the triangle or cymbals), or is it a duller, dryer sound (as with the sticks), or "scratchy" (as with the sandpaper blocks)? (to develop concepts about timbre)

4. Is the sound soft or loud, or can the instrument play both soft and loud sounds? (to develop concepts about dynamics)

5. Can the instrument play fast as well as slowly? (to develop concepts about tempo)

Nearly any favorite song can be enhanced by the discriminating use of rhythm instruments. The value of the activity, however, lies in the opportunity it affords the pupils *to develop their own powers of discrimination* by making suitable choices of instruments.

Use the same type of questions as those given above to examine the characteristics of a favorite song. For example, consider the well-known song "Oh Dear, What Can the Matter Be?"[2]

1. Is the song fast or slow? (Fast.)

2. Where are the *long tones?* (The long tones appear as dotted quarter notes in the book, but try to get the class to answer from what they can *hear* rather than what they can *see*.) Seven long tones in the first four phrases can be heard as follows:

> "Oh dear" at the beginning of the first phrase
> "Dear, dear" at the beginning of the second phrase
> "Oh dear" at the beginning of the third phrase
> "Fair" at the end of the fourth phrase

3. What kinds of instruments will sound best to *emphasize the long tones?* (Probably the drums, sand blocks, or struck tambourine.)

[2] Found in Book 2 of *The Spectrum of Music* Series, published by Macmillan Publishing Co., Inc.

4. What kinds of instruments can move lightly and fast enough for the short tones (eighth notes)? (Probably the triangles, sticks, sleigh bells, or shaken tambourine.)

5. So far, are there any phrases that are exactly alike in this song? (The first and the third are exactly alike; the second and fourth, different.) Perhaps we will want to try the same instruments for the phrases that are alike, and different instruments, for contrast, on those phrases that are different.

After listening to the rest of the song, some of the following kinds of questions can be used in directing attention to important aspects of the music:

6. Which phrases sound exactly alike in this part of the song? (The fifth and seventh are exactly alike; the sixth and eighth, different.)

7. Are there any *long tones?* (There is one long tone at the end of the eighth phrase, "hair." All the other tones are short tones. The short tones appear as eighth notes.)

8. What does the "D.C." mean at the end of the eighth phrase? (Go back to the beginning.)

9. Where does the song end? (At the end of the fourth phrase, "Johnny's so long at the fair.")

The class can be led to discover that this song has three parts:

First part: the first four phrases

Second part: phrases five through eight

Third part: the first four phrases again

In choosing appropriate rhythm instruments, the class can keep this three-part song form in mind and explore the concepts of similarity and contrast as brought out in the music. However, young children should not be kept at work on any activity beyond the point where they are interested and able to participate. Do only one part of this activity at a time if the class becomes restless.

Another easy way to use rhythm instruments is to ask some questions like this about the song:

1. Does the beat of the music move in twos or in threes? (In "Oh Dear, What Can the Matter Be?" the song moves in twos because it is written in a fast $\frac{6}{8}$ meter.)

2. Which instruments will sound best on the "one" (or strong beat) of each measure?

3. Which instruments can be used to play the second (or weak) beat of each measure? (In fast $\frac{6}{8}$ the dotted quarter gets one beat.)

4. Which instruments can be used to play the *long tones* (dotted quarter notes in this song) of the *rhythm pattern?*

5. Which instruments can play the *short tones* (eighth notes) of the *rhythm pattern* of this song? (In fast $\frac{6}{8}$ three eighth notes get one beat.)

In this way the pupils can explore the beat and the rhythm pattern of the words and choose suitable instruments. This kind of study of form, beat, and rhythm pattern also applies to the use of other informal instruments in the classroom—particularly Autoharps and tone bells.

One important essential for successful rhythm instrument experiences on each of these levels is appropriate song material. The text as well as the music should match the intellectual and emotional maturity of the children.

You will probably want to use instrumental selections as well as songs in your work with rhythm instruments. In addition to the material included in the current basic music series, you may find these books and records helpful (also see Appendix F):

BOOKS

Creative Rhythms and Accompaniments for Primary Grades, by Phoebe James

Make Music with the Bells (Melody instruments and xylophone), by McLaughlin and Dawley.

Sound Sketches with Rhythm Instruments (Would need to adapt material), by Vandevere.

SUGGESTED RECORDINGS FOR USE WITH RHYTHM INSTRUMENTS

Adventures in Rhythm (Jenkins)	Scholastic Records
"Air Gai" from *Iphigenie in Aulis* (Gluck)	RCA Adventures I

Rhythm Band Accompaniment "Concerto for Toys and Orchestra" (Hendl)	Rhythm Record RRC-1003 YPR-432
Exploring the Rhythm Instruments	Classroom Materials
Introducing the Rhythm Instruments	Classroom Materials
"Leap Frog" from *Children's Games* (Bizet)	RCA Adventures I
"March" from *Soirées Musicales* (Rossini-Britten)	RCA Adventures I
"Music for Rhythm Bands"	Album E-90, RCA Basic Record Library
"Nursery School Rhythms," *Creative Rhythms for Children* (James)	Phoebe James Records AED 20
"Outer Space" from *Play Time Rhythms* (White)	Rhythms Productions CC 618-2
"Parade" from Divertissement (Ibert)	RCA Adventures I
Piano and Instrument Sounds	Rhythm Record RRC-2003
"Rain" from *Play Time Rhythms* (White)	Rhythms Productions CC 618-2
Rhythm Instruments with Folk Music from Many Lands (White)	Rhythms Productions CC 614
Rhythms, Series One (Ed Durlacher)	Educational Activities 101 (Side A)
"Strike Up the Band"	CRG 5027
This Is Rhythm (Jenkins)	Scholastic Records
"Waltz of the Doll" from *Coppélia* (Delibes)	RCA Adventures I

MAKING RHYTHM INSTRUMENTS

Sometimes teachers like to make rhythm instruments. Frequently the children can help with this. There are many ways to make instruments.[3] Here is how two teachers did it.[4]

DRUM—DENIM HEAD

Materials: Gallon can, four circles of denim 3" larger than the can, 26 belt eyelets, leather strips for lacing heads to can, enamel paint, and shellac.

[3] The materials for making these instruments may be purchased at a lumberyard, hardware store, or variety store.

[4] Mrs. Esther Donley, former teacher at the Randall-Wachter School, Independence, Mo., and Mrs. Ann Banks, currently teaching kindergarten at this school, shared these suggestions for making rhythm instruments.

Paint the can. Cut four denim circles, fold under edges, and sew each pair of two circles together. Coat heavily with shellac. When the denim is dry, put in eyelets and lace onto the can with leather strips. Give both heads of the drum another coat of shellac and allow to dry.

DRUM—INNER TUBE HEAD

Materials: Gallon can, inner tube, leather strips, and enamel paint.

Paint the can. Cut two circles from the inner tube a little larger than the top of the can. With a paper punch, make holes around the edges of the circles, 2½-3″ apart. Lace heads on can with leather strips.

BEATER FOR DRUM

Materials: Dish mop, scrap of colored plastic, thin wire.

Cut away most of the string from the dish mop. Cover with plastic and secure with wire.

TAMBOURINE

Materials: Plywood, denim, roofing caps, thumbtacks, nails, paint, and shellac.

Saw two circles, 8″ in diameter, from ¼″ plywood and one circle, 8″ in diameter, from ¾″ plywood. Remove the centers of all three circles, leaving rings approximately ¾″ wide. Saw the ring of ¾″ plywood into 2″ blocks. Cover both sides of six of these blocks with Elmer's glue, and space them between the two complete rings, leaving five spaces approximately 1¾″ for the roofing caps and a larger space (3½″) for holding the tambourine. Clamps are helpful to hold the rings securely. Using 1¼″ finishing nails, nail the three pieces of wood together where you have the two-inch blocks of wood. (An electric drill is needed to bore these nail holes to keep the wood from splitting.) This frame should be painted and allowed to dry before the roofing caps are attached.

In the center of the 1¾″ spaces left for roofing caps, bore a nail hole. Drive a 1¼″ nail through one circle of plywood. Place two roofing caps with raised sides together over the end of the nail and continue driving the nail into the other ring.

Cut a circle of denim ½″ larger than the frame. Turn under ¼″ and hem with sewing machine. Decide which ring you want for the head of the tambourine. Cover the top and sides of this ring with Elmer's glue. Working from one side to the other, stretch the denim over the frame and secure firmly with a row of thumbtacks all the way around the frame. Be sure to leave no slack in the cloth. Give the denim two coats of shellac.

TRIANGLE

Materials: Steel rod 18″ long (rolled steel seems the hardest that can be bent without being heated), wooden knob, short piece of cord, and a spike nail.

Measure six inches from each end of the rod. Bend at these places until the ends nearly touch. Attach cord to wooden knob and put on triangle to hold it. Use nail to strike the triangle.

JINGLE BELLS

Materials: Scraps of colored plastic and bells.

Cut 8″ X 1″ strips of plastic and staple the ends to make a circle. Sew on three bells.

JINGLE CLOGS

Materials: ¼″ plywood, roofing caps, a screw, and paint.

Cut the piece of wood into the shape of a small paddle. Paint. Attach two roofing caps with screw.

SAND BLOCKS

Materials: Scraps of wood, wooden knobs, and fine sandpaper.

Cut blocks of wood 3″ X 5″. Attach knobs. Paint. When blocks are dry, cut pieces of sandpaper the width of the blocks and long enough to cover the undersides and both ends of the blocks. Secure the sandpaper to the wood with a staple gun.

RHYTHM STICKS

Materials: Dowel pins and paint.

Cut dowel pins into 12″ pieces. Sand ends. Paint.

MARACAS OR RATTLES

Materials: Light bulbs—75, 150, and 500 watt.

Cover bulbs with papier-mâché—one or two layers. Let dry thoroughly. Drop bulbs on a hard surface (so as to break them without damaging the outsides). Cover with more strips of paper and wallpaper paste. Let dry. Paint bright colors.

STORAGE BOX

It is wise to prepare some type of box with a hinged lid to hold the instruments. This helps to keep them assembled and in good condition.

Middle and Later Childhood
(Levels 3, 4, 5, and 6)

PLAYING INFORMAL
INSTRUMENTS

RHYTHM INSTRUMENTS. Although rhythm instruments were an essential part of the earlier music classes, they can still be used effectively. Many songs can still be enhanced by these instruments, particularly if a distinctive rhythm pattern is being emphasized. For example, consider this song:[5]

Tum Balalaika

[5] From Book 5 of *Growing with Music* Series, by Harry R. Wilson, Walter Ehret, Alice M. Snyder, Edward J. Hermann, and Albert A. Renna. Copyright, 1966 by Prentice-Hall, Inc., Englewood Cliffs, N.J. Reprinted with permission; also found in Book 6 of *Explor-*

TUM BALALAIKA. This song has an interesting tonality (D minor) and through the use of instruments (as scored) it can be gratifying to the class—both musically and educationally. The two rhythm patterns shown above the first staff can furnish a very satisfying experience with timbre and form as well as with meter.

ing Music Series, published by Holt, Rinehart and Winston, Inc., and in Book 6 of *The Spectrum of Music* Series, published by Macmillan Publishing Co., Inc.

Concepts about how triple meter sounds (STRONG, weak, weak in each measure) should normally be developed through past experience (see pages 93 and 109–119). The class should also understand that $\frac{3}{4}$ not only indicates triple meter (upper figure), but also designates the quarter note as the "one-beat note" (lower figure).

A careful study of the printed page should result in this important consideration: "Which instrument could make an appropriate sound on the STRONG beat (or "one") that is scored for a steady recurrence in the upper pattern? Experimentation can show the class that: 1) some of the rhythm instruments have a stronger tone than others, 2) some of the rhythm instruments can sustain a tone longer than others, and 3) some of the rhythm instruments can be manipulated faster and with greater precision of sound than others.

From looking at the patterns, the children can discover that no sustained sounds are required—since the quarter note is the "one-beat note" in this music, and because the rhythm patterns are made up entirely of:

1. "one-beat notes" (♩)
2. "one-beat rests" (𝄽)
3. two equal divisions of one beat (♫)

Pupils are capable of selecting an instrument with a STRONG tone for the strong beat, and they are also able to find a contrasting instrument for the second pattern. These skills are developed largely through opportunity. The class may conclude that a drum or a wood block would sound effective on the repeated downbeat of the top pattern, and that the castanets or finger cymbals can be tried for the second pattern.

Great variety is possible through using different pairs of instruments for:

1. an introduction or a coda, or both
2. the first stanza
3. the second stanza
4. the refrain

Of these four places in the music, can the class find a place where the *same instrumentation* would be suitable? The realization that the refrain could be played in an exact imitation can deepen the students' understanding of FORM.

Through reading the page *vertically,* it is also apparent that violins may be added. Substitutions of small wind instruments or voices could be made, if necessary. If the violin part is sung, an open, easily articulated neutral syllable (such as "TAH") can produce a beautiful effect. Singers will need to remember to sustain the tone three FULL beats each time they see the ♩. , to give a beautiful legato line to the melody.

RHYTHM EXPERIENCES.   Of particular interest to boys and girls at this age is the playing of percussion instruments with a recording. Choose a composition that lends itself well to this type of experience, such as *Concerto for Percussion and Small Orchestra,* by Milhaud, and write a percussion score that is not too complicated for your class to play. Here are some suggestions for planning such an experience:

1. Display the title of the composition and the name of the composer in a prominent place. Ask the class to listen to the entire composition to see how many percussion instruments they will be able to identify afterward. (Although this concerto has two movements, the division between the two is so slight that it seems continuous—and should be presented that way.)

2. Ask the students to name the percussion instruments that seemed to be prominent in the music. List these on the chalkboard:

    Drums:
      Bass
      Tenor
      Timpani
      Snare
    Tambourines
    Cymbals
    Castanets
    Triangle
    Maracas
    Gong

3. Tell the students that you have written a percussion score for only part of the concerto. (Sections of the first movement will probably be most appropriate.)

Suggest that they listen again to see if they can discover the places you chose, and the instruments you selected to play.

4. Select a student who you are confident can read the percussion score and perform successfully on one of the instruments. One by one, add other performers on other instruments.

As you explore with other compositions and your students become more experienced, you may want to give them the opportunity to assist with the writing of the percussion score. (See pages 109–119 for detailed help on this.)

"Performing" with a recording in this manner gives the students the excited feeling of playing with a "real" orchestra. This enjoyable experience can help to clarify and strengthen concepts about meter, rhythm pattern, tempo, and dynamics.

MELODY INSTRUMENTS

These simple instruments are excellent for helping children to distinguish *the high and the low* (or pitch) in music. Some teachers like to keep an inexpensive set of metal bells (the kind that are fastened together like a toy xylophone) hanging within reach of the children. The set is placed with the larger bars at the bottom, so that the children can discover which are the lower tones and which are the higher tones by simple experimentation. Bells of this type are played by striking with a small mallet.

In addition to this type, there are also tuned resonator bells in which each bar is mounted separately. Some of these can be passed out individually, one to a child, so that a few notes from a familiar melody can be played. Because bells of this type are made of high quality metal, and are each mounted on a separate block of wood that is hollowed out inside to form a resonating cavity, they have an unusually beautiful tone. Some tuned resonator bells come in a case with the black and white bars arranged like the black and white keys of the piano. These bells are also played by striking with a small mallet. A number of companies (see Appendix B) feature Orff instruments. A wide variety of tone bells are available: xylophones, resonator bells, glockenspiels, and metallo phones. These, too, are played by striking with mallets. They are unusually helpful aids in the study of the pentatonic scale.

*Under the direction of their teacher, some children are
shown playing Orff instruments.*

A third kind, Melode Bells, is an inexpensive set of eight plastic bells, usually in eight different colors, and rung by hand. Inside each colored plastic bell is a small tuned metal ball with a small metal clapper. Generally, these bells are constructed to play an F major scale in the octave above middle C, and are very useful and enjoyable in the classroom.

Early Childhood (Levels 1 and 2)

Here are some ways in which these informal melodic instruments can be used to help children develop their perception of pitch and their ability to remember tonal groups.

For experience in determining *melodic direction,* you may want to play on the xylophone the last phrase of "Hickory, Dickory, Dock." Ask the class if the mouse was going up or down the clock. Some of the inaccurate singers may not be aware that the

Melody instruments include (from top down) chromatic step bells, plastic Melode Bells, tuned resonator bells, and (at right) xylophone (photo by Ken Raveill).

general direction of this melody is *downward,* and this is one of the reasons they do not sing better.

Other children will be able to tell you that the mouse took one little step up, then came back down the clock.

Hick-o - ry, dick- o - ry, dock.

The purpose of this kind of activity is to give the class frequent experience with upward and downward melodic lines.

As these melodies are played on the xylophone the class will have the additional advantage of *seeing the direction of the tune* while they are listening to it.

With a set of tuned resonator bells, the teacher may give a C-bell to a child to strike as some of the class sings "one" (from "the clock struck one"). The singers will need to listen carefully to their own singing, to make sure it is exactly in tune with the C-bell when it is time for the "clock" to strike "one." Some teachers are successful in helping the out-of-tune singer by having him strike the tone bell and try matching it with his own voice by singing "bong" on the same pitch. As in all such remedial work, the child needs instruction after each try, to make sure he understands whether his sound was "too low," "too high," or "just right." It's even possible for him to match the pitch perfectly without realizing it himself.

Using a set of hand-rung melody bells, you may want to have six pupils line up in a row, each holding a bell from the low F to the D above. At first, the teacher may need to point to each child when it is his or her turn to play one of the notes:

Each child should be told to shake his bell rapidly when his turn comes. It's a good idea to select the child you think will be the most skillful to play the C-bell, because that bell has to sound twice in this song. Remind the children not to shake their bells until the director points to them. Later on, one of the more capable children will be able to direct the playing of a familiar pattern like this.[6]

In determining *melodic direction,* the class will need some experience with melodies that go up. There are many examples in the various music books. One well-known song, "Sing a Song of Sixpence,"[7] has an excellent example of *a tune that goes up.* This is the last phrase, the last six notes of the song:

To   set   be   fore   the   king.

Many children will discover that some tunes go up, and that others go down. There are also some tunes that go *straight across.* Two

[6] This same tune is also found in some versions of the singing game "Looby-Loo," in the fourth phrase: "All on a Sat-ur-day night."

[7] Found in the Kindergarten Book of *Exploring Music* Series, published by Holt, Rinehart and Winston, Inc.; and Book 1 of *This Is Music for Today* Series, published by Allyn and Bacon, Inc.; and in Book 2 of *Growing with Music* Series, published by Prentice-Hall, Inc.

These children are shown playing rhythm and melody instruments (photo by Ken Raveill).

well-known songs that have repeated notes (that "go straight across") are "Rig-a-Jig-Jig"[8] and "Jingle Bells."[9] There are many other songs with repeated tones, but they are not always as easy to hear as tones that go up or down. Children who cannot distinguish

[8] Found in Book 1 of *Discovering Music Together* Revised Series, published by Follett Publishing Co. (Teacher's edition only); Book 1 of *This Is Music for Today* Series, published by Allyn and Bacon, Inc.; Book 2 of *Growing with Music* Series, published by Prentice-Hall, Inc.; "Beginning Music" from *New Dimensions in Music* Series, published by American Book Co.; and in Kindergarten Book of *The Spectrum of Music* Series, published by Macmillan Publishing Co., Inc.

[9] Found in Book 2 of *Discovering Music Together* Revised Series, published by Follett

between *high and low* in music will not understand how some tunes can go "straight across." Making "pictures" in the air with our hands will help teach *melodic direction,* but repeated tones are a more advanced concept.

All three types of tone bells used in these early experiences can be used both melodically and harmonically. Like the piano, these bells can play notes *one at a time melodically,* or they can play chord tones *together harmonically.* After the children have become quite familiar with melodic direction you might want to try these new procedures.

USING THE BELLS
MELODICALLY

The following suggestions (except items 5, 6, and 10) will work with all three types of tone bells. The activities suggested in items 5, 6, and 10 require the sharps and flats found on some toy "xylophones" and in all sets of tuned resonator bells.

1. If possible, leave the bells out where all the children have an opportunity to try the instrument. During class, hold it high once so that all of the children can see it.

2. Then put it on a desk or table and play the bells from C to C, or F to F.

3. If there is a piano in your room that is in tune, invite one of the children to find and play the same tune on the piano.

4. Encourage the children to discover that the bells you used sound like the white keys of the piano.

5. Play C♯ (D♭), D♯ (E♭) through F♯ (G♭), G♯ (A♭), A♯ (B♭). Ask some child to play the same tune on the piano.

6. Help the children to discover that the bells you used this time sound like the black keys of the piano. The pupils can find alternating groups of twos and threes on the keyboard.

Publishing Co.; Book 2 of *This Is Music for Today* Series, published by Allyn and Bacon, Inc.; Book 1 of *Growing with Music* Series, published by Prentice-Hall, Inc.; Book 1 of *Silver Burdett Music Series,* published by General Learning Corporation (Teacher's edition only); Kindergarten Book and Book 1 of *The Magic of Music* Series, published by Ginn and Company; and Kindergarten Book of *The Spectrum of Music* Series, published by Macmillan Publishing Co., Inc.

7. Play an easy tune such as "Hot Cross Buns"[10] on the bells.

B	A	G
Hot	Cross	Buns,

B	A	G
Hot	Cross	Buns,

G	G	G	G
One	a	Pen -	ny,

A	A	A	A
Two	a	Pen -	ny,

B	A	G
Hot	Cross	Buns!

8. Give two or three children an opportunity to pick out the tune on the bells.

9. Let some try to find the tune on the piano, using only the white keys.

10. Invite the children to play the same tune on the bells and the piano, using only the black keys.

A♯	G♯	F♯
(B♭)	(A♭)	(G♭)
Hot	Cross	Buns,

A♯	G♯	F♯
(B♭)	(A♭)	(G♭)
Hot	Cross	Buns,

F♯	F♯	F♯	F♯
(G♭)	(G♭)	(G♭)	(G♭)
One	a	Pen -	ny,

G♯	G♯	G♯	G♯
(A♭)	(A♭)	(A♭)	(A♭)
Two	a	Pen -	ny,

A♯	G♯	F♯
(B♭)	(A♭)	(G♭)
Hot	Cross	Buns!

The bells should also be used frequently to play the melody pattern that you may teach as a part of the music reading readiness

[10] Found in Book 1 of *Exploring Music* Series, published by Holt, Rinehart and Winston, Inc. (Key of F—change BAG to AGF) (Melody 1); Book 2 of *This Is Music for Today* Series, published by Allyn and Bacon, Inc.; and in Kindergarten Book and Book 1 of *The Spectrum of Music* Series, published by Macmillan Publishing Co., Inc. (Key of C—change BAG to EDC).

program. In addition, they may be used in creative activities. Encourage the children to use the bells to make up their own tunes.

USING THE BELLS
HARMONICALLY

The Melode Bells and the tuned resonator bells can also be used to develop concepts about harmony by playing the *chord tones* of many of the songs in your music book.

If your text doesn't have the Autoharp chords marked, ask the music teacher in your building (or your music resource person) to write them in your book for you.

Here are some suggestions for an effective *harmonic* experience using the bells to play chord tones:

1. Play "Are You Sleeping?"[11] on the bells.

Are You Sleeping?

Old French Round

Are you sleep - ing, are you sleep - ing, Broth - er John,

Broth - er John? Morn- ing bells are ring - ing, morn-ing bells are ring - ing,

Ding, ding, dong, ding, ding, dong!

Ask the children to identify the song.

2. Since this song is in the key of G, play the G bell on the first beat of each measure as the children sing the song.

[11] Found in Book 2 of *Discovering Music Together* Revised Series, published by Follett Publishing Co. (Key of F); "Enjoying Music" (Book 2) from *New Dimensions in Music* Series, published by American Book Co.; Book 2 of *The Spectrum of Music* Series, published by Macmillan Publishing Co., Inc.; Book 2 of *This Is Music for Today* Series, published by Allyn and Bacon, Inc. (appears as "Frère Jacques"); Kindergarten Book of *The Magic of Music* Series, published by Ginn and Company; and Book 3 of *Exploring Music* Series, published by Holt, Rinehart and Winston, Inc.

3. Let someone play your bell. Choose for yourself the octave G bell above. Help the children to see that the larger bell has a lower tone. Lead them to the conclusion that the larger the bell, the lower the tone; the smaller the bell, the higher the tone.

4. Let the two bells play the song on the first beat of each measure as the children sing.

5. Continue with this same procedure until five bells are playing at once—low G, high G, B, low D, and high D.

Five bells play together.

6. Give other children a turn.

7. Discuss with the boys and girls the fact that these five bells sound well together. Let them discover that this is not true with all of the bells. Add to these five B♭ and A. The discord that results will tell you that these seven bells sound dissonant.

All of the G's, B's, and D's harmonize with this melody when the song is in the key of G major.[12] "Are You Sleeping?" ("Frère Jacques") is one of the few tunes that sounds well with *only one chord* repeated over and over. Most simple melodies require two or three different chords, but there are a great many songs of this type that you and the children will enjoy harmonizing. The early experiences will be easier, of course, if you select a song that needs only two chords for harmonizing. For example:

Oh Where, Oh Where Has My Little Dog Gone?[13]

German Song

---

[12] In the key of F major, use the F, A, and C bells instead.

[13] From Book 1 of *Exploring Music* Series, by Boardman and Landis, Copyright © 1966, published by Holt, Rinehart and Winston, Inc.

1. Choose seven children. Ask three of them to stand at one side of the room. Give them the F, A, and (high) C bells.
2. Ask the other four children to stand at the other side of the room. Give them the C, E, G, and B♭ bells.
3. Where the letter F is indicated in the music, point to the group of three children and have them play their bells together.
4. Where the letter C_7 is indicated, point to the group of four children and have them play their bells together.

Most music books use chord symbols to indicate simple harmony for some of the songs. The chords are usually marked in capital letters above the melody, and can be played by the bells, the Autoharp, and the piano. Children will also be able to sing these chords later on, when they have gained aural experience and vocal independence.

Middle Childhood (Levels 3 and 4)

EXTENDING CREATIVITY
THROUGH THE USE
OF TONE BELLS

Creating introductions and codas for songs with informal instruments can be a very meaningful, satisfying experience for boys and girls at this age. In the early stages of experimenting it is probably best to use melody or rhythm patterns from the song itself—or variations of these patterns. To be specific, let's consider creating a melody or melodies for the Scandinavian "Hiking Song" that could be played on the bells as an introduction or coda—or both.

You might find this plan helpful with your class:

1. Be sure the students know the song well and enjoy singing it before you begin the process of developing an introduction and coda.

Hiking Song[14]

Scandinavian Song   Words by Charles Winter

[14] From *Songtime 4*, by Vera Russell, John Wood, Lansing MacDowell, and Charles Winter. Copyright © 1963 by Holt, Rinehart and Winston, Inc. Reprinted by permission of Holt, Rinehart and Winston, Inc.

1. As   we   sing   the   songs   we   please   on   our   way,   Fa - le - ra!
2. But   we'll   sing   one   cho - rus   more   com - ing   in,   Fa - le - ra!

2. To begin this group experience in creativity, call attention to the first words of the song, "The morning is bright." Then ask the class what part of the melody (in the total song) reminds them of morning. There is a reminiscence of "reveille" in the tune for "The morning is bright." Some students will be aware of this, although they may not know the correct terminology.

3. Invite a student to play that part of the tune on the resonator bells or xylophone. Then ask the class if they would like to add a little more to this tune to make it sound "finished." (If they continue the melody or the phrase as it appears in the song they will not have a complete cadence.) It could be that the children will want to use just the short excerpt that has been played. If so, suggest that this is a little short for an introduction and ask what they could do to make it longer. Through motivated discussion they should discover that repetition may enhance the effect of this brief melody. If completed in this manner the last note would need to be a dotted quarter instead of a quarter. The introduction would then look like this:

Tune 1

While this brief tune would make a fitting introduction, there seems to be need for a greater feeling of "ending" in the coda. (The children can discover that the coda is a special ending added at the conclusion of the song.) Suggest to the children that they think of a few more notes to follow the introduction that will give a stronger feeling of having arrived "home." Their efforts might result in a coda similar to this tune:

Tune 2

To give the song a real "dressed-up air," Tune 1 could be used only as the introduction and Tune 2 as the coda. Several children could take turns performing these on the bells just before and after the class sings the song.

As the class develops skill in repeated experiences of this type, they will become freer in creating melodies that are not necessarily found in the song but are appropriate to use with it.

Introductions and codas involving rhythm patterns and percussion instruments can be developed in much the same manner as

In a learning center one student creates and rehearses an introduction and coda that he will later play in his music class (photo by Patrick Burke).

the one just described for melodies. A more detailed discussion of the use of percussion instruments can be found on pages 229–244.

EXPERIENCING MELODY. Some of the most useful of all the informal instruments are those we call the "small wind instruments": the Tonette, song flute, Flutophone, ocarina, fife, and recorder. The recorder has a lovely tone quality, but it is more expensive than the others. Tonettes, song flutes, and Flutophones are generally the most popular with teachers because they are inexpensive and easy to finger. However, manufacturers have developed serviceable plastic recorders that are now in the same general price range as the other small wind instruments (Aulos, Jensen, and Cambridge) if purchased in quantity orders. These are proving to be quite satisfactory. The German fingering featured on these instruments is the same as that on the Flutophone or Tonette.

When these melody instruments are handled wisely they can be an effective aid in teaching music. Learning the letter (pitch) names of notes can be accelerated by this method. Rhythmic awareness can be developed and strengthened. Part singing problems are greatly reduced when the class can *hear the parts* of a song played *simultaneously* through the use of small wind instruments.

The many skills that children can gain through this kind of activity will also help to indicate the potential talent they may have for learning to play a band or orchestral instrument.

PREPARATORY WORK. Although detailed instruction booklets can be purchased with each instrument, it is well to consider these things when planning for this activity:

1. Select a *single type of instrument* for use in your classroom. Although each of the small wind instruments serves the same functions musically, instructional problems will be much less if you are dealing

Close-up of a Tonette or song flute (photo by Ken Raveill).

with all song flutes, or all Flutophones, etc. To mix them up within a single class can create additional problems of fingering and playing in tune.

2. Make a rule that each child use only his or her own instrument. It is possible to sterilize the instruments (mouthwash that contains no alcohol will not damage the plastic), but without sterilization no one should ever share a wind instrument, any more than he would a toothbrush. If each individual child owns his own instrument, he should be sure his name is taped on it, and should keep his instrument clean.

3. When you first begin work on the small wind instruments, it is easier if you concentrate your efforts on them exclusively. Later on, when the class has some degree of mastery, you will have no trouble adding other types of instruments if you want special rhythmic or harmonic effects.

FINGERING.   Here are some suggestions for teaching the fingering of the small wind instruments:

1. Stand in front of the class with your back to the children, holding the instrument with the right hand near the bell (the end opposite the mouthpiece).

2. Find the single hole on the back of the instrument. This is the left-hand thumb hole. Place the left thumb over it.

3. Find the right-hand thumb guide near the center of the instrument. Place the right thumb on the thumb guide.

4. The illustration below shows the fingering for middle C and B (third line, treble staff):

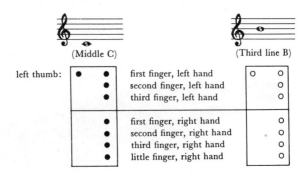

left thumb:	●	●	first finger, left hand	o	o
		●	second finger, left hand		o
		●	third finger, left hand		o
		●	first finger, right hand		o
		●	second finger, right hand		o
		●	third finger, right hand		o
		●	little finger, right hand		o

Dots indicate holes to be covered; circles indicate holes to be left open.

Your instruction booklet will give about fifteen fingerings for all the chromatic tones that are found in a little more than an octave above middle C.

PLAYING IN TUNE.   Just as in singing, it is up to the performer to make the music sound in tune. Almost any instrument can be played out-of-tune (and often is!). Emphasize to the children the importance of "training their ears" in order to play in tune. Use your melody bells to check the pitch. They are always in tune— unlike the piano and the Autoharp. Unless a person is handicapped, he can learn to listen to the bells attentively and match the pitch with his instrument.

If the instrument sounds higher than the tone bells, pull the mouthpiece out slightly, and it will lower the pitch. Conversely, pushing in the mouthpiece will raise the pitch. Keep any joints in the instrument fitted together snugly.

Also, remind the children to blow softly. "Over-blowing" the instrument is a common cause of poor intonation. Here are some other hints for proper playing:

1. Sit tall and breathe deeply.
2. Breathe through the mouth.
3. Hold the mouthpiece lightly between the lips.
4. Whisper "too" on each note.
5. Keep *"snug fingers"* on the tone holes to be covered.

Close-up of a recorder (photo by Patrick Burke).

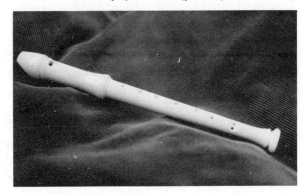

6. Keep *"high fingers"* on the tone holes to be left open.

PLAYING FAMILIAR MUSIC. The early experiences will be more successful if familiar music is used. As the children learn to play the instrument, they can also learn to read some simple unfamiliar music. For the beginning experiences, try these suggestions:

1. Ask the class to study the note values (quarter, eighth, half, and whole notes) and count them out silently.
2. Establish a steady, audible beat with an appropriate tempo.
3. Have the class clap or tap the rhythm pattern of the note values exactly in time with the beat. Emphasize the need for precision and accuracy.
4. Ask the class to study the pitch names of the melody silently.
5. Ask the class to finger the instrument (without blowing) while counting the note values silently.
6. Now they should be able to play successfully and musically, but when mistakes occur, be sure the class has the opportunity to discover them and to analyze how to correct them.

A good instruction booklet will provide simple beginning music that will present one problem at a time. A piece may feature a new fingering or a different kind of note value. When the beginner can play this piece *in tune and in rhythm,* a new problem will be presented. In other words, a good instruction booklet will not "throw everything at the learner at once."

PLAYING UNFAMILIAR MUSIC. As soon as children gain some proficiency on the instrument, you will find that experiences with unfamiliar music will help to develop reading readiness and independent sight playing.

In all activities involving the use of the small wind instruments, the outstanding advantage is probably the appeal these instruments have for children. The enjoyment they derive from successful performance adds much to the acquisition of musical skills.

Later Childhood (Levels 5 and 6)

TUNED RESONATOR BELLS

On these levels the resonator bells are particularly helpful in many types of music experiences—creating accompaniments for songs, strengthening intonation skills, reinforcing the sense of melodic direction, and as a teaching aid in presenting chords. For a detailed discussion on this last use of the bells, see pages 103-107 in Chapter 3.

*THE SMALL WIND
INSTRUMENTS*

On these levels you may want to plan activities using these instruments to develop sight singing skills and to provide MELODIC EXPERIENCES. There are usually several songs in your basic music series books that can be played on these instruments. The more difficult songs should be presented first by rote before the class tries playing them on the small winds. With simpler songs, plan a complete reading process. (The types of songs that are suitable for initial reading experiences are discussed on page 90.)

When you plan this type of reading experience, you may want the class to clap the rhythm of the notes—or chant the rhythm of the words of the song—before they attempt to play the melody. Of course, there are many ways to plan reading activities, but if you will ask the group to consider one thing at a time, your teaching will be more effective.

A discussion of the time signature (when considering rhythm) and the key signature (when considering melody) is an essential part of the initial presentations. After the class has learned to play a song fairly well, plan to have part of the group sing while the others play.

As the students become more skilled you might want to select a few of the better ones to play the descants or chants that appear with some of the songs in the students' songbooks. In addition to giving variety to the experience, it could also be a useful tool in assisting those who are attempting to sing these special parts.

Toward the end of the year, or whenever your pupils become quite skillful, you may want to try playing rounds. Perhaps the class should first sing the round in unison, then in parts. Duplicate this experience with the instruments.

A suggestion should probably be given here. When the students are learning to play the instrument, be sure that they are learning to read *notes,* not just the *fingering.* Because it is easier, teachers are sometimes tempted to write the fingering on the board, eliminating the notes. However, one of the essential, educational purposes of the instrument is to assist in the reading of notes.

HARMONY INSTRUMENTS

The harmony instruments—such as the Autoharp, ukulele, guitar, and others—are used on the elementary levels to play *chords.*

Early and Middle Childhood
(Levels 1, 2, ad 3)

THE AUTOHARP

The soft, harplike quality of chords played on the Autoharp makes an excellent accompaniment for children's singing.

On the first level the Autoharp is more often played by the teacher than by the pupils, although it is a very simple instrument to play. You need only to push the small chord button, hold it

Close-up of an Autoharp (photo by Ken Raveill).

down *firmly,* and strum the strings with a small pick held in the other hand.

Most Autoharps have two kinds of picks to be used in strumming: a plastic pick, and a felt pick. Children enjoy discovering the difference in the *loud and soft sounds* made by the two kinds of picks.

There are many simple songs with accompaniments made up of only two chords. Most music books show the names of the chords, with capital letters placed right above the notes where a chord is to be changed. If your book does not have these chord symbols, perhaps you can get one of the music teachers to mark them in for you.

A very easy song to start with is "Row, Row, Row Your Boat."[15] You need to change the chord only twice during the entire song—once just before the word "life" (G₇ chord), and then back again just before the word "dream," to the C chord you started with.

Hold down the button marked "C major" (or just "C"). Keep pressing it down *firmly.* Strum at the places marked by asterisks in the example below, but never strum unless you are holding down one of the buttons. (If you do, you'll be playing all the strings at once, and the effect will be entertaining, but not very musical.)

(*Keep holding the C button*)	Row,	row,	row your	boat
	*	*	*	*
	Gent-ly	down the	stream .	. . . . .
	*	*	*	*
	Merr-i-ly,	merr-i-ly,	merr-i-ly,	merr-i-ly
	*	*	*	*
(*Now hold the G₇ button*)	Life is	but a (C)	dream .	. . . . .
	*	*	*	*

Another children's song with an easy Autoharp accompaniment is "The Farmer in the Dell."[16] Begin by holding the G button down firmly. You will not have to change to the D₇ button until just before the last "in." Keep holding the G button and strum on the words marked by asterisks, as follows:

[15] Found in Book 6 of *The Spectrum of Music* Series, published by Macmillan Publishing Co., Inc.

[16] Found in Book 3 of *This Is Music for Today* Series, published by Allyn and Bacon, Inc.; "Music for Early Childhood" from *New Dimensions in Music* Series, published by American Book Co. Also found in Kindergarten book of *Exploring Music* Series, published by Holt, Rinehart and Winston, Inc.

(Keep holding the G button)	The farm-er	in the	dell	
	*	*	*	*
	The farm-er	in the	dell	
	*	*	*	*
	Heigh	ho, the	der-ry	o
	*	*	*	*
(Get ready to change twice)	The farm-er (D₇)	in the (G)	dell	
	*	*	*	*

1. Strum the Autoharp steadily where the asterisks appear.

2. Chord changes are shown immediately *before* the word they're sung with. Press the chord button quickly and hold it down firmly. Never strum before the chord button is held down, but keep strumming steadily in time with the rhythm.

You will enjoy playing accompaniments on the Autoharp, and the children will like to sing with it. Notice, in these examples, that we have suggested strumming steadily on the strong beat (first beat) of each measure. But don't be afraid to experiment and try some other ways.

After the pupils have had many happy experiences with the Autoharp, encourage them to discover that the long, thick strings have low "voices"; the short, thin strings have high "voices." Show the class that when you press the various buttons on the Autoharp bars you get different combinations of musical sounds, or chords.

Try to help the children learn to *recognize the sounds* that result when two or more tones are played or sung together simultaneously (chords). Contrast this with the melodic "line" of single tones played or sung in succession (tune). Point out that when people talk about *harmony* in music they are referring to the *chords.* When people talk about the *melody,* they mean the *tune.* Melody is made up of single notes heard one after another; *harmony* is made up of groups of notes heard together at the same time.

Some children are able to use the terms "melody," "chords," and "harmony" correctly through repeated successful opportunities to identify these words with the corresponding musical sounds.

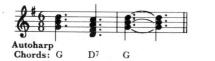

Autoharp
Chords: G   D⁷   G

Melody: Three blind   mice.___

If you play the chords marked G, D₇, G on the Autoharp (as shown on the staff above), *harmony* will result. If you sing the words "Three blind mice," *melody* will result. If you both sing and play the Autoharp, *music* will result. Children can be led to realize that although *melody* and *harmony* are all right by themselves, they really become more interesting and satisfying when they are put together (with rhythm)—as is usual in music.

STRUMMING TO THE BEAT OF THE MUSIC.   Although children on the first two levels are not usually expected to play the Autoharp by themselves, some teachers like to press the appropriate chord buttons while the children take turns strumming the strings. The pupils with the best sense of *beat* will be able to strum the best. You may have to help some of them find how many beats there are in the measure of the song, and remind them which is the strong beat. For example, some easy ways to strum are:

In $\frac{2}{4}$ meter, strum: *STRONG, weak* for each measure.

In $\frac{3}{4}$ meter, strum: *STRONG, weak, weak* for each measure

In $\frac{4}{4}$ meter, strum: *STRONG, weak, less weak, weak* for each measure; or: *STRONG, weak* (as in $\frac{2}{4}$ meter).

In most $\frac{6}{8}$ meter, strum: *STRONG, weak* for each measure.

In very slow $\frac{6}{8}$ meter, strum: *STRONG, weak, weak, less weak, weak, weak* for each measure.

The experience of strumming the Autoharp can also help to develop a *sense of rhythm,* which can lead to an understanding of three concepts about rhythm: the beat, the meter, and the pattern of the note values.

By the third level your class should be mature enough to attempt the entire process of playing the Autoharp by themselves. Whenever a child accompanies the class in a song it is wise to

Miss Aleta Runkle, author, manipulates the chord buttons on an Autoharp while children take turns strumming the strings (photo by Patrick Burke).

suggest that he find the specific chords on the instrument before beginning. In addition, he will have a more successful experience if he does a "trial run" of the chords by himself once or twice before the class "joins in." You may need to assist at first by pointing to the chords in the book as the student familiarizes himself with the printed page. Above all, stress needs to be given the necessity for maintaining a *steady beat* and accurate rhythm.

**Middle and Later Childhood
(Levels 4, 5, and 6)**

THE AUTOHARP

Chord markings for the harmony instruments can be found in most songbooks. At times, however, you may want deliberately to avoid using music with chord indications. A good activity that brings genuine satisfaction and strengthens basic music skills is playing the Autoharp "by ear."

The experience could be planned in this manner:

1. Choose a familiar folk song that has only the three basic chords: I, IV, and V₇. (The song will need to

be one that the students know, since they will not be using books.)

2. Have the class name the key in which the song is written. Have one of the students write the scale on the board, with both letters and numbers. (If the key were G it would look like this:)

G	1
F$\sharp$	7
E	6
D	5
C	4
B	3
A	2
G	1

3. Next, decide the letters for the three chords:

	C	
D	A	G
B	F$\sharp$	E
G	D	C
I	V$_7$	IV

4. Ask the students to name the root of each chord:

I	G
V$_7$	D
IV	C

5. Remind the class that these three chords are the only ones needed for this song, and ask a student to go to the Autoharp and locate the corresponding chord buttons or bars. (Normally, sixth graders have little trouble understanding that the chord bars are lettered to match the PITCH, or LETTER name of the ROOT OF THE CHORD. Be sure the players realize the D$_7$ bar is needed—not the D.)

6. Ask the class which chord is found at the end of the song (the tonic chord, or "key" chord—which in this case happens to be G Major). Suggest that the student hold this chord button down and strum in rhythm while the class begins the song. When he feels that he should change to another chord he should do so. Until that time he should keep press-

ing the G bar firmly. This experience should include discussions of CADENCE, in order to reinforce the knowledge that the concluding chord progression of many songs is the V_7 to I.

7. Give as many students as possible the opportunity to test their musical sensitivity in this manner.

Another *homophonic** experience that you might try is the tuning of the Autoharp by one of your more musical students. (Perhaps two or three could share in this experience.) The instruments to which the Autoharp is best tuned are the tuned resonator bells and the piano. One method that has proved successful for many teachers is tuning the Autoharp by chords. This keeps the instrument "in tune with itself." For example, the pitch of the lowest string on most Autoharps is F. Tune the F, A, and C strings. Now that the C is tuned, use this note as the root of the next chord and tune C, E, and G. From there proceed with G, B, and D, and so on. After the tuning is completed, it may be necessary to go back and check the F chord once again. (Since most of us don't possess absolute pitch, there is usually a slight deviation from the first chord to the last.) *Tune the chords in this order:*

F	A	C
C	E	G
G	B	D
D	F♯	A
A	C♯	E
E	G♯	B
B	D♯	F♯
F♯	A♯	C♯

If the chord button is held down firmly during the tuning, the correct strings are easier to locate. (This results from the fact that the nearby strings—the ones not being tuned at the time—are thereby prevented from sounding clearly.)

An excellent recording is available called, "Tuning Your Autoharp with Meg Peterson."[17] The first nine bands are for inexperienced people, and bands ten through fourteen are for those who are more advanced. There are also many helpful suggestions for playing the Autoharp and for keeping it in tune.

*This term relates to the study of chords or harmony.

[17] This recording is available from Oscar Schmidt-International, Inc., Garden State Rd., Union, N.J. 07083. See Appendix F for other valuable materials about Autoharps.

THE GUITAR AND UKULELE

These harmony instruments are becoming increasingly popular with today's boys and girls. The guitar, particularly, seems to be at an all-time "high." Because of its widespread use with both rock and folk singing groups it has spiraled to fame as the instrument of the people. The wise teacher will take advantage of this in the music class.

Perhaps two examples here will serve as a stimulus for your own creative planning. One music teacher brought his own guitar to school and accompanied a fourth level class in its singing.[18] When the students questioned him about how he knew where to put his fingers on the strings, he called attention to the chord markings in the song, then demonstrated the position of his fingers for each chord. This led to a discussion of chords with the two in a specific song (I and V_7) spelled out on the chalkboard in letters: G B D (I) and D F♯ A C (V_7.) The teacher then suggested that he would play only the chord ROOTS. Thus he played G (root of the G B D chord) and D (root of the D F♯ A C) for the two chords throughout the song. Since G and D are both open strings on the guitar, this was very simple. The teacher then gave the guitar to various students and let them accompany the class by playing G and D.

The strings on the guitar are tuned to these pitches:

E A D G B E (low to high—reading left to right)

Another music teacher had equal success with students on the sixth level by using techniques that were somewhat more difficult.[19] She, too, brought her own guitar to school to excite interest. Then she invited the students in all three classrooms on the sixth level to bring their guitars from home provided they had permission from their parents. There was an astonishing response. Between fifteen and twenty guitars showed up! With this number the teacher could give one instrument to every two children. (She established a "transportation corps" to take the guitars from one room to another for each music class.) In each class her procedure was similar. After teaching the basic chords (I and V_7) and demonstrating the position of the fingers in each case, she divided the

[18] Mr. Keith Schult, elementary vocal music teacher at the McCoy School, Independence, Mo.

[19] Mrs. Pamela Simmons, elementary vocal music teacher at the Alton School, Independence, Mo.

Mrs. Pamela Simmons conducts an extra session in guitar techniques for some of her students (photo by Patrick Burke).

entire class into two groups. To one group she assigned the I chord to play, to the other, the V_7. Thus, once the children had their fingers in the right position on the strings, they did not change them throughout the song. The one child in each pair who was not actually playing the guitar each time, placed his fingers on an "imaginary" guitar and appropriately "strummed" in time. After both partners had had an opportunity to really play the guitar, the teacher switched sides on the chords. The group that had played

Close-up of a ukulele (photo by Ken Raveill).

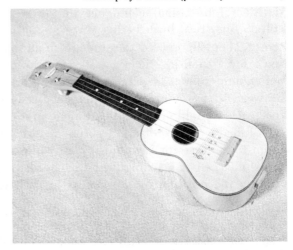

the I chord before now played the V_7, and vice versa. The same procedure was repeated. Finally, after much practice with responsibility for only one chord, the entire class played both chords throughout the song. The technique seemed to work well, with enthusiasm remaining at a high peak.

In both of these examples the students seem to gain a rather quick understanding of chords, keys, and other basic information through this motivational approach.

Some teachers might find it easier to "round up" soprano ukuleles than guitars. However, the same general procedures could be followed. The most current tuning for the ukulele is A D F♯ B.

The ukulele was also very popular with the college students of the 1920s. When tuning the "uke," they used to sing:

My   dog   has   fleas!

EXPERIENCING TIMBRE
(TONE COLOR/TONE QUALITY)

Early and Middle Childhood
(Levels 1, 2, and 3)

The children's first acquaintance with timbre will probably be through singing and instrumental experiences. As you sing there will be many songs that "invite" the accompaniment of one or several instruments. For example, the children can scarcely hear a song or record about a duck without "quacking." Here is a natural opportunity to suggest that some of the youngsters experiment with instruments, to find which one would sound most like the "quack" of a duck. You may need to guide them in matching the tone color of the instrument with the sound they want to produce. The castanets will make a much better "quack" than the drum, but the children should be given an opportunity to experiment as fully as possible, and to identify the name of the instrument with the kind of sound it makes.

Music is fun at this school, with Mrs. Ruth Napper as the teacher (photo by Patrick Burke).

CREATING MUSICAL STORIES

Frequently stories can provide the setting for exploring with timbre. Interesting sound effects for musical stories can be created in this manner. To illustrate, suppose you had finished reading the story of "Jack and the Beanstalk" to your class. You could review with them the plot of the story and ask them to suggest an appropriate instrument for each action. The final list might be something like this:

Jack climbing the beanstalk	Xylophone or bells
Giant walking	Drum or tom-tom
Hen clucking	Castanet or wood block
Jack descending the beanstalk	Xylophone

Harp	Autoharp
Moneybag	Tambourine or jingle clogs
Chopping the beanstalk	Triangle or wood block
Beanstalk falling	Crash of cymbals

Use any appropriate instruments. Let the children explore, suggest, and discover which are best. Of course, avoid using the same instrument to represent two different things.

EXPERIMENTING WITH
DYNAMICS AND TONE COLOR/
TONE QUALITY/TIMBRE

As they mature the children can also find satisfaction from this experience: let them experiment with the plastic pick and the felt pick that are used for strumming the strings. Through informal exploration they can improve their ability to distinguish which sound is louder, and which is softer (dynamics). They can also compare the tone quality (tone color) (timbre) of the two sounds by considering the questions:

> "Which sounded more mellow?" (The use of the felt pick.)
>
> "Which sounded brighter?" (The use of the plastic pick.)

Many times children will give vivid descriptions of tone quality (tone color) (timbre) in their own words, and of course, should be encouraged to do so.

Middle and Later Childhood
(Levels 4, 5, and 6)

EXPERIENCING TIMBRE
(TONE COLOR)

In well-planned listening activities attention is customarily given to the instruments of the band and orchestra. Each has, of course, its distinctive tone color, or timbre. It is easy to distinguish the difference between the sound of a violin and the sound of a trumpet, even if they are playing exactly the same melody.

It is not always so easy to describe this difference in words, however, because tone color in music often goes beyond the expressive limitations of language. However, it is possible to distinguish tone color as a recognizable element in music, and provide opportunities for children to respond to it.

Informal instruments can also be of practical use in developing children's ability to hear and distinguish tone color (timbre). Simple questions such as these can direct their attention to tone color:

1. What is the difference between the sound when the Autoharp is strummed with:

   a. a plastic pick?
   b. a felt pick?
   c. the fingers?
   d. the fingernails?
   e. the eraser end of a pencil?

2. Can you tell with your eyes shut—*just by listening carefully to the sound*—what's being used to strum the Autoharp?

3. Which instruments can make a tinkling sound?

4. Which instruments boom? Crash? Clang? Swish?

5. Can you distinguish these sounds with your eyes closed, and name the instrument that is being played?

INCREASING MUSICAL DISCRIMINATION WITH INFORMAL INSTRUMENTS

Children normally respond expressively to the *mood* of music even before they are old enough to go to school. As they grow, they are capable of controlled responses to *rhythm,* and are able to appreciate the rise and fall of *melodies.* Many children are also aware of the subtleties of *harmony* and *tone color.* Early experiences in determining the similarities and differences between phrases can help children understand basic *design* in music.

Middle and Later Childhood
(Levels 4, 5, and 6)

EXPERIENCING FORM

Probably the most important part of this kind of activity is the *consideration of the music* itself. Before any instruments are chosen or played, ask the class to study the music to learn:

1. Its *mood:*
   a. "How does the music make you feel?"
   b. "How can we show this feeling with our instruments?"
2. Its *design:*
   a. "Are there any places where the music is *repeated exactly?*"
   b. "Are there any places where the music is very *different*—in order to provide contrast?"
   c. "Are there some other places where the music is *similar,* but is not an exact repetition of any other part?"
   d. "Can we show this design on the chalkboard?"
   e. "How can we use our instruments to show this design clearly?"
   f. "Does our performance express the mood and musical design so well that the listener can understand and appreciate the message of the music?"
3. Its *rhythm:*
   a. "Where are the strong beats? Does the music move in twos, threes, or fours?"
   b. "Can we 'scan' the text to find out which syllables of the words are accented?"
   c. "Are there any interesting places where the accented words do not fall on the strong beat?" (syncopation)
   d. "Which instruments shall we use to show the beat?"

e. "Which ones shall we use to show the rhythm pattern of the accent of the words?"

This consideration of the music is a sensitive activity. Do not let the discussion take up so much time that the joy of performance may be lost.

EXPLORING PITCH CONCEPTS
AT THE PIANO

Early and Middle Childhood
(Levels 1, 2, and 3)

Although the piano is not an informal instrument, the children should be encouraged to become acquainted with it in a relaxed, informal atmosphere. On these levels they should have opportunities to discover some of its capabilities in expressing mood and dynamics. At the piano, a child should have the opportunity to find out for himself how to make "heavy dinosaur music" and "light butterfly music." Some children are aware that the notes toward the left are lower notes, and the ones to the right are higher notes; but, most important, the young children can explore the difference between high and low sounds, fast and slow sounds, and loud and soft sounds. His awareness of these concepts needs to be associated with the appropriate terms, so that he can express himself as he develops discrimination in music.

It is a good idea to leave the child as free as possible at the keyboard. Remember, you are not trying to teach him to play the piano. If he shows little interest in *experimenting with sounds,* do not insist. This is a good policy to follow for all music activities: the child who hangs back and seems unwilling to participate should be encouraged, but if the music fails to motivate him, be patient. *Conformity is not our goal.* Sooner or later, most children will join in with the others. If left alone the nonparticipant will at least be free to go on his own way. Perhaps he would rather do finger painting at that particular time. Good teachers try to encourage sincere expression in all the arts, in order to help the child realize the *importance of honestly being himself* all his life. The courage to *be ourselves* often grows out of effective early experience in music and the other arts.

After this initial experience with the piano, the children might discover the black and white keys as they attempt to reproduce tunes they have heard. (A detailed explanation of this is given on pages 249 and 250.) At this point it might be well to discuss some other specific ways that can be used to acquaint children of this age with the piano:

1. Let the class discover that sounds on the piano are produced by playing the keys. In some classrooms it is possible to remove a section of the piano and show the children how the felt-covered hammers strike the strings when the piano keys are played.

2. Have a child demonstrate by playing several keys— one at a time—some in the middle, and some at each extreme end of the keyboard. Play a little "game" with the children, who (with eyes closed) try to determine if the sounds are high, low, or in the middle.

3. Have another child experiment while the group watches, to determine in which direction the low sounds are played, and where the keys are located that produce the high sounds. As many children as possible should have a "turn" at playing and discovering that the low sounds come from the keys toward the left-hand side, and that the high sounds come from the keys toward the right-hand side of the keyboard.

4. Another kind of discovery can be made by observing the groups of black keys. The children can see that some of them are found in groups of two and some are found in groups of three. Let some of the children play all the groups of two black keys they can find on the *entire* keyboard. Then let some others play all the groups of three black keys they can find on the *entire* keyboard.

5. When the children have learned how these groups of black keys alternate (both on the piano keyboard and on the colored chromatic sets of tone bells), show them how to *place* (not play) the index finger and the third finger on any group of

two black keys. The thumb will fall naturally on the white key directly to the *left* of this group of two black keys. The name of this white key (where the thumb is) is always C!

6. How many C's can the children locate in this manner? If the class will count them as they are played, they will find there are eight C's on the standard piano keyboard. Children often enjoy playing "all the C's there are" and can also discover that the highest C is the very last white key at the extreme right of the keyboard.

7. When additional exploration of this type seems desirable, ask someone in the class (who perhaps hasn't had a "turn" yet) to locate any group of three black keys and to place (not play) his index finger, his third finger, and his fourth finger on the group of three black keys. The thumb will then fall naturally on the white key directly to the left of this group of three black keys. The name of this white key is always F!

8. How many F's can your class discover in this manner? There are seven that can be found on the standard piano keyboard.

9. If a picture of the piano keyboard is available in the pupil's book of your basic music series, the entire class can explore how the alternating groups of two and three black keys can teach us the names of all the white keys.

10. As the children become more familiar with the piano keyboard, encourage them to begin on any C and play all the white keys until they reach the next C. This sequence will automatically, of course, give them the sound of the major scale.

11. Individual students can also find pleasure and accomplishment in picking out tonal patterns and simple, short songs like "Hot Cross Buns."

These explorations at the keyboard will reinforce the understanding of "high" and "low," and the concept of the octave. Experiences of this kind can form a basis for understanding not only the traditional tonalities, but also the whole-tone and twelve-tone systems that make twentieth century music so exciting.

PARTICIPATION IN THE ELEMENTARY
ORCHESTRA AND BAND

Middle and Later Childhood
(Levels 4, 5, and 6)

Although the orchestral and band instruments (and, of course, piano) are not in the same category with those that are classed as "informal," still it would be well to discuss them, because some of your students are interested and are learning to play them. Many schools conduct an instrumental program that begins on the fourth or fifth level. Special music teachers give instrumental instruction to individuals who are generally selected for one of the performance groups by means of tests and interviews. Although you may not be involved in the actual teaching, you can assist immeasurably by providing opportunity for these students to perform occasionally in your classroom. Be sure to include the piano student as well. Your encouraging attitude will speed their progress and will help to make their experience a happy one.

Children who are able to play a band or orchestral instrument can act as resource people for the class when these instruments are discussed in the regular listening lessons. A child with a real instrument is more stimulating than the finest charts and pictures, and will be remembered more vividly and pleasurably. Demonstrations of the technique required to manipulate an instrument can give the class some appreciation of the accomplishments of the skilled performer whose playing often seems so effortless to the untutored.

SUGGESTED INDIVIDUAL AND
SMALL GROUP PROJECTS
FOR METHODS COURSES

Levels 1 through 6

1. Make a set of simple rhythm instruments, permitting the class to help as much as possible. Use these instruments throughout the year.

2. Write out a set of simple directions about how you made each instrument. Let individual children make their own instruments by following the directions.

3. Make an evaluation of the tone bells currently being sold. Are they diatonic bells, or chromatic bells? How can you tell? Can individual tone bars be removed and used separately, or are they fixed in the case? Which type do you prefer, and why? What uses can be made of each type? What material is used in their construction? Compare prices and durability.

4. Choose a group of songs suggested for beginning part singing experiences. Write out the fingering for small wind instruments so that these songs can be played as well as sung.

5. Teach a friend or relative to play the recorder. Which tones will you teach first? Describe how you will tell him or her to hold the instrument; how to blow into the mouthpiece.

6. List the songs in each of the books in a current series that can be played on the Flutophone, Tonette, song flute, or recorder.

An upper level student created tone bells by cutting steel pipe into varying lengths and suspending them on strong cord (photo by Patrick Burke).

7. Select a simple song that cannot be played on the Flutophone, Tonette, song flute, or C recorder, and transpose it to a key that it can be played in.

8. Evaluate the different types of song flutes and recorders that are on the market, listing the advantages and disadvantages of each.

7

Bicentennial Program Helps

This Bicentennial period in America has been celebrated with much pageantry. However, the commemorative events are not completely over, but according to plans will continue for at least two or three more years. The school can be a key center for this expression of patriotism. As a teacher you may be involved in presenting programs of one type or another. Your responsibility could range from the simple preparation of two or three patriotic songs for your students to sing at PTA to a pageant involving your entire class—or perhaps the entire school.

Recently the elementary vocal music department of the Independence, Mo., public schools presented a citywide Bicentennial concert for the community, featuring a sixth grade choir, narration, vignettes, and assisting high school musicians. The program lasted about an hour and a quarter. The script is presented here in the hope that you might be able to use the pageant as is, adapt it for different grade levels or other unique needs, use only selected parts, or be stimulated to write your own script. Detailed explanations appear at the end of the script.

"SPIRIT OF '76"

Narrator: I speak to all—both young and old. Children of the Republic, who gave you freedom? The mighty cries of many before you rise in answer. It was purchased on bloody fields, in constitution halls, and in the hearts and homes of lonely women.

283

"The Spirit of '76" is a vital part of the Bicentennial pageant described in this chapter (photo by Patrick Burke).

The solemn declaration on July 4, 1776, officially voiced the unbounded, surging desire to be free. For themselves and all of the sons and daughters who would follow, the freedom fighters stood spiritually and physically erect. For YOU they were a wall against tyranny. Their battle cry was embodied in the dramatic roll of their drums.

Drum fanfare in $\frac{2}{4}$ meter

Spot immediately when drums begin (Upstage right)

Children for portrait, "Spirit of '76" march (in time with the drum) on stage in spotlight, assume still position, and remain until song "Yankee Doodle" is finished, then march back to places.

Chorus: "YANKEE DOODLE" (Piccolo and Drum)

Narrator: No mind or body can bear prolonged tension without snapping. In the revolutionary period there were moments of gay laughter and lighthearted singing—bringing therapeutic relief. One of the nonsense songs was the still-popular "Pop Goes the Weasel."

Chorus: "POP GOES THE WEASEL"

Narrator: The victory of the colonists in the Revolutionary War was not to go unchallenged. Once again they were enmeshed in a mighty struggle with England in the War of 1812. Their anxieties about the outcome were dramatically caught up in the experience of Francis Scott Key. From the deck of a gunboat offshore he watched through the long, dark hours of night to see if the flag was flying. By dawn the answer was clear. America was still free.

Tonight, many years later, WE can say, "America is still free." In appreciation of the rich heritage that has blessed us with this truth, shall we all sing together Francis Scott Key's grateful words—our NATIONAL ANTHEM. We shall sing only the first stanza and follow that with the PLEDGE OF ALLEGIANCE to our flag.

Spot on flag (Upstage, center)

Subdued house lights on

Audience and Chorus: Sing first stanza of NATIONAL ANTHEM and repeat PLEDGE OF ALLEGIANCE.

House lights off

Spot off flag (Upstage center)

Narrator: There were to be other wars for America. In the developing young nation, brother was pitted against brother in an agonizing strife over the slave issue. One of the most moving songs of this period was the martial "Battle Hymn of the Republic."

Chorus: "BATTLE HYMN OF THE REPUBLIC"

Narrator: Before Africans were brought to America as slaves, blacks were imported from the West Indies to work in the fields. The rhythms were an intriguing mixture of black culture and the calypso influence of their Spanish conquerors. From the West Indies comes the nonsense song "Down in Trinidad."

Chorus: "DOWN IN TRINIDAD" (Flute, Bongos, Maracas)

Narrator: In sharp contrast to the sparkling mood of the calypso, the black slave music mirrored the utter despair of those in bondage. The poignant heartbreak of "Sometimes I Feel Like a Motherless Child" is felt by all sensitive spirits.

Solo: "SOMETIMES I FEEL LIKE A MOTHERLESS CHILD"

Narrator: United in their common misery, the blacks sang of their only hope—life after death and the sustaining power of God in their present plight. From this setting comes one of their loveliest spirituals, "Let Us Break Bread Together."

Chorus: "LET US BREAK BREAD TOGETHER"

Narrator: While those in the East were involved with the slave question, adventurers were pushing West to explore its vast resources. With the cry of "Gold," wagons were hastily outfitted and began rolling toward the "land of promise."

Chorus: "ROLL ON WAGONS" (Temple blocks, Cocoanut shells)

Narrator: The goal was bright, but the way was rough. Many disasters common to the westward trek are humorously expressed in the traditional folk song "Sweet Betsy from Pike."

Chorus: "SWEET BETSY FROM PIKE"

Narrator: The excitement of the westward rush of the mid-1880s was succeeded by the Gay Nineties. The entertainment world was starred during this time, giving impetus to the development of varying musical forms. One that had its birth then and was later revived in the 1930s, was the "barber-shop" style. The nostalgic "Oh, Mister Moon" is a favorite of quartets.

Barbershop Quartet, directed by Mrs. Jeanne Borden (photo by Patrick Burke).

Spot (Upstage center)

Stand microphones live

Barbershop Quartet: "OH, MISTER MOON"

Quartet back to places

Stand microphones dead

Spot off

Narrator: While "barbershop" was enjoying its popular role, another style was emerging that was destined to make a significant impact on the American culture. This was the rise of Afro-American jazz. By the late 1800s this style had evolved into the slow, mournful blues. Although the white, Appalachian folk song, "Every Night When the Sun Goes In" is not strictly blues, with its dissonances and recorder accompaniment it *is* typical of the plaintive, haunting quality of the blues.

Chorus: "EVERY NIGHT WHEN THE SUN GOES IN" (Recorders)

Narrator: It was during World War I that an exuberant type of jazz—Dixieland—gradually began to replace the blues. Though a number of cities were centers of interest, New Orleans became the permanent home of Dixieland jazz. Remember the immortal "When the Saints Go Marching In"?

Chorus: "WHEN THE SAINTS GO MARCHING IN" (Dixieland Band)

Narrator: America survived the shock and aftermath of World War I, endured the Great Depression of the 1930s, suffered the blow of Pearl Harbor in the 1940s, then later agonized over the Korean and Vietnam conflicts. In spite of these periods of national testing, there *was* progress in many areas of American life. In the 1960s America stepped into a new day—the Space Age. On May 5, 1961, Alan Shepard, in Freedom 7, broke the bonds of earth.

Poem: "HIGH FLIGHT"

Narrator: The contemporary scene is characterized by constant sudden changes. In the midst of shifting sands, many seek for a point of reference that is stable and sure. In the two current folk style songs, "Joy Is Like the Rain," and "Morning Has Broken," the authors suggest the Infinite as the Source for inner peace.

Chorus: "JOY IS LIKE THE RAIN" (Guitar and Piano)

Special Group: "MORNING HAS BROKEN" (Flute and Piano)

Narrator: Although in the twentieth century art forms are constantly changing, Broadway show tunes are constantly popular. The sprightly "Wells Fargo Wagon" from *The Music Man* and the lyric "River Song" from *Tom Sawyer* have an exciting appeal for all ages.

Chorus: "THE WELLS FARGO WAGON"

Chorus: "RIVER SONG"

Narrator: Today America has taken its place in the sun. During its 200 years from birth to adulthood it has struggled, matured, and been refined. But now—what of the future?

Chorus: "GEE, I'M LOOKING FORWARD TO THE FUTURE"

Narrator: Children of the Republic, who gave you freedom?

Drum Fanfare

Spot immediately *when drum begins (Upstage right) and spot (Downstage center) Children for portrait "Spirit of '76" march on stage in spotlight, assume still position, and remain until end of program.*

Narrator: Children of the Republic, what have you done with your freedom?

Drum fanfare

Spot immediately *when drum begins (Upstage left)*

Children for portrait "Spirit of 1976" walk on stage in spotlight, assume still position, and remain until end of program.

Chorus and Reader: "THIS IS MY COUNTRY" (Brass Ensemble)

END

VIGNETTES:

"Spirit of '76" portrait (1776)

Three children were costumed in identical manner to those in the famous painting "Spirit of '76." (The artist was Archibald Willard, 1837–1918.) Every effort was made to be so meticulous in duplication that all of those in the audience would immediately recognize the scene. Style and color of costumes, wigs that were used, bandages, drums and fife, flag, etc., were authentically portrayed.

"Spirit of 1976" portrait

Centered in this group and to the back was a TALL rocket in launch position. On one side was an astronaut with authentic gear; on the other was a girl wearing the white coat of a scientist, holding a beaker and test tube. She was seated on a tall stool. In front and to the right of the scientist were children representing areas of interest in American life today. One was wearing a complete baseball uniform, standing in batting position with the bat poised and ready. Another was seated on a small, folding campstool before an easel, holding a pallette and brush, and working on an uncompleted painting. The third was seated cross-legged, appearing to play a guitar.

In front and to the right of the astronaut were two children: a girl dressed as a career businesswoman (holding an attaché case), and a boy garbed as a carpenter with appropriate tools.

SPECIAL MUSICIANS:

SPECIAL GROUP: About forty selected sixth grade children.

BARBERSHOP QUARTET: Four fifth grade boys who sang in HARMONY, "Oh, Mister Moon." They were authentically costumed: red vests, straw hats, moustaches, canes, etc., and did a dance routine following the song.

DIXIELAND JAZZ BAND: Most of this group were senior high school musicians who improvised as they played. They were authentically costumed.

Shown here is another typical scene of Americana from the Bicentennial pageant (photo by Patrick Burke).

OTHER MUSICIANS: Those playing the piccolo, flute, recorder, bongos, guitar, brass instruments, and parade drum were high school musicians.

The pianists were elementary vocal music teachers.

Sixth grade students played the temple blocks, cocoanut shells, and maracas.

NARRATOR: The narrator was a sixth grade teacher.

*SOURCES FOR MUSIC USED
(IN ORDER OF APPEARANCE ON THE PROGRAM):*

For addresses of publishers not listed here, see Appendix L.

"Yankee Doodle": Book 6, *Discovering Music Together* (Revised), Follett Publishing Company; piccolo melody from recording of this song in Follett Album S603R-2B

"Pop Goes the Weasel" (S.A., arranged by Margaret Shelly Vance): Belwin-Mills Publishing Corp.

"Star Spangled Banner": Book 6, *Discovering Music Together* (Revised), Follett Publishing Company.

"Battle Hymn of the Republic": Book 6, *Discovering Music Together* (Revised), Follett Publishing Company

"Down in Trinidad" (S.A., 312-40498; calypso song, arranged by Emile Schillio): Theodore Presser Company; instrumental parts for flute and string bass

"Sometimes I Feel Like a Motherless Child" (arranged by Burleigh): Belwin-Mills Publishing Corp.

"Let Us Break Bread Together": Book 6, *Exploring Music*, Holt, Rinehart and Winston, Inc.

"Roll On Wagons": Book 5, *This Is Music*, Allyn and Bacon, Inc.

"Sweet Betsy from Pike": Book 5, *Discovering Music Together* (Revised), Follett Publishing Corp.

"Every Night When the Sun Goes In": Book 6, *Making Music Your Own*, Silver Burdette; recorder accompaniment on song recording in album accompanying Book 6

"When the Saints Go Marching In" (From *Fred Waring Collection*, compiled and arranged by Hawley Ades); Shawnee Press, Inc.

"Joy Is Like the Rain" (by Medical Mission Sisters): Vanguard Music Corp.

"Morning Has Broken" (arranged by Cat Stevens): available in most music stores or from Irving Music, Inc. (BMI), Hollywood, Calif.

"The Wells Fargo Wagon" (from *The Music Man*): Book 6, *Making Music Your Own*, Silver Burdett

"River Song" (theme from *Tom Sawyer*), by Richard M. and Robert B. Sherman): available as sheet music in most music stores and from Unart Music Corp., New York, N.Y.

"Gee, I'm Looking Forward to the Future" (by Cates and Allen from *Up with People*): available in most music stores and from the Heritage Music Press, Dayton, Ohio 45401

"This Is My Country" (by Raye, Jacobs, and Scott): Shawnee Press, Inc.

POEM:

"High Flight" (by John Gillespie Magee, Jr., from *The Treasure Chest*): Harper and Row, Publishers, New York, N.Y.

Appendixes

APPENDIX A

CURRENT BASIC SERIES
OF MUSIC BOOKS

(listed alphabetically by publisher)

(Addresses for the sources of these materials can be found in Appendix L)

Addison-Wesley Publishing Co.
The Comprehensive Musicianship Program

The authors are music and educational specialists from the United States and New Zealand, including: Leon Burton, Dorothy Gillett, Brent Heisinger, William Hughes, Vernon Read, Malcolm Tait, William Thomson, and Allen Trubitt.

Although designed for grades Kindergarten through 12, the traditional grading system has been replaced by five zones:

Zone 1—Kindergarten and Grade One

Zone 2—Grades Two and Three

Zone 3—Grades Four, Five, and Six

Zone 4—Junior High

Zone 5—High School

This series is sponsored by the College of Education Curriculum Research and Development Group at the University of Hawaii. It is:

Behaviorally oriented: each unit concludes with evaluation activities related to the behavioral objectives of that unit.

Music has been selected from various cultures, historical periods, and styles to develop seven basic concepts of music: rhythm, melody, harmony, texture, tone, tonality, and form.

Spiral curriculum is the basis for procedures for organizing large group, small group, and individual experiences.

Allyn and Bacon, Inc.
This Is Music for Today

AUTHORS: William R. Sur, Adeline McCall, Mary R. Tolbert, William R. Fisher, and Charlotte DuBois.

This is a series of music texts for grades one through eight, organized in such a way that it can be used by the elementary classroom teacher as well as the special music educator. The program is based on child interest centers and on the structure of music.

Books are numbered from Kindergarten and Nursery School to eight, and the Teachers' Editions are spiral bound. The page numbers in the Teachers' Editions are the same as those in the pupils' book. Teaching suggestions are on blue pages and are found directly beside the music they are to be used with.

Record albums for listening, singing, and rhythmic movement are available.

American Book Co.
New Dimensions in Music

AUTHORS: Dr. Robert A. Choate, Dr. Richard C. Berg, Dr. Lee Kjelson, and Dr. Eugene Troth.

Special consultants include William Anderson (Music of China, Korea, and Japan), Moshe Jacobson (Music of Israel), Rosemary Hallum (Early Childhood), Sally Monsour (Music of the Middle East), Barbara Reeder (Music of Africa), Harold Schramm (Music of India), Benjamin Suchoff (Music of Bartók).

The series is organized into seven levels:

Level A—1: Music for Early Childhood
"Looking at Music" (the big book: 19" x 24½")
"Music for Early Childhood" (teacher's professional book)
Song Albums (all songs recorded)
Listening Album

Level A—2: Beginning Music
"Introducing Music" (Pupil's Book)
"Beginning Music" (Teacher's Edition)
Song Albums (all songs recorded)
Listening Albums

Level B—"Enjoying Music": Pupil's Book and Teacher's Edition by the same name, Song Albums, and Listening Albums

Level C—"Expressing Music": Pupil's Book, Teacher's Edition, Song Albums, and Listening Albums

Level D—"Investigating Music": Pupil's Book, Teacher's Edition, Song Albums, and Listening Albums

Level E—"Experiencing Music": Pupil's Book, Teacher's Edition, Song Albums, and Listening Albums

Level F—"Mastering Music": Pupil's Book, Teacher's Edition, Song Albums, and Listening Albums

Music is presented in cultural context with architecture, sculpture, literature, dance, painting, and poetry to develop the understanding of music and the other arts as expressions of man—"his ideas, feelings and emotions, values, relations with other men, and reactions to the time and place in which he lives."

Follett Publishing Co., Educational Division
Discovering Music Together (Revised)

AUTHORS: Dr. Charles Leonhard, Beatrice Perham Krone, Irving Wolfe, and Margaret Fullerton.

Each book (Grades 1-6) is numbered, and contains a section called "Let's Read Music" using both tone syllables and rhythm syllables. The hand signals developed in England by John Curwen are included. Sixteen large charts are an integral part of the first grade program. Teacher's Editions are interleaved, all songs are recorded, and Listening Albums are also available.

The series also provides an expanded humanities program, grades one through eight and Junior/Senior High School.

Ginn and Company
The Magic of Music

AUTHORS: Lorraine E. Waters, Louis J. Wersen, Wm. C. Hartshorn, Eileen L. McMillan, Alice Gallup, and Frederick Bechman.

The kindergarten level of this series includes a professional text for the teacher, recordings, and charts. Other levels, graded one through six, provide texts for pupils, teacher's guides, and recordings.

Holt, Rinehart and Winston, Inc.
Exploring Music (Revised)

AUTHORS: Eunice Boardman (K-6), Beth Landis (K-12), and Lara Hoggard (The Junior Book).

CONSULTANTS: Milton Babbitt, Keith Baird, Bjornar Bergethon, Dr. Robert Buggert, Chou Wen-Chung, Harry Coopersmith, Dorothy Gillette, Lucrecia Kasilag, Egon Kraus, Alan Lomax, Kurt Miller, Juan Orego-Salas, Elena Paz, Virginia Stroh Red, Kurt Stone, David Ward-Steinman, and Henrietta Yurchenco.

The series emphasizes the structure and basic concepts of music. The revised edition also contains additional material for improvisation and creative activities. The humanities approach not only points up the relationship of the other arts to music, but also the role of the related arts in the life of man.

At the kindergarten level a musical activity kit and an easel display board are available in addition to the set of recordings and the teacher's reference book that contains teaching procedures and accompaniments.

Exploring Music, Book One is a pupil's text. There is also a Jumbo Book, an enlargement of the Pupil's Book One. Recordings and a Teacher's Reference Book are also available at this level.

Levels Two through Six each have a textbook for the pupil, a Teacher's Edition, and corresponding record albums.

Exploring Music Instrumental Accompaniments (Grades 4-6) are contained in five books by Edward B. Jurey that provide selected songs for performance by elementary instruments. These supplementary books are available for C Instruments (Violins and Flutes), B Flat Instruments (Clarinets and Trumpets), Saxophones (E Flat Alto and B Flat Tenor), Bass Instruments (Trombone, Cello, and Double Bass), and Percussion Instruments (Bells, Drums, and Rhythm Instruments).

The Macmillan Company, Inc.
The Spectrum of Music
with Related Arts

AUTHORS: Mary Val Marsh, Carroll A. Rinehart, Edith J. Savage, Ralph G. Beelke, and Ronald H. Silverman.

CONSULTANTS: William Brohn (Rock and Popular Music), Venoris Cates (Afro-American Music), Lois Choksy (Kodály Material), Wayne Johnson (Musicology), Walter E. Purdy (Music Education), John Rouillard (American Indian Music), Anna Mae Stine (Curriculum Coordination Notes), Jose Villarino (Mexican-American Music), Lawrence Wheeler (Orff Schulwerk Material), and David L. Wilmot (Teacher's Annotated Editions).

Pupil's books are not numbered, but are color-coded by levels, Kindergarten through Grade 6. They are organized into four major sections: 1) Media, 2) Components, 3) Structure, and 4) Perspectives.

Teacher's Annotated Editions contain:

1. Charts of Concepts, Competencies, and Content, Grades K-6
2. Color reproductions of all the pages in the pupil's book of the corresponding level, with specific annotations for the teacher concerning the music and related art
3. A Teacher's Guide that includes a six-point plan for every musical experience
4. Piano accompaniments

All music materials have been recorded in stereophonic sound, available on both phonograph discs and tape cassettes.

Prentice-Hall, Inc.
Growing with Music

AUTHORS: Harry R. Wilson, Walter Ehret, Alice M. Knuth, Edward J. Hermann, and Albert A. Renna.

SPECIAL CONTRIBUTORS: Chrystal Bachtell, Emily Batluck, Patricia Bond, Janet Mehling, Donna Rustand, Helen Socolofsky, Judith Stein, and Dorothy Ward. Orff and Kodály Procedures: Arnold Burkhart and Lois Choksy.

In addition to a complete series of recordings and special Teacher's Editions, for K through 8, the *Growing with Music* Series has a set of large Concept Charts with a special Teacher's Guide and recordings for K through 2.

Silver Burdett, General Learning Corp.
Making Music Your Own

Authors:

Levels 1-6:   Beatrice Landeck, Elizabeth Crook, Harold
C. Youngberg, and Otta Luening. Special
Consultants: Lawrence Eisman and Eliza-
beth Jones

Kindergarten: Mary Tinnin Jaye and Imogene Hilyard

Grades 7 and 8: Raymond J. Malone

Recordings and Cassettes: Dr. Merrill Staton

The series offers the following:

Kindergarten: Teacher's Book, Chart-size Picture Packet, Records, and Cassettes

Grade One: Pupil's Book, Chart-size Pupil's Book,
Teacher's Edition, Records, and Cassettes

Grades 2-8: Pupil's Book, Teacher's Edition, Records,
and Cassettes

The complete program includes:

*Orff Instrument Source Book for Making Music Your
Own,* by Elizabeth Nichols. Selected songs from Books
1-6 are arranged for Orff instruments. The emphasis is
on improvisation. Two Teacher's Volumes are available

Listen, Look, and Sing, by Aden G. Lewis. Chart-size
Pupil's Books and three volumes of Teacher's Editions
for grades 1 through 6. Based on the Kodály techniques
and cross referenced to *Making Music Your Own*

Making Music Your Own Choral Series: Treble Voices
(grades 4-9)

Pick-a-Track Recordings and Cassettes for *Making Music
Your Own* permit the separation of voices and instrumentation when played on stereo machines

APPENDIX B

SPECIALIZED TEACHING METHODS: JAQUES-DALCROZE, KODÁLY, LABAN, MONTESSORI, ORFF, AND OTHER TECHNIQUES

(Addresses for the sources of these materials can be found in Appendix L)

Adam, Jeno. *Growing in Music with Movable DO*, edited by Georgiana Peterson and translated by Dr. Louis Boros, 1971. Available from Dr. Boros, 359 D Crowells Park, Highland Park, N.J. 08904.

Aronoff, Frances Webber. *Music and Young Children*. New York: Holt, Rinehart and Winston, 1969. Based on Bennett Reimer in aesthetic education, Jerome Bruner in conceptual learning, and Emile Jaques-Dalcroze in eurhythmics.

Bachman, Tibor. *Reading and Writing Music* (based on Kodály Method with liquid duplicating materials available). Elizabethtown, Pa.: The Continental Press, Inc.

Bachman, Tibor, and Getz, Russell. *Songs to Read* (Kodály Method). Elizabethtown, N.J.: The Continental Press, Inc.

Barnett, Elise Braun. *Montessori & Music: Rhythmic Activities for Young Children*. New York: Schocken Books.

Bartalus, Ilona. *The Soul of Hungary* (Kodály Method). London, Ontario, Canada: University of Western Ontario. Videotape.

Burakoff, Gerald, and Wheeler, Lawrence. *Music Making in the Elementary School*. New York: Hargail Music, Inc. Teacher and student editions based on Orff and Kodály.

Busse, Bernard W. *Basic Elements of Music*. Raleigh, N.C.: Classroom World Publications. For upper elementary grades.

Carabo-Cone, Madeleine. *The Playground As Music Teacher*. New York: Harper and Row, 1959.

———. *A Sensory-Motor Approach to Music Learning*. New York: Carabo-Cone Method Center, 1971.

Carabo-Cone, Madeleine, and Royt, Beatrice. *How to Help Children Learn Music*. New York: Harper and Row, 1955.

Choksy, Lois. *The Kodály Method*. Englewood Cliffs, N.J.: Prentice-Hall, 1974. A thorough and authoritative treatment of the subject with an abundance of song material, predominantly American folk songs.

Cox, Kenneth. *Music for Me*. London: London Press, Limited. Three workbooks and Teacher's Guide.

Curriculum for Elementary Grades, Wellesley, Mass.: The Kodály Musical Training Institute, Inc. A two-volume curriculum for elementary grades, based on Kodály.

Daniel, Katinka S. *Kodály Approach Workbooks*. Belmont, Calif.: Fearon Publishers, Lear Siegler, Educational Division. Three workbooks.

Doolin, Dr. Howard A. *A New Introduction to Music, Levels One, Two, and Three* (Teacher's Score/Manual and Pupil's Easel available for each). Park Ridge, Ill.: Neil A. Kjos Music Co. Practical materials for developing skills and concepts. Well organized, easy to use.

Encyclopedia of Child Guidance. Ralph B. Winn (editor). New York: Philosophical Library, 1943. Article "Rhythm" (with particular reference to Dalcroze Eurhythmics) by Bertha K. Somer.

Faunt, Edith. *The Staff-Syllable Method of Teaching Sight-Singing*. Vancouver, British Columbia, Canada: Edith Faunt.

Findlay, Elsa. *Rhythm and Movement: Applications of Dalcroze Eurhythmics*. Evanston, Ill.: Summy-Birchard Co., 1971.

Hancock, Preston. *Let's Have Fun with Music*. Raleigh, N.C.: Classroom World Productions. Tape units for developing basic musical concepts through aural and physical play experiences in kindergarten and primary grades.

Hoenack, Peg. *The Peg Hoenack Method: Songs I Can Play* (Grades K-2) and *Let's Sing and Play Together* (Grades 2-4). Chevy Chase, Md.: Music for Young Children.

Jaques-Dalcroze, Emile. *Rhythm, Music and Education*. New York: G. P. Putnam's, 1921.

Keeping Up with Orff-Schulwerk in the Classroom, Arnold Burkhart (editor). Published five times yearly. This publication focuses on the adaptation and application of Orff methods and philosophy.

Kersey, Robert. *Just Five*. Westminster, Md.: The Westminster Press. Pentatonic songs for use with the Kodály approach.

Kodály for Beginning Levels, Vols. 1 and 2. Wellesley, Mass.: Kodály Musical Training Institute, Inc.

Kuhmerker, Lisa. *We Sing and Read: A Multisensory Program for Beginning Readers*. New York: John Day Co., 1972. Original songs focused on such basic concepts as time, colors, and weather to aid in beginning reading in the classroom.

Land, Lois Rhea, and Vaughan, Mary Ann. *Music in Today's Classroom: Creating, Listening, Performing*. New York: Harcourt Brace Jovanovich, Inc. A textbook for elementary education majors. A four-record set of listening selections is available from the publisher.

Landis, Beth, and Carder, Polly. *The Eclectic Curriculum in American Music Education: Contributions of Dalcroze, Kodály, and Orff*. Washington, D.C.: Music Educators National Conference, 1972.

Let's Read Music. Scotia, N.Y.: Dickson-Wheeler, Inc.

Lewis, Aden G. *Listen, Look and Sing* (Kodály Method). Morristown, N.J.: Silver Burdett Co.

McNair, Murray, and Nash, Grace C. *Choristers' Manual*. Chicago: Kitching Educational Division of Ludwig Industries. Songs and speech ensembles with accompaniments.

Nash, Grace C. *Creative Approaches to Child Development through Music, Language, and Movement.* Port Washington, N.Y.: Alfred Publishing Co.

_____. *Today with Music* (utilizing the principles of Orff, Kodály, and Laban). Port Washington, N.Y.: Alfred Publishing Co.

_____. Film 1: *Introduction;* Film 2: *Musical Forms;* Film 3: *Expressing Note Values;* Film 4: *Music in Action.* Chicago: Kitching Educational Division of Ludwig Industries. Films with children in classroom settings.

_____. *Rhythmic Speech Ensembles.* Chicago: Kitching Educational Division of Ludwig Industries.

_____. *Teacher's Book with Introduction and Principles of Procedure* (Series I); *Teacher's Book with Glossary of Terms, Techniques, and Tools* (Series II); *Classroom Book for Teachers and Students* (Series III). Chicago: Kitching Educational Division of Ludwig Industries.

_____. *Verse and Movement.* Kitching Educational Division of Ludwig Industries.

Nichols, Elizabeth. *Orff Instrument Source Book.* Morristown, N.J.: Silver Burdett Co.

Peterson, Georgiana. *Getting to Know Music.* Boston: Allyn and Bacon, Inc., 1969.

Richards, Mary Helen. *The Child in Depth* (Reading Readiness through Singing Games). Portola Valley, Calif.: Richards Institute of Music Education and Research.

_____. *Language Arts Through Music.* Portola Valley, Calif.: Richards Institute of Music Education and Research.

_____. *Threshold to Music.* Palo Alto, Calif.: Fearon Lear Siegler Publishers. *Teacher Training* Record; Graded *Experience Charts; Teaching Music through Songs, Hand Singing, and Inner Hearing; Songs in Motion; The Fourth Year; Upper Grades, Book I.*

Rosenstrauch, Henrietta. *Percussion, Movement and the Child.* Far Rockaway, N.Y.: Carl Van Roy, 1964. Material based on the Jaques-Dalcroze philosophy.

Stecher, Miriam B., McElheny, Hugh, and Greenwood, Marion. *Music and Movement Improvisations.* New York: The Macmillan Company, Threshold Division.

Szabo, Helga. *The Kodály Concept of Music Education.* Records available. Oceanside, N.Y.: Boosey and Hawkes, 1969.

Wheeler, Lawrence, and Raebeck, Lois. *Orff and Kodály Adapted for the Elementary School.* Dubuque, Iowa: Wm. C. Brown Company, Publishers, 1972.

APPENDIX C

MULTIMEDIA TEACHING MATERIALS
AND AIDS FOR
INDIVIDUALIZED INSTRUCTION

(Specific references for teachers appear at end of this appendix; addresses for the sources of these materials can be found in Appendix L.)

Allyn and Bacon, Inc. Graded record albums for use with the basic music series *This Is Music for Today* and *The Play-Game Song Book* and recordings.

American Book Company. Graded record albums for use with the basic music series *Music for Young Americans* and *ABC Music Series;* also additional rhythm, dance, and music appreciation recordings.

Angel Records (*See* Capitol Records Distributing Corporation).

Batcheller, John M. *Musical Notation.* Chicago: Encyclopedia Britannica Press, 1964. A program with separate worksheets designed for use at the fifth grade level introduces the beginner to the fundamentals of music notation.

Biographies of Great Composers. Filmstrips and thirty-minute narrations on record or cassette, and Teachers Guide. Glendale, Calif.: Bowmar Records, Inc.

Bond, Dorothy. *Enjoy Music More* (Teacher's Guide and Student's Book available, also four recordings). New York: Project Publications, 1968. Designed to teach music fundamentals.

Bowmar Records, Inc. Selections include recordings dealing with rhythms, part singing, and folk songs. *The Bowmar Orchestral Library,* containing selected compositions with charts and suggestions for the teacher, is featured.

Capitol Records Distributing Corporation. Producers of children's records, also Capitol and Angel labels.

Challenge. A series of individualized instructional materials, with Teacher's Guide and Answer Guide. Rapids City, Ill.: Multi-Media Learning Co.

Childcraft Records (*See* Mercury Record Productions, Inc.).

Children's Music Center, Inc. Selection of recordings deals with rhythms, biographical stories, orchestral instruments, music listening, with theme charts and recordings of music for exceptional children. Library also includes "Leonard Bernstein's Young People's Concerts."

Children's Record Guild (*See* Greystone Corporation).

Cohn, Arthur. *Music Quizzical.* New York: MCA Music. Music puzzles, crosswords, crostics, anagrams, and cryptograms.

Columbia Records, Educational Dept. Recordings of instrumental stories, such as *Tubby the Tuba,* children's song albums, and Benjamin Britten's *The Young Person's Guide to the Orchestra;* also a general catalogue of standard works.

Decca Records. Song stories and a general catalogue of standard works.

Educational Audio-Visual, Inc. Very large selection of music education materials, including music appreciation, sing-a-long, rhythms, dance, acoustical and biographical recordings, as well as standard classics.

Elektra Records. Many ethnic selections and folk songs.

Epic Records (*See* Columbia Records). A general catalogue of standard works.

Exploring the Arts, Exploring the Arts, Publisher. Interdisciplinary experiences in music, art, drama, and movement. Demonstration lessons with cassette available.

Fearon/Lear Siegler, Inc. (*See Threshold to Music*).

Folkraft Records. Recordings for use in elementary schools.

Folkways Records and Service Corporation. A large catalogue of ethnic, educational, and folk music.

Follett Educational Corporation. Graded record albums for use with the basic music series *Discovering Music Together;* also *The Development of Jazz,* folk song albums, etc.

The Gift of Music. Sound Book Press Society, Inc., North Plainfield, N.J. An introduction to music for preschool and primary grade children based on singing as the heart of children's early music. Includes six recordings.

Ginn and Company. Graded record albums for use with the basic music series *The Magic of Music* and *Dance a Story* albums. The company also serves as the educational sales agent for RCA Victor educational recordings (*Adventures in Music, Instruments of the Orchestra,* etc.).

Golden Records (*See* Simon and Schuster, Inc.).

Greystone Corporation, Institutional Division. Library includes Young People's Records, Children's Record Guild, American Recording Society, and other recorded material for educational purposes.

Holt, Rinehart and Winston, Inc. Graded record albums for use with the basic music series *Exploring Music;* also *Exploring Music,* a record album including all the listening recordings available for use as a basic listening program with any elementary music series.

Individualized Music Activities Packet. Fullerton, Calif.: The California State University, Fullerton, Joseph W. Landon, chairman, Music Division, 1974. This packet was designed by Dr. Landon to accompany the text *How to Write Learning Activity Packages for Music Education* (*see* Landon, Joseph W., under "Specific References for Teachers").

Instrumental Odyssey. Taped series with accompanying scripts highlighting the development of instruments up to modern times. Chicago: American Music Conference.

Instruments of the Orchestra. Teaching guide by Charles W. Walton. New York: RCA Records.

Jam Handy Corporation. Color films of the stories of great masterpieces with related recordings.

Keyboard Jr. Publications, Inc. (*See* Keyboard Publications, Inc.).

Keyboard Magic. Atlanta, Ga.: Educational Productions, Inc. An audiovisual program covering thirty-two weeks of material aimed at musical understanding and development of skills.

Keyboard Publications, Inc. Publishers of *Young Keyboard, Jr., Keyboard Junior,* and *Music of Man.* The latter is subtitled *From Bach to Rock.* Teacher's Guides and monthly magazines. Also publishes art appreciation materials and other publications.

Know the Orchestra. Stories by Inez Schubert and Lucille Wood. Music by Edward B. Jurey. Glendale, Calif.: Bowmar Records, Inc.

Landon, Joseph W. *Strategies for Opening the Traditional Classroom.* Vienna, Va.: *Music Educators Journal* 60, No. 8 (April 1974). Pointers on reaching the individual through small group music strategies (SGMS), "star" activities, quest activities, contracts, and learning activity packages (LAPS).

Man and His Music. New Haven, Conn.: Keyboard Publications, 1974. Student magazines, sound filmstrips, listening records, and teacher guides suitable for middle school. Program contains: *Rhythm: from Rock to Bach; Melody: "Turning on" to the Tune; The Roots of Democracy,* and *Careers in Music.*

McLaughlin, Roberta, and Schliestett, Patti. *The Joy of Music* (five recordings also available). Evanston, Ill.: Summy-Birchard Publishing Co., 1967. Good material for middle school children.

Mercury Record Productions, Inc. The *Childcraft-Playcraft* series; also a general catalogue of standard works.

Monitor Recordings, Inc. Library includes many folk and ethnic albums.

Music Education Record Company. Wheeler Becket's *The Complete Orchestra,* which deals in great detail with instruments of the orchestra and their functions.

Music Experiences—Grand Canyon Suite and *Music Experiences—Mississippi Suite* (films for intermediate and junior high grades). Hollywood, Calif.: AIMS Instructional Media Services.

Musical Sound Books, Inc. (*See* Sound Book Press Society, Inc.). Lillian Baldwin materials.

Orchestral Library. Recordings of 317 basic compositions with Theme Charts and Lesson Guides. Glendale, Calif.: Bowmar Records, Inc.

Peripole Record Corporation. *Here, There and Everywhere,* a recording of children's songs sung by Marais and Miranda with Carol Merrill; *Theatre Music for Young People;* five record albums; also special recordings to accompany song collections and singing games (*see* Appendix D).

Pioneer Record Sales, Inc. (*See* Folkways Records and Service Corporation).

Pipeline. Jane Beethoven (editor). Morristown, N.J.: Silver Burdett Co. Monthly subscription program containing a fourteen-minute record, illustrated student newsletters, and teaching guide for discovering music concepts in current popular hits, with parallels in classic music compositions.

Pop Hit Listening Guides. Memphis, Tenn.: Pop Hits. Monthly guide with teacher's supplement. Permission given for unlimited copying. Monthly recording.

Portraits of Composers. Reproductions of original paintings by Jean Keuterick. Miniature study prints also available. Glendale, Calif.: Bowmar Records, Inc.

Prentice-Hall, Inc. Graded record albums for use with the basic music series *Growing with Music;* also sing-a-long albums, etc.

RCA Victor Educational Sales. Recordings especially made for music education, notably *Adventures in Music* by Gladys Tipton and *Instruments of the Orchestra,* both complete with teaching guides, as well as *RCA Victor Basic Library for Elementary Schools* and rhythmic activities recordings; also a general catalogue of standard works. Ginn and Company serves as educational sales agent for RCA Victor educational recordings.

REP. *Reading Enrichment Program,* Unit I: "American Composers." New Haven, Conn.: Keyboard Publications. Recordings, filmstrips, booklets, teacher's guides, and response sheets packaged for small group or individualized instruction. Eight American composers are represented.

Rhythms Productions. This firm specializes in material devoted to the use of rhythm instruments and produces recordings designed for this purpose.

Richards, Mary Helen (*See Threshold to Music*).

Scriptographic Study Booklets. Channing L. Bete Company, Inc., 45 Federal St., Greenfield, Mass. 01301. *What Everybody Should Know about Brass Instruments; What Everybody Should Know about Percussion and Keyboard Instruments; What Everybody Should Know about Reading Music; What Everybody Should Know about Stringed Instruments; What Everybody Should Know about "Woodwind" Instruments.*

Shetler, Donald (consultant). *The Guitar from Stone Age Through Solid Rock; The Beats Go On; Percussion: From Pleistocene to Paradiddle; The Pretty Lady and the Electronic Musicians.* Stamford, Conn.: Xerox Films.

Silver Burdett Company. Graded record albums for use with the basic music series *Making Music Your Own* and *Music for Living.* In addition, the Lillian Baldwin *Musical Soundbook* record albums.

Simon and Schuster, Inc. Library includes *A Child's Introduction to the Orchestra* and other *Golden Records.*

Simpson, Betty, and Simpson, Cecil. *I Wonder What I'll Be.* Songbook with record, song sheets and activity sheets (liquid duplicator). Delaware Water Gap, Pa.: Shawnee Press. Activities and songs for beginning career education.

Sound Book Press Society, Inc. Lillian Baldwin's library of music selections for young people, from *Tiny Masterpieces* and *Music for Young Listeners* to *Music to Remember (Also see* Silver Burdett).

SVE (Society for Visual Education). Sound filmstrips in full color portraying musical skills, holiday music, music of our American heritage, and black American folk music.

Threshold to Music. A five-year program for elementary grades (and adult beginners) by Mary Helen Richards. Based on the philosophy of Zoltán Kodály and available through Fearon/Lear Siegler, Inc.

Time-Life Records. Extensive catalogue of classical music by periods. Includes material on the times with pictures in color.

Vanguard Recording Society, Inc. A general catalogue of standard works.

Vox Productions, Inc. *Music Master* series, presenting the composer's biography with a background of his best known works; also a general catalogue of standard works.

Westminster Recording Company, Inc. A general catalogue of standard works.

White, Ruth. *Library of Basic Activities* (records and teacher suggestions). Hollywood, Calif.: Highland Music Company.

Wood, Lucille F. (editor). *Bowmar Small Musician: First Experiences for the Very Young.* Glendale, Calif.: Bowmar Records, Inc. Includes *Small Singer Book; Small Singer Records; Small Player; Small Dancer; Small Listener.*

Wurlitzer. *The Mobile Music Learning Center.* Consists of eight 44-note electric piano keyboards mounted on a table that folds up for moving and storage. Can be used with the Wurlitzer Key/Note Visualizer, a six-foot-high panel showing both treble and bass staffs. Notes on staff light up as they are played on instructor's console.

Young Keyboard (*See* Keyboard Publications, Inc.).

Young People's Records (*See* Greystone Corporation).

SPECIFIC REFERENCES FOR TEACHERS

(Concerning Individualized and Multimedia Materials)

Andrews, J. Austin, and Wardian, Jeanne Foster. *Introduction to Music Fundamentals.* New York: Appleton-Century-Crofts, 1964. A programmed textbook for the elementary classroom teacher.

Ashford, Theodore H. A. *A Programmed Introduction to the Fundamentals of Music.* Dubuque, Iowa: William C. Brown, 1969. Material is presented in ordinary prose, then in a linear program to develop specific skills. Topics include sound, scales, intervals, keys, and chords.

Barnes, Robert A. *Fundamentals of Music.* New York: McGraw-Hill, 1964. A program for self-instruction in the elementary aspects of music, including rhythm, the keyboard, major and minor keys, intervals, and syllables.

Brethower, Dale M. *Programmed Instruction: A Manual of Programming Techniques.* Chicago: Educational Methods, 1963.

Carlsen, James C. *Melodic Perception* (tape recordings available). New York: McGraw-Hill, 1965. A program for self-instruction to develop a student's ability to listen perceptively to melodic materials.

Clough, John. *Scales, Intervals, Keys and Triads.* New York: W. W. Norton, 1964. A text that applies the procedures of programmed instruction to the basic elements of music theory.

Colwell, Richard, and Colwell, Ruth. *Concepts for a Musical Foundation.* Englewood Cliffs, N.J.: Prentice-Hall, 1974. Basic self-instructional music book for beginners and potential music teachers. Recordings, musical examples, complete songs, and a programmed workbook format.

Cram, David. *Explaining "Teaching Machines" and Programming.* Palo Alto, Calif.: Fearon Publishers, 1961.

Dallin, Leon. *Introduction to Music Reading.* Glenview, Ill.: Scott, Foresman, 1966. A programmed method of self-instruction that teaches students to read music, pick out simple melodies on the piano, follow printed music as it is played, and use the basic terminology in talking and writing about music.

DeGrazia, Alfred, and Sohn, David A. (editors). *Programs, Teachers, and Machines.* New York: Bantam Books, 1964.

Fry, Edward. *Teaching Machines and Programmed Instruction.* New York: McGraw-Hill, 1963.

Guide Book, a publication of the *Agency for Instructional Television* (AIT). Bloomington, Ind.: AIT Headquarters. Publication of an organization created to strengthen education through television and other technologies. Television course materials available on a rental basis to educational institutions.

Hargiss, Genevieve. *Music for Elementary Teachers.* New York: Appleton-Century-Crofts, 1967. A programmed text in basic theory and chording for classroom teachers.

Hughes, John L. (editor). *Programmed Learning: A Critical Evaluation.* Chicago: Educational Methods, 1963.

Landon, Joseph W. *How to Write Learning Activity Packages for Music Education.* Costa Mesa, Calif.: Educational Media Press, 1973. Individualized Music Activities Packet to accompany the book is available from The California State University, Fullerton, Calif. 92634.

Mager, Robert F. *Preparing Objectives for Programmed Instruction.* Palo Alto, Calif.: Fearon Publishers, 1962.

Martin, Gary M. *Basic Concepts in Music.* Belmont, Calif.: Wadsworth Publishing, 1966. A branching program in music fundamentals with self-test and a review index at the end of each chapter.

O'Brien, James P. "Packaging the One-Concept Music Period," *Music Educators Journal* 60, No. 1 (September 1973): 41-43.

Schubert, Inez. *The Craft of Music Teaching.* Morristown, N.J.: General Learning Press (Silver Burdett), 1974 edition. Fifty-one fully written-out lesson plans that can be successfully used by elementary education majors who have not specialized in music. Twelve-inch LP record accompanies book.

Thomas, George, and Crescimbeni, Joseph. *Individualizing Instruction in the Elementary School.* New York: Random House, 1967.

APPENDIX D

ACTION SONGS, DANCING GAMES, AND MATERIALS FOR CREATIVE RHYTHMIC MOVEMENT

(Addresses for the sources of these materials can be found in Appendix L)

Agatz, Grethe. *Rhythmic Games* (recording available). Far Rockaway, N.Y.: Peripole Publishing Co.

_____. *Rhythmic Songs* (recording available). Far Rockaway, N.Y.: Peripole Publishing Co.

Andrews, Gladys E. *Creative Rhythmic Movement for Children.* Englewood Cliffs, N.J.: Prentice-Hall, 1954.

Barlin, Anne, and Barlin, Paul. *The Art of Learning Through Movement.* Los Angeles: Ward Ritchie.

Barlow, Betty M. *Do-It-Yourself Songs.* Delaware Water Gap, Pa.: Shawnee Press.

Boorman, Joyce. *Creative Dance in the First Three Grades.* New York: David McKay.

Stanley Bowmar Co., Inc. Folk songs and dances, rhythms, singing games, square and social dances.

Cherry, Clare. *Creative Movement for the Developing Child.* Palo Alto, Calif.: Fearon.

Diamondstein, Geraldine. *Children Dance in the Classroom.* New York: Macmillan.

Doll, Edna, and Nelson, Mary Jarman. *Rhythms Today!* (recordings available). Morristown, N.J.: Silver Burdett.

Fletcher, Helen Jill. *Action Songs.* New York: McGraw-Hill, Inc.

Gelineau, R. Phyllis. *Songs in Action.* New York: McGraw-Hill, Inc.

Gray, Vera, and Percival, Rachel. *Music, Movement, and Mime for Children.* New York: Oxford University Press.

Humphreys, Louise, and Ross, Jerrold. *Interpreting Music through Movement.* Englewood Cliffs, N.J.: Prentice-Hall.

Jones, Genevieve. *Seeds of Movement.* Pittsburgh, Pa.: Volkwein Bros., Inc., 1972.

Kraus, Richard G. *Folk Dancing: A Guide for Schools, Colleges, and Recreation Groups.* New York: Macmillan.

_____. *A Pocket Guide of Folk and Square Dances and Singing Games for the Elementary School.* Englewood Cliffs, N.J.: Prentice-Hall.

Mendoza, Anne. *Eight Dancing Songs.* New York: Chappell.

Nash, Grace C. *Creative Approaches to Child Development Through Music, Language, and Movement.* Port Washington, N.Y.: Alfred Publishing Co.

Nordoff-Robbins. *Children's Play Songs,* Vols. 1 and 2. Bryn Mawr, Pa.: Theodore Presser Co.

Paris, Leo, and Herschel, Lee. *Captain Kangaroo's Dance-A-Long Songs.* New York: Sam Fox Publishing.

Pitcher, Gladys. *Swing Your Partner.* New York: Harold Flammer.

Rohrbough, Lynn. *Handy Folk Dance Book.* Delaware, Ohio: Cooperative Recreation Service.

———. *Handy Square Dance Book.* Delaware, Ohio: Cooperative Recreation Service.

———. *Play Party Games.* Delaware, Ohio: Cooperative Recreation Service.

Rowen, Betty. *Learning Through Movement.* New York: Bureau of Publications, Teachers College, Columbia University.

Russell, Joan. *Creative Dance in the Primary School.* London: W. W. Norton; material can be obtained from their agency at 500 Fifth Ave., New York, N.Y. 10036.

Saffran, Rosanna B. *First Book of Creative Rhythms.* New York: Holt, Rinehart and Winston.

Stuart, Frances R., and Ludlam, John S. *Rhythmic Activities,* Series I (Grades Kindergarten to 3) and Series II (Grades 4 to 6). Minneapolis: Burgess Publishing.

Tolman, Newton F. *Quick Tunes and Good Times.* Dublin, N.H.: William L. Bauhan, Publisher, 1972. Survey of square dance melodies with personal anecdotes of specific performers in an historical account of little-known New England folk music.

Weiner, Jack, and Lidstone, J. *Creative Movement for Children: A Dance Program for the Classroom.* New York: Van Nostrand Reinhold.

White, Ruth. *Library of Music for Dance* (records and suggestions for use). Hollywood, Calif.: Highland Music Co.

Wiseman, Herbert, and Northcote, Sydney. *Singing Games.* New York: Oxford University Press.

APPENDIX E

SONG COLLECTIONS FOR
VARIOUS AGE GROUPS,
PART SINGING, PERFORMING GROUPS,
AND SPECIAL OCCASIONS

(Addresses for the sources of these materials can be found in Appendix L)

Ades, Hawley. *Little Folk Songs.* Delaware Water Gap, Pa.: Shawnee Press, Inc.

_____. *One for the Melody* (record album available). Delaware Water Gap, Pa.: Shawnee Press, Inc.

_____. *Sugar and Spice* (three-part treble). Delaware Water Gap, Pa.: Shawnee Press, Inc.

_____. *Sugar and Spice for Christmas* (three-part treble). Delaware Water Gap, Pa.: Shawnee Press, Inc.

_____. *Three to Make Music* (mixed voices: high, medium, low). Delaware Water Gap, Pa.: Shawnee Press, Inc.

_____. *Two for the Holiday Song.* Delaware Water Gap, Pa.: Shawnee Press, Inc.

_____. *Two for the Song.* Delaware Water Gap, Pa.: Shawnee Press, Inc.

Alfred Burt Carols. Delaware Water Gap, Pa.: Shawnee Press, Inc.

Appleby, William, and Fowler, Frederick. *Firsts and Seconds: An Introduction to Two-Part Singing* (voice parts only, or voice parts with piano accompaniment available). New York: Oxford University Press.

Bacon, Denise. *46 Two-Part American Folk Songs.* Wellesley, Mass.: The Kodály Musical Training Institute. An a cappella song collection for elementary grades.

Balkin, Alfred. *We Live in the City.* Bryn Mawr, Pa.: Theodore Presser Co.

Beckman, Frederick. *More Partner Songs.* Boston: Ginn.

_____. *Partner Songs.* Boston: Ginn.

Brand, Oscar. *Singing Holidays.* New York: Alfred A. Knopf.

Cacavas, John. *City Children.* New York: M. Witmark & Sons.

Carmichael, Hoagy. *Songs for Children.* New York: Simon and Schuster.

Christmas Carols (A Little Golden Book). New York: Golden Press.

Coleman, Satis N., and Thorn, Alice G. *Another Singing Time.* New York: John Day.

Continental Choral Selections. Two- and three-part selections for elementary choruses on liquid duplicating masters. Make as many copies as you need. Music arranged by James H. Burden and Ellis Carter. Available from Continental Press.

Coward, Barbara E. (editor). *Relax and Harmonize,* Books I and II. Boston: Boston Music Co.

Cox, Kenneth. *Six Traditional Songs.* New York: Chappell.

Crowninshield, Ethel, and Grant, Louise. *A Child's World,* Vols. 1, 2, and 3. Melville, N.Y.: Belwin Mills.

Dale, Ralph A. *Sound the Round* (Choral Series, Book 6). Englewood Cliffs, N.J.: Prentice-Hall.

Dallin, Leon, and Dallin, Lynn. *Heritage Songster.* Dubuque, Iowa: William C. Brown.

Ehret, Walter. *The Youthful Chorister.* New York: Edward B. Marks Music. Program material.

———. *Yule-Tidings.* New York: Edward B. Marks Music. Christmas carols with descants.

Foltz, David, and Murphy, Arthur. *Descants to Sing for Fun.* New York: Mills Music.

Foltz, David, and Shelley, Margaret. *More Descants to Sing for Fun.* New York: Mills Music.

Garlid, Georgia E., and Olson, Lynn Freeman. *For Our Small World* (Teacher's Book and Child's Book available). Minneapolis: Schmitt, Hall and McCreary.

Gearhart, Livingston. *Belles and Beaus* (SA and boys). Delaware Water Gap, Pa.: Shawnee Press, Inc.

———. *A Christmas Singing Bee.* Delaware Water Gap, Pa.: Shawnee Press, Inc.

———. *Once Upon a Song* (three-part treble). Delaware Water Gap, Pa.: Shawnee Press, Inc.

———. *A Singing Bee* (record album available). Delaware Water Gap, Pa.: Shawnee Press, Inc.

Harris, Jerry W. *Songs for Fun* (two-part voices). New York: Harold Flammer.

Hobbs, Barbara M. *Morning Glories.* Minneapolis: Schmitt, Hall and McCreary.

Howard, John T. (editor). *A Treasury of Stephen Foster.* New York: Random House.

Hutson, Wihla, and Zaninelli, Luigi. *Youth Praises* (Red Book, Unison; Yellow Book, S(A); Green Book, SA; Blue Book, S(S)A, with record album available for each book). Delaware Water Gap, Pa.: Shawnee Press, Inc.

Ives, Burl. *The Burl Ives Song Book.* New York: Ballantine Books.

Koch, Mary Blatt. *Little Musicland Express.* New York: Plymouth Music.

Krone, Beatrice Perham. *Songs to Sing with Descants.* Park Ridge, Ill.: Neil A. Kjos.

Krone, Beatrice Perham, and Krone, Max. *Descants and Rounds for Special Days.* Park Ridge, Ill.: Neil A. Kjos.

———. *Descants for Christmas.* Park Ridge, Ill.: Neil A. Kjos.

———. *From Descants to Trios.* Park Ridge, Ill.: Neil A. Kjos.

———. *Growing Up with Music.* Book I (for the lower grades): *Jerry and Janet on a Farm, Come Let Us Make a Garden,* and *Songs of Travel and*

Transport; Book II (for the upper grades): *Music of the Troubadours, Minstrels and Minnesingers, The Music of Early Greece,* and *Christmas, Its Origins, Music and Traditions.* Park Ridge, Ill.: Neil A. Kjos. (Also available separately.)

_____. *Intermediate Descants.* Park Ridge, Ill.: Neil A. Kjos.

_____. *Our First Songs to Sing with Descants.* Park Ridge, Ill.: Neil A. Kjos.

_____. *Our Third Book of Descants.* Park Ridge, Ill.: Neil A. Kjos.

_____. *Sing We All Noel.* Park Ridge, Ill.: Neil A. Kjos.

_____. *Songs for Fun with Descants.* Park Ridge, Ill.: Neil A. Kjos.

_____. *Very Easy Descants.* Park Ridge, Ill.: Neil A. Kjos.

Kvamme, Torstein O. *Christmas Caroler's Book: In Song and Story.* Minneapolis: Schmitt, Hall and McCreary.

Landeck, Beatrice. *More Songs to Grow On.* New York: Edward B. Marks Music.

_____. *Songs to Grow On.* New York: Edward B. Marks Music.

_____. *Songs My True Love Sings.* New York: Edward B. Marks Music.

Landeck, Beatrice, and Crook, Elizabeth. *Wake Up and Sing.* New York: Edward B. Marks Music.

Langstaff, John, and Langstaff, Carol. *Shimmy Shimmy Coke-Ca-Pop!* Garden City, N.Y.: Doubleday & Co. Street calls of the American city.

Lefebvre, Channing. *Fourteen Folk Tunes for Young Men.* New York: Galaxy Music.

_____. *Old Carols for Young Men.* New York: Galaxy Music.

Leisy, James. *The Good Times Song Book.* Nashville: The Abingdon Press, 1974. 160 songs for informal singing.

Lloyd, Norman. *The New Golden Song Book.* New York: Simon and Schuster.

McCall, Adeline. *Timothy's Tunes.* Boston: Boston Music.

MacCartney, Laura. *Songs for the Nursery School.* Cincinnati: Willis Music.

_____. *Up and Down We Go.* Cincinnati: Willis Music.

McLaughlin, Roberta. *Sing a Song.* Englewood Cliffs, N.J.: Prentice-Hall.

Marks, Gerald. *Sing a Song of Safety.* New York: Irving Caesar.

Marquis, Margaret Hurley. *Songs for All Seasons and Rhymes without Reason.* New York: Edward B. Marks Music.

Marsh, Mary Val. *Here a Song, There a Song.* Delaware Water Gap, Pa.: Shawnee Press, Inc.

Morgan, Haydn M. (editor). *Songs for Young Gleemen.* Minneapolis: Schmitt, Hall and McCreary.

Mysels, George. *Aesop's Fables in Song.* Delaware Water Gap, Pa.: Shawnee Press, Inc. Record-songbook combination.

Nelson, Mary Jarman, and Tipton, Gladys. *Music for Early Childhood.* Morristown, N.J.: Silver Burdett.

Nordoff-Robbins. *Songs for Children.* Bryn Mawr, Pa.: Theodore Presser Co. Special arrangements with resonator bells.

Nye, Robert E.; Nye, Vernice T.; Aubin, Neva; and Kyme, George. *Singing with Children*, 2nd Ed. Belmont, Calif.: Wadsworth.

Nye, Robert E.; Nye, Vernice T.; and Nye, Virginia. *Toward World Understanding with Song in the Elementary School.* Belmont, Calif.: Wadsworth.

Obenshain, Kathryn Garland. *Holiday Songbag.* Delaware Water Gap, Pa.: Shawnee Press, Inc.

Paris, Leo, and Herschel, Lee. *Captain Kangaroo's Riddle-A-Diddle Songs.* New York: Sam Fox Publishing.

Parry, W. H. *Christmas Day and Every Day.* New York: Chappell.

Pearse, John, and Copley, I. A. *Eight Fun Songs.* New York: Chappell.

Pitcher, Gladys. *People and Songs, Unusual Folk Songs Arranged for SSA.* New York: Harold Flammer.

_____. *Playtime in Song.* New York: M. Witmark.

Pooler, Marie. *Concert Time for Treble Voices.* Minneapolis: Schmitt, Hall and McCreary.

The Prince Street Players Songbook. New York: Associated Music Publishers.

Reichenbach, Herman. *Easy Canons.* Bryn Mawr, Pa.: Theodore Presser.

_____. *Modern Canons.* Bryn Mawr, Pa.: Theodore Presser.

Reton, Ellen Borchard, and Castagnetta, Grace. *Holiday Harmony.* Boston: Boston Music.

Richter, Ada. *My First Song Book.* Bryn Mawr, Pa.: Theodore Presser.

Richter, Ada, and Borie, Lysbeth Boyd. *Let's Stay Well.* Bryn Mawr, Pa.: Theodore Presser.

Riegger, Wallingford. *Harold Flammer Choral Collection for Two-Part Boys' Voices.* New York: Harold Flammer.

Rinehart, Carroll, and Rinehart, Marilyn. *Folk Songs with Descants.* Park Ridge, Ill.: Neil A. Kjos.

_____. *Sacred Songs of Praise.* Park Ridge, Ill.: Neil A. Kjos.

Ritchie, Jean. *Jean Ritchie's Swapping Song Book.* New York: Henry Z. Walck.

Robbins Choral Collection. New York: Robbins Music. Twelve numbers for two-part SA or TB; single arrangements are also available.

Ruff, Edna M. *It's Fun to Sing!* Minneapolis: Schmitt, Hall and McCreary.

Ruff, Edna M., and Smith, Herman F. *High, Low—Together Go!* Minneapolis: Schmitt, Hall and McCreary.

Seeger, Ruth Crawford. *Animal Folk Songs for Children.* Garden City, N.Y.: Doubleday.

Seuss, Dr. *The Cat in the Hat Song Book.* New York: RCA Educational Sales.

Sewell, Helen, and Noble, T. Tertius. *A Round of Carols.* New York: Henry Z. Walck.

Seymour, Brenda Meredith. *First Carols.* New York: Henry Z. Walck.

_____. *First Hymns.* New York: Henry Z. Walck.

Siegmeister, Elie. *Work and Sing.* New York: William R. Scott.

Simeone, Harry. *Have Songs—Will Sing* (SAB). Delaware Water Gap, Pa.: Shawnee Press, Inc.

———. *Hello Tomorrow*. Delaware Water Gap, Pa.: Shawnee Press, Inc.

———. *Rise and Shine*. Delaware Water Gap, Pa.: Shawnee Press, Inc.

———. *Youth Sings* (SAB). Delaware Water Gap, Pa.: Shawnee Press, Inc.

———. *Youth Sings at Christmas* (SAB). Delaware Water Gap, Pa.: Shawnee Press, Inc.

———.(arranger). *Teach the World to Sing*. Delaware Water Gap, Pa.: Shawnee Press, Inc. A Choral collection for upper elementary, middle school, and junior high choruses.

Songs Children Like—Folk Songs from Many Lands (Bulletin No. 63). Washington, D.C.: Association for Childhood Education International. ·

Stickles, William. *On Wings of Song: Community Song Book*. New York: Edwin H. Morris.

Stickley, Eileen (arranger). *25 Carols from The Oxford Book of Carols* (unison and guitar). New York: Oxford University Press.

Surer, Verna Meade, and Epler, E. D. *Let's Make Believe*. Bryn Mawr, Pa.: Theodore Presser.

Tobitt, Janet E. *Our World in Song*. New York: Plymouth Music.

Upshur, Claire. *Springtime for the Very Young*. New York: Harold Flammer.

Watson, Wendy. *Fisherman Lullabies*. Cleveland: World Publishing.

Weil, Paul, and Weil, Esther. *First Steps in Part Singing*. New York: G. Schirmer.

Werner, Elsa Jane. *Hymns* (A Little Golden Book). New York: Golden Press.

Wessells, Katherine T. *Golden Song Book*. New York: Simon and Schuster.

Wheeler, Opal. *Sing for Christmas: A Round of Christmas Carols and Stories of the Carols*. New York: E. P. Dutton.

———. *Sing Mother Goose*. New York: E. P. Dutton.

Whelan, Florence O'Keane. *All through the Year*. Minneapolis: Schmitt, Hall and McCreary.

Whitaker, Helen Hart. *Sing and Celebrate*. Morristown, N.J.: Silver Burdett.

Whitmer, Mary Elizabeth. *Joyous Carols*. New York: Carl Fischer.

Wiechard, Angela C. *Today's Tunes for Children*. Minneapolis: Schmitt, Hall and McCreary.

Wiedinmyer, Clement. *Play-Sing-Chord Along* (scored for classroom chord or melody instruments). Bryn Mawr, Pa.: Shawnee Press, Inc.

Wilson, Harry R. *Old and New Rounds and Canons*. Bryn Mawr, Pa.: Shawnee Press, Inc.

Wilson, Harry R. (editor). *Three-Part Choruses for Male Voices*. Minneapolis: Schmitt, Hall and McCreary.

Wilson, Mabel. *Sing a Round* (voice parts only, or voice parts with piano accompaniment). New York: Oxford University Press.

Winters, Geoffrey. *Rejoice and Be Merry*. New York: Chappell.

Wolfe, Richard. *Old Mother Hubbard: A Royal Collection of 20 Play Party Songs* (recording available from MGM dealer). New York: Big Three Music Corp.

Wood, Lucille F., and Scott, Louise B. *More Singing Fun.* St. Louis: Webster Publishing.

_____. *Singing Fun.* St. Louis: Webster Publishing.

Wright, Don. *Pre-Teen Song Settings.* New York: Robbins Music. A collection for Grades 5, 6, and 7; sixty selections for two-part, some three-part, and rounds.

_____. *Youthful Voices,* Book I, Revised. New York: Robbins Music. More than sixty-five selections for any conceivable vocal combination from unison to four-part, all boys, all girls, unchanged, changing, and changed.

Young, Percy M. *Animal Alphabet.* New York: Mills Music.

Zaninelli, Luigi, and Hutson, Wihla. *Youth Praises.* Delaware Water Gap, Pa.: Shawnee Press, Inc. Four anthem collections, unison and two-part.

Zimmerman, George H. *Seasons in Song.* New York: Music Publishers Holding Corp.

APPENDIX F

MATERIALS FOR MAKING AND PLAYING
CLASSROOM INSTRUMENTS

(Addresses for the sources of these materials can be found in Appendix L)

Bachman, Tibor. *Reading and Playing Musical Patterns* (for use with recorder, Tonette, song flute, and Flutophone). Elizabethtown, Pa.: The Continental Press, Inc.

The Beginner's Method for Soprano and Alto Recorders, in duet. New York: Hargail Music, Inc.

Bergmann, Walter. *Compositions for Voices, Recorders, Piano and Orff Instruments.* New York: Hargail Music, Inc.

_____. *The Drummer Boy.* London, Eng.: Schott, and Company (available from Associated Music Publishers).

_____. *Sixteen American Folksongs* (for soprano recorder and piano; easy). New York: Hargail Music, Inc.

Bouchard, Robert. *Let's Play the Recorder.* Boston: Bruce Humphries.

Buchtel, Forrest L. *Buchtel Class Ensemble Book for Tonettes.* Park Ridge, Ill.: Neil A. Kjos.

_____. *Highways to Music.* Park Ridge, Ill.: Neil A. Kjos.

_____. *Melody Fun: For Singing and Playing with the Tonette.* Park Ridge, Ill.: Neil A. Kjos.

_____. *Tooter Talent.* Park Ridge, Ill.: Neil A. Kjos.

Burakoff, Gerald, and Wheeler, Lawrence. *Music Making in the Elementary School* (music for the recorder, available in Teacher's Edition and Student's Edition). New York: Hargail Music, Inc.

Creating Music with Melody Instruments, Creating Music with Guitar, Creating Music with Melody and Rhythm Instruments. Port Washington, N.Y.: Alfred Music Co.

Davis, Henry W. *Tonette Tunes and Technic.* Chicago: Rubank.

Dinn, Freda. *First Tunes: Method for Alto Recorder.* New York: Associated Music Publishers.

Dolmetsch, C. *Start My Way* (for soprano recorder). New York: Associated Music Publishers.

Duschenes, M. *Method for the Recorder* (Vols. I and II). New York: Associated Music Publishers.

Eisenkramer, Henry E. *Guitar in the Classroom.* Evanston, Ill.: Summy-Birchard Co.

Elliott, Helen L. *Guitar Magic,* an audiovisual teaching method. Atlanta: Educational Productions, Inc.

Foglia, Rudolph, and Guertin, Robert. *The Graphic Guitar.* San Antonio: Southern Music Company. A course for individual and class study.

The Follow-Up Book for the Soprano Recorder. New York: Hargail Music, Inc.

Francis, James. *Familiar Rings for Handbells*. Cincinnati: World Library Productions.

Giesbert, F. J. *Method for Alto Recorder*. New York: Associated Music Publishers.

Goodman, Lisa. *Color a Song*. New York: Hargail Music, Inc. A soprano recorder method for the very young.

Guitar Class Method, with cassette tape. Kirkwood, Mo.: Mel Bay Publications, Inc.

Have Fun with Music on the Autoharp. Union, N.J.: Oscar Schmidt-International.

Hood, Marguerite V. *Teaching of Rhythm and Classroom Instruments*. Englewood Cliffs, N.J.: Prentice-Hall.

Huang, Cham-Ber. Pamphlet on how to play the Hohner Chordominica. Hicksville, N.Y.: M. Hohner, Inc. (Instructional cassette recording available.)

Instructor for the Autoharp. Union, N.J.: Oscar Schmidt-International.

Krone, Beatrice Perham, and Krone, Max. *Harmony Fun with the Autoharp*. Park Ridge, Ill.: Neil A. Kjos.

_____. *Harmony Fun with the Harmolin*. Park Ridge, Ill.: Neil A. Kjos.

Langill, Roxane. *Anyone Can Play the Guitar*. New York: Charles Scribner's Sons.

Learning Unlimited Audio-Visual Recorder Series, with records, cassettes, and manuals. Milwaukee: Hal Leonard Publishing Corp.

Lively Craft Cards, Set 2: Making Musical Instruments. England: Mills & Boon Limited; available from Magnamusic-Baton, Inc., St. Louis, Mo. 63130.

Mandel, Muriel, and Wood, Robert E. *Make Your Own Musical Instruments*. New York: Sterling Publishing, 1959.

The Many Ways to Play the Autoharp, Vols. I and II (Vol. II: *Advanced Techniques*). Union, N.J.: Oscar Schmidt-International.

Mistak, Margaret Warren. *The Guitar Goes to School*. Chicago: M. M. Cole Publishing Co.

Music for Everyone on the Autoharp. Union, N.J.: Oscar Schmidt-International.

Nash, Grace C. *Recorder Book for Beginners*. Kitching Educational Division of Ludwig Industries.

Newman, Harold. *The Follow-Up Book*. New York: Hargail Music, Inc. A soprano technique book for advanced beginners, with Orff accompaniments.

_____. *Hargail Melody Method: Music Around the Clock*, for soprano recorder. New York: Hargail Music, Inc.

_____. *In the Beginning: The Recorder*. New York: Hargail Music, Inc. A book for third grade and young beginners on the soprano recorder.

_____. *Recorder Playing in the Elementary School*. New York: Hargail Music, Inc.

Newman, Harold, and Kolinski. *On Holiday with Two Alto Recorders*. New

York: Hargail Music, Inc. A musical trip through nine countries.

Nordoff, Paul. *Fun for Four Drums.* Bryn Mawr, Pa.: Theodore Presser.

Nye, Robert E., and Peterson, Meg. *Teaching Music with the Autoharp.* Union, N.J.: Music Education Group.

Rast, Lawrence R. *Keyboard Magic.* Atlanta: Educational Productions Incorporated. A structured audiovisual program for class piano, including audio cassettes and color filmstrips.

Recorder Playing for the Beginner, Alto. New York: Hargail Music, Inc.

Sebastian, John. *A Chromatic Harmonica Instruction Course.* Hicksville, N.Y.: Hohner, Inc.

Silverman, Jerry. *Graded Guitar Method/Work Books.* New York: Big Three Music Corp. Workbooks may be used to supplement the graded guitar method books.

Slind, Lloyd H. *Melody, Rhythm, and Harmony for the Elementary Grades* (Teacher's Book and Student's Book available). New York: Mills Music.

———. *More Melody, Rhythm, and Harmony.* New York: Mills Music.

Snyder, Alice M. *Sing and Strum.* Melville, N.Y.: Belwin Mills.

Targ and Dinner, Inc. Distributor of general music merchandise, tone bells, Elenick (formerly Jensen) recorders, and teaching aids. Distributor for Designers for Education, Inc., 2955 Altgeld, Chicago, Ill. 60647.

Thomas, Max. *Play Time: Self Instructor for the Tonette.* Park Ridge, Ill.: Neil A. Kjos.

Timmerman, Maurine, and Griffith, Celeste. *Folk Music and the Guitar in the Classroom.* Dubuque, Iowa: William C. Brown Company, Publishers.

———. *Guitar in the Classroom.* Dubuque, Iowa: William C. Brown Company, Publishers.

Twittenhoff, W. *How to Play the Recorder.* New York: Associated Music Publishers.

Vaughan Williams, Ralph. *March-Past of the Kitchen Utensils.* London, Eng.: Schott and Company.

The VIP Method for Guitar (includes manuals and cassette lesson tapes). Lincolnwood, Ill.: Chicago Musical Instrument Company (CMI).

Wiedinmyer, Clement. *Play-Sing-Chord Along.* Delaware Water Gap, Pa.: Shawnee Press, Inc.

Winters, Geoffrey. *A Diabelli Suite.* New York: Chappell.

Woelflin, Leslie E. *Classroom Melody Instruments.* Glenview, Ill.: Scott, Foresman. Fingering diagrams, photographs, simple note patterns, familiar melodies, and graphic representation of rhythmic values are used in this program, which teaches students to play the recorder, Flutophone, song flute, and Tonette.

Yamaha Guitar Course. Buena Park, Calif.: Yamaha International Corp.

Young, J. E., and MacKnight, C. B. *Reading and Playing Musical Patterns.* Elizabethtown, Pa.: Continental Press. An aural-visual approach for recorder (C Soprano, C Tenor), Tonette, song flute, and Flutophone.

APPENDIX G

REFERENCE BOOKS,
STANDARDIZED MUSIC TESTS,
AND PERIODICALS
FOR THE TEACHER'S USE

(Addresses for the sources of these materials can be found in Appendix L)

Andress, Barbara L.; Heimann, Hope M.; Rinehart, Carroll A.; and Talbert, E. Gene. *Music in Early Childhood.* Washington, D.C.: Music Educators National Conference, 1973.

Austin, Virginia. *Learning Fundamental Concepts of Music: An Activities Approach.* Dubuque, Iowa: William C. Brown, 1969.

Bailey, Eunice. *Discovering Music with Young Children.* New York: Philosophical Library, 1958.

Baird, Forrest J. *Music Skills for Recreation Leaders.* Dubuque, Iowa: William C. Brown, 1963.

Barzun, Jacques. *Music in American Life.* Bloomington: Indiana University Press, 1962.

Basescu, Bernard. *Music Reading for Beginners.* Bryn Mawr, Pa.: Theodore Presser, 1973.

Batcheller, John, and Monsour, Sally. *Music in Recreation and Leisure.* Dubuque, Iowa: William C. Brown, 1972.

Beard, Ruth M. *An Outline of Piaget's Development,* for Students and Teachers. New York: Basic Books, 1969.

Beegle, Charles W., and Brandt, Richard M. *Supervision and Curriculum Development: Observational Methods in the Classroom.* Washington, D.C.: Association for Supervision and Curriculum Development.

Beer, Alice S., and Hoffman, Mary E. *Teaching Music: What, How, Why.* Morristown, N.J.: Silver Burdett General Learning Corp., 1973. Records are included.

Bergethon, Bjornar, and Boardman, Eunice. *Musical Growth in the Elementary School.* New York: Holt, Rinehart and Winston, 1963.

Birge, Edward Bailey. *History of Public School Music in the United States,* 1939 Ed. Available from M.E.N.C. Publication Sales, paperback, Stock No. 321-10268.

Boney, Joan, and Rhea, Lois. *A Guide to Student Teaching in Music.* Englewood Cliffs, N.J.: Prentice-Hall, 1970.

Broudy, Harry S. *Enlightened Cherishing; An Essay on Aesthetic Education.* Urbana, Ill.: The University of Illinois Press, 1972.

Browder, Lesley H., Jr. *An Administrator's Handbook on Educational Accountability.* Arlington, Va.: American Association of School Administrators.

Butler, Jack. *New Dimensions.* Cincinnati: Willis Music, 1965.

A Career in Music Education. Washington, D.C.: Music Educators National Conference, 1965.

Careers in Music, Revised. Washington, D.C.: Music Educators National Conference, 1968.

Carpenter, Thomas H. *Televised Music Instruction.* Washington, D.C.: Music Educators National Conference, 1973.

Cheyette, Irving, and Cheyette, Herbert. *Teaching Music Creatively in the Elementary School.* New York: McGraw-Hill, 1968.

The Child's Bill of Rights in Music. Washington, D.C.: Music Educators National Conference, 1950.

Church, Joseph. *Language and the Discovery of Reality.* New York: Random House/Vintage Books, 1961.

Clarkson, E. Margaret. *Let's Listen to Music.* New York: Robbins Music (Big Three Music Corp.). 100 complete lesson outlines for school and home.

CMP Publications. Washington, D.C.: Music Educators National Conference (*see* Gary and Landis).

CMP: *Comprehensive Musicianship, the Foundation for College Education in Music,* 1965.

CMP: *Experiments in Musical Creativity,* 1966.

CMP: *Creative Projects in Musicianship,* 1967.

CMP: *Comprehensive Musicianship: An Anthology of Evolving Thought,* 1971.

CMP: *Comprehensive Musicianship and Undergraduate Music Curricula,* 1971.

CMP: *Source Book of African and Afro-American Materials for Music Educators,* 1972.

CMP: *What Is Music?* (sound and color film), 1973.

The Code for the National Anthem of the United States of America. Washington, D.C.: Music Educators National Conference.

Creative Approach to School Music: A Compendium of Viewpoints and Innovative Solutions. Chicago: American Music Conference, 1967.

Creative Arts in Education. Washington, D.C.: Music Educators National Conference, 1959.

Curriculum Balance, American Association of School Administrators. Resolution stressing the importance of a well-rounded, well-balanced curriculum. Washington, D.C.: Music Educators National Conference, 1973.

Davis, Marilyn K. *Music Dictionary.* Garden City, N.Y.: Doubleday, 1956.

Elliott, Raymond. *Learning and Teaching Music,* 2nd Ed. Columbus: Charles E. Merrill, 1966.

Ellison, Alfred. *Music with Children.* New York: McGraw-Hill, 1959.

Engleman, Finis. *Music and Public Education.* Washington, D.C.: Music Educators National Conference, 1961.

Ewen, David. *Home Book of Musical Knowledge.* Englewood Cliffs, N.J.: Prentice-Hall, 1954.

_____. *Opera: Its Story Told Through the Lives and Works of Its Foremost Composers.* New York: Franklin Watts, Inc., 1972.

Finn, William Joseph. *The Art of the Choral Conductor* (Vols. I and II). Evanston, Ill.: Summy-Birchard, 1960.

Fleming, William, and Veinus, Abraham. *Understanding Music.* New York: Holt, Rinehart and Winston, 1958.

Gary, Charles L. *Vignettes of Music Education History.* Washington, D.C.: Music Educators National Conference, 1964.

Gary, Charles L. (editor). *Music Buildings, Rooms and Equipment.* Washington, D.C.: Music Educators National Conference, 1966.

Gary, Charles L., and Landis, Beth. *The Comprehensive Music Program.* Washington, D.C.: Music Educators National Conference, 1973.

Gaston, E. Thayer. *An Analysis, Evaluation and Selection of Clinical Uses of Music in Therapy.* Lawrence: University Press of Kansas, 1965.

Gerzina, Frank. *Developmental Music in the Elementary School.* Philadelphia: Dorrance, 1966.

Gesell, Arnold, and Ilg, Frances L. *Child Development.* New York: Harper and Brothers, 1948.

Gillies, Emily. *Creative Dramatics for All Children.* Washington, D.C.: Association for Childhood Education, 1973. Suggestions for creative drama activities in the classroom, with special sections devoted to children who are emotionally disturbed or brain-injured, or for whom English is a second language.

Ginsberg, Herbert, and Opper, Sylvia. *Piaget's Theory of Intellectual Development.* Englewood Cliffs, N.J.: Prentice-Hall, 1969.

Goldhammer, Keith, and Taylor, Robert E. *Career Education.* Columbus: Charles E. Merrill, 1972.

Goodlad, John I., and Shane, Harold G. *The Elementary School in the United States: The Seventy-Second Yearbook of the National Society for the Study of Education, Part II.* Chicago: University of Chicago Press, 1973.

Gordon, Edwin (editor). *Experimental Research in the Psychology of Music,* eighth compendium. Iowa City, Iowa: University of Iowa Press, 1972. Series of experimental research studies in music.

Gordon, Roderick D. *Doctoral Dissertations in Music and Music Education, 1968-1971.* Washington, D.C.: Music Educators National Conference.

Gould, A. Oren. *Developing Specialized Programs for Singing in the Elementary School.* Macomb, Ill.: Western Illinois University Press, 1970.

Grant, Parks. *Music for Elementary Teachers.* New York: Appleton-Century-Crofts, 1960.

Greenberg, Marvin, and MacGregor, Beatrix. *Music Handbook for the Elementary School.* New York: Parker Publishing Co., Inc., 1972.

Grindea, Carola. *We Make Our Own Music.* New York: Alexander Broude, Inc. An approach to the keyboard for children, requiring original composition by them.

Guidelines in Music Education: Supportive Requirements. Vienna, Va.: Music Educators National Conference, 1972. A service book prepared by the National Council of State Supervisors of Music.

Hartsell, O. M. *Teaching Music in the Elementary School: Opinion and Comment.* Washington, D.C.: Music Educators National Conference, 1963.

Heffernan, Charles W. *Teaching Children to Read Music.* New York: Appleton-Century-Crofts, 1968.

Henry, Nelson B. (editor). *Basic Concepts in Music Education.* 56th Yearbook, Part I, National Society for the Study of Education. Chicago: University of Chicago Press, 1958.

Hermann, Edward J. *Supervising Music in the Elementary School.* Englewood Cliffs, N.J.: Prentice-Hall, 1965.

Hertzberg, Alvin, and Stone, Edward F. *Schools Are for Children.* New York: Schocken Books, 1971. An American approach to Open Education. Suggested activities, materials, ideas, inspiration, and step-by-step instructions.

Hewes, Dorothy, and Hartman, Barbara. *Early Childhood Education: A Workbook for Administrators.* San Francisco: R. and E. Research Associates.

Hickok, Dorothy, and Smith, James A. *Creative Teaching of Music in the Elementary School.* Boston: Allyn and Bacon, Inc., 1974.

Hill, Frank W., and Searight, Roland. *A Study Outline and Workbook in the Elements of Music,* 5th Ed. Dubuque, Iowa: William C. Brown, 1972.

Hood, Marguerite V. *Teaching Rhythm and Using Classroom Instruments.* Englewood Cliffs, N.J.: Prentice-Hall, 1970.

Hoppock, Anne S. *All Children Have Gifts* (Bulletin No. 100). Washington, D.C.: Association for Childhood Education International, 1958.

House, Robert W. *Administration in Music Education.* Englewood Cliffs, N.J.: Prentice-Hall, 1973.

Hughes, William O. *A Concise Introduction to Teaching Elementary Music.* Belmont, Calif.: Wadsworth Publishing Co., 1973.

Hunter, Hilda. *Growing Up with Music.* Old Tappan, N.J.: Hewitt House, 1970.

Ingram, Madeline D., and Rice, William C. *Vocal Technique for Children and Youth.* Nashville: Abingdon Press, 1962.

Instructional Objectives in Music. Vienna, Va.: Music Educators National Conference, 1974. Resources for planning instruction and evaluating achievement, compiled by J. David Boyle for the National Commission on Instruction (Stock No. 321-09928).

Jenkins, Ella. *This Is Rhythm.* New York: Oak Publications, 1962.

Jones, Betty Jensen. *What Is Music for Young Children?* Washington, D.C.: National Association for Nursery Education, 1959.

Kaplan, Max. *Foundations and Frontiers of Music Education.* New York: Holt, Rinehart and Winston, Inc., 1966.

Kaplan, Max, and Steiner, F. J. *Musicianship for the Classroom Teacher.* Chicago: Rand McNally, 1966.

Konowitz, Bert. *Music Improvisation as a Classroom Method.* Port Washington, N.Y.: Alfred Publishing Co., 1973. Emphasis on performance of their own music by elementary children. Sample lessons based on author's contributions to Manhattanville Curriculum.

Kowall, Bonnie C. (editor). *Perspectives in Music Education (Source Book III).* Washington, D.C.: Music Educators National Conference, 1966.

Kreitler, Hans, and Kreitler, Shulamith. *Psychology of the Arts.* Durham, N.C.: Duke University Press, 1972.

Krone, Beatrice Perham, and Krone, Max. *Music Participation in the Elementary School.* Park Ridge, Ill.: Neil A. Kjos, 1952.

Krone, Beatrice Perham, and Miller, Kurt R. *Help Yourselves to Music,* 2nd Ed. Belmont, Calif.: Wadsworth Publishing Co., 1968.

Krone, Max. *Expressive Conducting,* Revised. Park Ridge, Ill.: Neil A. Kjos, 1949.

Labuta, Joseph A. *Guide to Accountability in Music Instruction.* West Nyack, N.Y.: Parker Publishing Co., Inc., 1974.

Land, Lois Rhea, and Vaughan, Mary Ann. *Music in Today's Classroom: Creating, Listening, Performing.* New York: Harcourt Brace Jovanovich, Inc., 1973.

Lawler, Vanett. *The Arts in the Educational Program in the Soviet Union.* Washington, D.C.: Music Educators National Conference, 1961.

_____. *How Can Music Promote International Understanding?* Washington, D.C.: Music Educators National Conference, 1957.

Leach, John Robert. *Functional Piano for the Teacher.* Englewood Cliffs, N.J.: Prentice-Hall, 1968.

Leonhard, Charles, and House, Robert W. *Foundations and Principles of Music Education,* Revised. New York: McGraw-Hill, 1972.

Livingston, James A.; Poland, Michael D.; and Simmons, Ronald E. *Accountability and Objectives for Music Education.* Costa Mesa, Calif.: Educational Media Press, 1972.

McGehee, Thomasina (revised by Alice D. Nelson). *People and Music.* Boston: Allyn and Bacon, Inc., 1973.

McLaughlin, Roberta (editor). *Music in Everyday Living and Learning.* Washington, D.C.: Music Educators National Conference, 1960.

McMillan, L. Eileen. *Guiding Children's Growth through Music.* Boston: Ginn, 1959.

Markel, Roberta. *Parents' and Teachers' Guide to Music Education.* New York: Macmillan, 1972.

Marvel, Lorene. *The Music Consultant at Work.* New York: Bureau of Publications, Teachers College, Columbia University, 1960.

Matthews, Paul W. *You Can Teach Music.* New York: E. P. Dutton, 1960.

Montessori, Maria. *The Absorbent Mind.* New York: Holt, Rinehart and Winston, Inc., 1967.

Morgan, Hazel Nohavec (editor). *Music in American Education (Source Book II).* Washington, D.C.: Music Educators National Conference, 1955.

Moustakas, Clark. *Teaching as Learning.* New York: Ballantine Books, 1972.

Music Education for Elementary School Children. Washington, D.C.: Music Educators National Conference, 1960.

Music for Your School. Washington, D.C.: Music Educators National Conference, 1960.

"Music in Open Education," *Music Educators Journal* 60, No. 8 (April 1974). Vienna, Va.: Music Educators National Conference, 1974. The entire issue is devoted to music in Open Education, with articles by a galaxy of experts in music and education. Also extensive bibliographies.

Music in the Informal School, Vol. VIII of "Current Issues in Music Education." Columbus: The Ohio State University. One of the reports of the 1973 Current Issues in Music Education Symposium. Publication can be ordered from Music Education Division, The Ohio State University, Columbus, Ohio 43210.

Mussen, Paul H.; Conger, John J.; and Kagen, Jerome. *Child Development and Personality,* 3rd Ed. New York: Harper and Row, 1969.

Myers, Louise Kifer. *Teaching Children Music in the Elementary School,* 3rd Ed. Englewood Cliffs, N.J.: Prentice-Hall, 1961.

Nallin, Walter E. *The Musical Idea: A Consideration of Music and Its Ways.* New York: Macmillan, 1968.

Nielsen, Floraine, and Folstrom, Roger J. *Music Fundamentals: A Creative Activities Approach.* Reading, Mass.: Addison-Wesley, 1969.

Nordholm, Harriet. *Learning Music: Musicianship for the Elementary Classroom Teacher.* Englewood Cliffs, N.J.: Prentice-Hall, 1970.

_____. *Singing in the Elementary Schools.* Englewood Cliffs, N.J.: Prentice-Hall, 1966.

Nye, Robert E. *Music for Elementary School Children.* New York: Center for Applied Research in Education, 1963.

Nye, Robert E., and Bergethon, Bjornar. *Basic Music: Functional Musicianship for the Non-Music Major,* 4th Ed. Englewood Cliffs, N.J.: Prentice-Hall, 1973.

Nye, Robert E., and Nye, Vernice T. *Essentials of Teaching Elementary School Music.* Englewood Cliffs, N.J.: Prentice-Hall, 1974. A recent book based on their more comprehensive text to fit the needs of the big-volume misses, for use in short courses. Aspects of Dalcroze, Orff, and Kodály are incorporated.

_____. *Exploring Music with Children.* Belmont, Calif.: Wadsworth Publishing Co., 1966.

_____. *Music in the Elementary School: An Activities Approach to Music Methods and Materials,* 2nd Ed. Englewood Cliffs, N.J.: Prentice-Hall, 1964.

The Open Classroom—Informal Education in America. Dayton, Ohio: Institute for Development of Educational Activities, Inc. (I/D/E/A)

Opera Repertory U.S.A., directory giving coverage to opera performances, children's operas, Christmas operas, and selected operas for young audiences. New York: Central Opera Service, Metropolitan Opera, Lincoln Center.

Pace, Robert L. *Music Essentials.* Belmont, Calif.: Wadsworth Publishing Co., 1968.

Paynter, John. *Hear and Now.* London, Eng.: Universal Edition, Ltd., 1972. Suggestions for creative music experiences.

Paynter, John, and Aston, Peter. *Sound and Silence.* Cambridge, Eng.: Cambridge University Press, 1970. Suggestions for creative experiments.

Pelz, William. *Basic Keyboard Skills.* Boston: Allyn and Bacon, Inc., 1963.

Piaget, Jean. *Play, Dreams and Imitations in Childhood.* New York: W. W. Norton, 1962.

Portnoy, Julius. *Music in the Life of Man.* New York: Holt, Rinehart and Winston, 1963.

The Power of Music. Washington, D.C.: Music Educators National Conference, 1971.

Raebeck, Lois, and Wheeler, Lawrence. *New Approaches to Music in the Elementary School,* 2nd Ed. Dubuque, Iowa: William C. Brown, 1970.

Reimer, Bennett. *The Market for Music Teachers.* Washington, D.C.: Music Educators National Conference, 1963.

———. *A Philosophy of Music Education.* Englewood Cliffs, N.J.: Prentice-Hall.

Rinderer, Leo. *Music Education: A Handbook for Music Teaching in the Elementary Grades.* Park Ridge, Ill.: Neil A. Kjos, 1961.

Schubert, Inez, and Wood, Lucille F. *The Craft of Music Teaching in the Elementary School* (recording available). Morristown, N.J.: Silver Burdett, 1964.

Sidnell, Robert. *Building Instructional Programs in Music Education.* Englewood Cliffs, N.J.: Prentice-Hall, Inc., 1973.

Silberman, Charles E. *The Open Classroom Reader.* New York: Random House, 1973. An overview of the subject designed to give a judicious balance between the practical and the theoretical.

Slind, Lloyd H., and Davis, D. Evan. *Bringing Music to Children: Music Methods for the Elementary School Teacher.* New York: Harper and Row, 1964.

Smith, Carleton Sprague, and Hartshorn, William C. *The Study of Music: An Academic Discipline.* Washington, D.C.: Music Educators National Conference, 1963.

Smith, Ralph A. *Aesthetic Concepts and Education.* Urbana: University of Illinois Press.

Snyder, Alice M. *Creating Music with Children.* New York: Mills Music, 1957.

———. *Music in Our World.* New York: Mills Music, 1962.

Snyder, Keith D. *School Music Administration and Supervision,* 2nd Ed. Boston: Allyn and Bacon, Inc., 1965.

Starr, William, and Starr, Constance. *Basic Piano Technique for the Classroom Teacher.* Dubuque, Iowa: William C. Brown, 1971.

Sunderman, Lloyd Frederick. *New Dimensions in Music Education*. Metuchen, N.J.: The Scarecrow Press, Inc., 1972.

Swanson, Bessie R. *Music in the Education of Children*, 3rd Ed. Belmont, Calif.: Wadsworth Publishing Co., 1969.

The Synthesizer Primer. Vernon, N.Y.: Electronic Laboratories, Inc. A short, easy to read guide to understanding synthesizers.

Werder, Richard H. (editor). *Music Pedagogy*. Washington, D.C.: Catholic University of America Press, 1963.

_____. *Procedures and Techniques of Music Teaching*. Washington, D.C.: Catholic University of America Press, 1962.

Weyland, Rudolph H. *A Guide to Effective Music Supervision*. Dubuque, Iowa: William C. Brown, 1960.

_____. *Learning to Read Music*. Dubuque, Iowa: William C. Brown, 1961.

Wilkie, Richard W., and Otis, Gladys B. *Quest for the Creative: An Analytical Report of a Seminar in Creative Music and the Related Arts for Elementary School Children*. Albany: Capital Area School Development Association, University of New York at Albany, 1964.

Winslow, Robert W., and Dallin, Leon. *Music Skills for Classroom Teachers*, 3rd Ed. Dubuque, Iowa: William C. Brown, 1971.

Wisler, Gene C. *Music Fundamentals for the Classroom Teacher*, 3rd Ed. Boston: Allyn and Bacon, Inc., 1971.

Zimmerman, Alex H.; Hayton, Russell; and Priesing, Dorothy. *Basic Piano for the College Student*. Dubuque, Iowa: William C. Brown, 1969.

Zimmerman, Marilyn Pfleder. *Musical Characteristics of Children*. Washington, D.C.: Music Educators National Conference, 1971.

STANDARDIZED TESTS AND MEASUREMENTS

Colwell, Richard. *Elementary Music Achievement Test*. Chicago: Follett Publishing, 1967.

Gordon, Edwin. *The Musical Aptitude Profile* (tapes, answer sheets, record sheets, scoring masks, etc.). Boston: Houghton Mifflin.

Kwalwasser, Jacob. *Kwalwasser Music Talent Test*. New York: Mills Music, 1953. This test is available in two forms of differing difficulty. Form B is for Grades 4 through 6.

Lehman, Paul R. *Tests and Measurements in Music*. Englewood Cliffs, N.J.: Prentice-Hall, 1968. Part of the Foundations of Music Education Series.

Miller, Lela, and Torgerson, T. L. *Diagnostic Tests of Achievement in Music*. Monterey, Calif.: California Test Bureau, 1950. In ten parts, covers rudiments from Grades 4 through 12.

Seashore, Carl E. et al. *Seashore Measures of Musical Talents*, Revised. New York: Psychological Corporation, 1939. These phonographically presented tests measure pitch, loudness, time, timbre, rhythm, and tonal memory. Abilities measured are fundamental to development of musical proficiency, and the scores are relatively unrelated to the amount of formal training.

Wing, Herbert. *Wing Standardized Tests of Musical Intelligence*, Revised. Sheffield, Eng.: City of Sheffield Training College, 1958. Seven measures, including chord analysis, pitch change, memory, rhythmic accent, harmony, intensity, and phrasing. Ages 7 to adult.

PERIODICALS

American Orff Schulwerk Association (Mrs. Ruth Pollack Hamm). Cleveland Heights, Ohio.

The American Record Guide (James Lyons, editor). The American Record Guide, Inc., New York, N.Y.

Billboard (Lee Zhito, editor-in-chief). Billboard Publishing Company, Cincinnati, Ohio.

Down Beat (Don DeMichael, editor). Maher Publications, Chicago, Ill.

The Folk Harp Journal. Mt. Laguna, Calif. A magazine devoted to the varieties of harps and harp literature.

The Gifted Child Quarterly, published by the National Association for Gifted Children (NAGC), Cincinnati, Ohio.

High Fidelity (Roland Gelatt, editor). The Billboard Publishing Company, Great Barrington, Mass.

Journal of Research in Music Education, published by the Society for Research in Music Education, Music Educators National Conference, Vienna, Va.

Journal of the Society for Ethnomusicology, published by the Society for Ethnomusicology, Ann Arbor, Mich.

The Journal of Teacher Education, published by the American Association of Colleges for Teacher Education (AACTE), Washington, D.C.

Junior Keynotes (Phyllis L. Hanson, editor). National Federation of Music Clubs, Worcester, Mass.

Junior Musician, published by the Sunday School Board, Southern Baptist Convention, Nashville, Tenn.

Keeping Up with Kodály (Prof. Arnold Burkhart). Muncie, Ind.

Keeping Up with Music Education (Prof. Arnold Burkhart). Muncie, Ind.

Keeping Up with Orff (Prof. Arnold Burkhart). Muncie, Ind.

Keyboard Junior (*see Young Keyboard Junior* below, and *Keyboard Publications* in Appendix L).

Kodály Envoy, published by the Organization of American Kodály Educators, Pittsburgh, Pa. Information concerning conferences, workshops, and materials.

Kodály Techniques, published by the Organization of American Kodály Educators, Pittsburgh, Pa.

Musart (Rt. Rev. Msgr. Sylvester J. Hotel, editor). National Catholic Music Educators Association, Washington, D.C.

Music Educators Journal (Malcolm E. Bessom, editor). Music Educators National Conference, Reston, Va.

Music Journal (Robert Cumming, editor). The Music Journal, Inc., New York, N.Y.

The Musical Quarterly (Paul Henry Lang, editor). G. Schirmer, Inc., New York, N.Y.

News Parade, A Weekly Reader. Xerox Educational Materials, Middletown, Conn.

Opera News (Frank Merkling, editor). The Metropolitan Opera Guild, Inc., New York, N.Y.

The Orff Echo (Mrs. Ruth Pollack Hamm). Cleveland Heights, Ohio. Back issues are available. Supplementary articles are also available, as well as information on conferences, workshops, and instruments.

State Music Education Periodicals. Official magazines of the respective federated state units of the Music Educators National Conference. See the complete list in the current issue of their *Official Directory,* which will be sent on request. Write M.E.N.C., Vienna, Va.

Variety (Abel Green, editor). Variety, Inc., New York, N.Y.

The World of Music (Egon Kraus, Jack Bornoff, and John Evarts, editors). International Music Council, Paris, France.

Young Keyboard Junior: The Magazine for Young Musicians (Sam Mininberg, editor). Young Keyboard Junior Magazine, New Haven, Conn.

APPENDIX H

BOOKS FOR THE SCHOOL LIBRARY

(Addresses for the sources of these materials can be found in Appendix L)

An excellent source is available from the Music Educators National Conference: *Music Books for the Elementary School Library,* by Peggy Flanagan Baird. The list is organized by topics, is annotated, and suggests grade level as well as the author's list of outstanding books (MENC catalogue no. 321-10478, 1972, 48 pages).

Appleby, William, and Fowler, Frederick. *Nutcracker and Swan Lake: Stories of the Ballets.* New York: Henry Z. Walck, 1968.

———. *The Sleeping Beauty and the Firebird: Stories of the Ballets.* New York: Henry Z. Walck, 1965.

Balet, James B. *What Makes an Orchestra?* New York: Oxford University Press, 1951.

Bernstein, Leonard. *Leonard Bernstein's Young People's Concerts for Reading and Listening.* New York: Simon and Schuster, 1962.

Bonner, Mary G. *Wonders of Musical Instruments.* New York: Lantern Press, 1963.

Britten, Benjamin, and Holst, Imogen. *The Wonderful World of Music.* Garden City, N.Y.: Garden City Books, 1958.

Brown, Margaret W. *The Little Brass Band.* New York: Harper and Row, 1955.

Buchanan, Fannie R. *How Man Made Music.* Chicago: Follett Publishing, 1959.

———. *Short Stories of American Music.* Chicago: Follett Publishing, 1959.

Bulla, Clyde Robert. *More Stories of Favorite Operas.* New York: Thomas Y. Crowell, 1965.

———. *Ring and the Fire: Stories from Wagner's Nibelung Operas.* New York: Thomas Y. Crowell, 1962.

———. *Stories of Favorite Operas.* New York: Thomas Y. Crowell, 1959.

———. *Stories of Gilbert and Sullivan.* New York: Thomas Y. Crowell, 1968.

Chappell, Warren. *Coppelia.* New York: Alfred A. Knopf, 1965.

Chissel, Joan. *Chopin.* New York: Thomas Y. Crowell, 1965.

Close, Elizabeth R. *The Magic Ring: Children's Tales from Richard Wagner.* New York: Carlton Press, 1964.

Crozier, Eric. *The Magic Flute.* New York: Henry Z. Walck, 1965.

———. *The Mastersingers of Nuremburg.* New York: Henry Z. Walck, 1964.

Dobrin, Arnold. *Aaron Copland: His Life and Times.* New York: Thomas Y. Crowell, 1967.

Ewen, David. *The Book of European Light Opera*. New York: Holt, Rinehart and Winston, 1962.

_____. *Complete Book of the American Musical Theater*, Revised. New York: Holt, Rinehart and Winston, 1959.

_____. *Composers for the American Musical Theater*. New York: Dodd, Mead, 1968.

_____. *Famous Conductors*. New York: Dodd, Mead, 1966.

_____. *Famous Instrumentalists*. New York: Dodd, Mead, 1965.

_____. *Famous Modern Conductors*. New York: Dodd, Mead, 1967.

_____. *A Journey to Greatness*. New York: Holt, Rinehart and Winston, 1956.

_____. *Panorama of American Popular Music*. Englewood Cliffs, N.J.: Prentice-Hall, 1957.

_____. *The Story of Arturo Toscanini*, Revised. New York: Holt, Rinehart and Winston, 1960.

_____. *The Story of George Gershwin*. New York: Holt, Rinehart and Winston, 1943.

_____. *The Story of Irving Berlin*. New York: Holt, Rinehart and Winston, 1950.

_____. *The Story of Jerome Kern*. New York: Holt, Rinehart and Winston, 1953.

_____. *Tales from the Vienna Woods*. New York: Holt, Rinehart and Winston, 1944.

_____. *With a Song in His Heart: The Story of Richard Rodgers*. New York: Holt, Rinehart and Winston, 1963.

_____. *The World of Great Composers*. Englewood Cliffs, N.J.: Prentice-Hall, 1962.

_____. *The World of Jerome Kern*. New York: Holt, Rinehart and Winston, 1960.

Ewen, David (editor). *The New Book of Modern Composers*, 3rd Ed. New York: Alfred A. Knopf, 1961.

Forsee, Aylesa. *Pablo Casals: Cellist for Freedom*. New York: Thomas Y. Crowell, 1965.

Freeman, Lydia, and Freeman, Don. *Chuggy and the Blue Caboose*. New York: Viking Press, 1951.

Gelatt, Roland. *The Fabulous Phonograph*. New York: Appleton-Century Press, 1966.

Gibson, Enid. *The Golden Cockerel*. New York: Henry Z. Walck, 1963.

Goss, Madeline. *Beethoven: Master Musician*, Revised. New York: Holt, Rinehart and Winston, 1956.

Gough, Catherine. *Boyhoods of Great Composers* (Books I and II). New York: Henry Z. Walck, 1960, 1965.

Hentoff, Nat. *Journey into Jazz*. New York: Coward-McCann, 1968.

Holst, Imogen. *Bach*. New York: Thomas Y. Crowell, 1965.

Hosier, John. *The Sorcerer's Apprentice and Other Stories.* New York: Henry Z. Walck, 1961.

Hughes, Langston. *Famous Negro Music Makers.* New York: Dodd, Mead, 1955.

———. *The First Book of Jazz.* New York: Franklin Watts, 1955.

Jackson, Jacqueline. *The Orchestra Mice.* Chicago: Henry Regnery Company, 1971.

Kaufmann, Helen. *Anvil Chorus: The Story of Giuseppe Verdi.* New York: Hawthorn Books, 1964.

Keats, Ezra Jack. *The Little Drummer Boy.* New York: Macmillan, 1968.

Kettelkamp, Larry. *Drums, Rattles and Bells.* New York: William Morrow, 1960.

———. *Flutes, Whistles and Reeds.* New York: William Morrow, 1962.

Kyle, Elisabeth. *The Swedish Nightingale: Jenny Lind.* New York: Holt, Rinehart and Winston, 1965.

LaMont, Violet. *Book about Ballet.* Chicago: Follett Publishing, 1953.

Lenski, Lois. *At Our House* (music by Clyde Robert Bulla). New York: Henry Z. Walck, 1959.

———. *Frank Luther Sings Lois Lenski Songs* (music by Clyde Robert Bulla). New York: Henry Z. Walck, 1960. (A recording of *All the Songs of Mr. Small* and the *Read and Sing* books are also available.)

Lingg, Ann M. *John Philip Sousa.* New York: Holt, Rinehart and Winston, 1954.

Montgomery, Elizabeth Rider. *The Story behind Musical Instruments.* New York: Dodd, Mead, 1953.

———. *The Story behind Popular Songs.* New York: Dodd, Mead, 1958.

Moore, John T. *Story of Silent Night.* St. Louis: Concordia Publishing House, 1965.

Nelson, Alice D. *People and Music,* Revised. Boston: Allyn and Bacon, Inc., 1968.

Newman, Shirlee P. *Marian Anderson: Lady from Philadelphia.* Philadelphia: Westminster Press, 1966.

Pauli, Hertha E. *Handel and the Messiah Story.* New York: Meredith Press, 1968.

Peare, Catherine O. *Stephen Foster: His Life.* New York: Holt, Rinehart and Winston, 1952.

Peters, Roberta, with Biancolli, Louis. *A Debut at the Met.* New York: Meredith Press, 1967.

Posell, Elsa. *This Is an Orchestra.* Boston: Houghton Mifflin, 1950.

Reynolds, William J. *A Survey of Christian Hymnody.* New York: Holt, Rinehart and Winston, 1963.

Ritchie, Jean. *From Fair to Fair.* New York: Henry Z. Walck, 1966.

Sadie, Stanley. *Beethoven.* New York: Thomas Y. Crowell, 1967.

Seligmann, Jean, and Danziger, Juliet. *The Meaning of Music: The Young Listener's Guide.* Cleveland: World Publishing, 1966.

Watson, Jack M., and Watson, Corinne. *A Concise Dictionary of Music: An Introductory Reference Book.* New York: Dodd, Mead, 1965.

Westcott, Frederic. *Bach.* New York: Henry Z. Walck, 1967.

Wheeler, Opal. *Adventures of Richard Wagner.* New York: E. P. Dutton, 1960.

_____. *Paganini: Master of Strings.* New York: E. P. Dutton, 1950.

_____. *The Story of Tchaikowsky.* New York: E. P. Dutton, 1964.

Wicker, Ireene. *Young Music Makers: Boyhoods of Famous Composers.* Indianapolis: Bobbs-Merrill, 1961.

Wilder, Laura Ingalls. *The Laura Ingalls Wilder Song Book.* New York: Harper and Row, 1968.

Woodford, Peggy. *Mozart.* New York: Henry Z. Walck, 1966.

Young, Patricia. *Great Performers.* New York: Henry Z. Walck, 1967.

APPENDIX I

SPECIAL MUSIC MATERIALS
FOR EXCEPTIONAL CHILDREN

(Addresses for the sources of these materials can be found in Appendix L)

Alvin, Juliette. *Music for the Handicapped Child.* London, Eng.: Oxford University Press, 1965.

Antey, John. *Sing and Learn.* New York: John Day, 1965. Includes teaching instructions for retarded children.

Basic Songs for Exceptional Children, Basic Enrichment Songs for Exceptional Children, and *Basic Training in Auditory Perception.* Long Island, N.Y.: Concept Records.

Best Records and Books for Exceptional Children (illustrated brochure). Los Angeles: Children's Music Center.

Betten, Bette, and Manning, Ardelle. *Basic Music for Retarded Children.* Ardelle Manning Publications, P.O. Box 125, Palo Alto, Calif.

Braun, Elsie. *Music for Active Children.* New York: Frederick Ungar Publishing, 1957.

Cole, Frances. *Songs for Children with Special Needs.* Glendale, Calif.: Bowmar Publishing.

Coleman, Satis N. et al. *Music for Exceptional Children.* Evanston, Ill.: Summy-Birchard Publishing, 1964.

The Council for Exceptional Children (CEC) supplies cassettes on teaching the exceptional child, among them:
Teacher Training in Special Education
Career Education—Its Nature and Need
The Right to Education
Leadership Training Institute for Special Education

Dobbs, J. P. B. *The Slow Learner and Music: A Handbook for Teachers.* New York: Oxford University Press, 1966.

Gillies, Emily. *Creative Dramatics for All Children.* Washington, D.C.: Association for Childhood Education, 1973. Suggestions for creative drama activities in the classroom, with special sections devoted to creative dramatics for children who are emotionally disturbed or brain-injured or for whom English is a second language.

Ginglend, David R., and Stiles, Winifred E. *Music Activities for Retarded Children.* Nashville: Abingdon Press, 1965.

Library of Congress. Free music instruction on many instruments and musical notes in forms other than normal print for visually and physically handicapped students.

Music for the Mentally Retarded Child, Vol. VI of "Current Issues in Music Education." Columbus, Ohio: The Ohio State University. One of the reports of the 1973 Current Issues in Music Education Symposium. This can be ordered from Music Education Division, The Ohio State University, Columbus, Ohio 43210.

Nordhoff, Paul, and Robbins, Clive. *Therapy in Music for Handicapped Children.* New York: St. Martin's Press, 1972.

The Role of Music in the Special Education of Handicapped Children. Albany, N.Y.: Publications Distribution Unit, State Education Department, 1971.

Syphers, Dorothy F. *Gifted and Talented Children: Practical Programming for Teachers and Principals.* Arlington, Va.: The Council for Exceptional Children.

APPENDIX J

ETHNIC MUSIC MATERIALS

(Addresses for the sources of these materials can be found in Appendix L)

1. General
2. The Americas:

> Afro-American
> American Indian
> Latin American
> Other American Folk Music

3. Africa
4. Asia
5. Europe
6. Oceania (Hawaii and Australia)

Some of the most delightful ethnic materials are found in the Basic Series of Music Books (Appendix A, page 295). *Also see* Appendix D for Folk and Square Dances (page 310).

GENERAL

Music in World Cultures, a bibliography and discography of the eight regions of the world, is to be found in the October 1972 issue of the *Music Educators Journal,* published by the Music Educators National Conference. Also included is a highly selective filmography and glossary. Articles on each region, bound-in sound-sheets, and a section on ethnic musics in education, covering instruction from the elementary school level through the university level, are also included.

Babin, Stanley, and Babin, Resa. *Dance Around the World.* New York: MCA Music.

Buchner, Alexander. *Folk Music Instruments of the World.* New York: Crown Publishers.

Folk Dance Costume Folios. Hollywood, Calif.: Highland Music Co.

Folk Dances from 'Round the World (records and instruction book). Hollywood, Calif.: Highland Music Co. (*Also see* Appendix D for other titles.)

Folkways Records. An excellent source of ethnic materials.

Haywood, Charles. *Folk Songs of the World.* New York: John Day.

Kasschau, Howard. *Folk Tune Time.* New York: Sam Fox Publishing.

Kaufman, William I. *UNICEF Book of Children's Songs.* Harrisburg, Pa.: Stackpole Books.

Monitor Recordings, Inc. Their library includes many folk and ethnic albums.

Niles, John Jacob, and Smith, Helen Louise. *Folk Ballads for Young Actors.* New York: Holt, Rinehart and Winston, 1962.

———. *Folk Carols for Young Actors.* New York: Holt, Rinehart and Winston, 1962.

Recording Laboratory, Music Division, Library of Congress, Washington, D.C. 20540. Albums issued by the Archive of Folk Song of the Library of Congress, such as *Music of Morocco*, edited by Paul Bowles.

Thomas, Edith L. *The Whole World Singing.* New York: Friendship Press.

Tobitt, Janet E. *The Yellow Book of Singing Games and Dances from around the World.* Evanston, Ill.: Summy-Birchard Publishing, 1960. (*Also see* Appendix D for other titles.)

THE AMERICAS

Afro-American

Afro-American Music, Its Heritage (film). Hollywood, Calif.: Communications Group West.

Black Music Calendar, Black Music Center, School of Music, Indiana University, Bloomington, Ind. 47401.

Cook, Bruce. *Listen to the Blues.* New York: Charles Scribner's Sons, 1973.

Courlander, Harold. *Negro Folk Music, U.S.A.* New York: Columbia University Press.

Emery, Lynne Fauley. *Black Dance in the United States from 1679 to 1970.* Palo Alto, Calif.: National Press Books, 1972.

Goddard, Tom. *Pops Foster: The Autobiography of a New Orleans Jazzman.* Berkeley, Calif.: University of California Press, 1971.

Haas, Robert Bartlett. *William Grant Still, and the Fusion of Cultures in American Music.* Los Angeles: Black Sparrow Press, 1972.

Hentoff, Nat, and McCarthy, Albert (editors). *Jazz.* New York: Holt, Rinehart and Winston, 1959.

Jones, Bessie, and Hawes, Bess Lomax. *Step It Down.* New York: Harper & Row, Publishers, 1972. Games, plays, songs, and stories from the Afro-American heritage.

Landeck, Beatrice. *Echoes of Africa in Folk Songs of the Americas*, Revised. New York: David McKay.

Lovell, John, Jr. *Black Song: The Forge and the Flame.* New York: Macmillan, 1972.

"Music of Black Americans," bibliography, *Music Educators Journal* (February 1974): 82.

Nordhoff, Paul. *Spirituals for Children to Sing and Play.* Bryn Mawr, Pa.: Theodore Presser Co.

Roach, Hildred. *Black American Music: Past and Present.* Boston: Crescendo Publishing Co. An illustrated text containing a chronological list of black composers and their publishers, a discography, and a selective bibliography.

Roberts, John Storm. *Black Music in Two Worlds.* New York: Praeger Publishers, 1972.

Schafer, William J. *Rock Music: Where It's Been, What It Means, Where It's Going.* Minneapolis: Augsburg Publishing House, 1972.

Shapiro, Nat, and Hentoff, Nat. *The Jazz Makers.* New York: Holt, Rinehart and Winston, 1957.

Songs of Black America (filmstrip/records). Chicago: Society for Visual Education.

Southern, Eileen. *The Music of Black Americans.* New York: W. W. Norton & Co., Inc., 1970.

Standifer, James A., and Reeder, Barbara. *Source Book of African and Afro-American Materials for Music Educators.* Stock No. 321-10460-MENC Publication Sales, 1972.

Stickley, Eileen (arranger). *10 Negro Spirituals* (unison voices and guitar). New York: Oxford University Press.

Wehrmann, Henri. *Creole Songs of the Deep South.* New Orleans: Philip Werlien.

American Indian

American Indians—Yesterday and Today. Elgin, Ill.: David C. Cook Publishing Company.

Dawley, Muriel, and McLaughlin, Roberta. *North American Indian Songs.* Hollywood, Calif.: Highland Music, 1965.

Densmore, Frances. *The Music of the North American Indians.* New York: DaCapo Press, Inc.

Discovering American Indian Music. Santa Monica, Calif.: BFA Educational Media.

Hofmann, Charles. *American Indians Sing.* New York: John Day Co. The culture of fourteen Indian nations is revealed through their music, dance, and ceremonials. A recording is available.

Krone, Beatrice Perham, and Krone, Max. *Songs and Stories of the American Indians.* Park Ridge, Ill.: Neil A. Kjos.

The Legend of Twelve Moons, an audiovisual program tracing the history of the American Indian. Port Chester, N.Y.: Michael Brent Publications, Inc.

Literature on the American Indian: 1970 and 1971. San Francisco: Indian Historical Press.

Oklahoma Indian Chants for the Classroom, record with booklet on tribal culture, song analyses, and dance diagrams. Santa Fe, N.M.: Southwest Music Publications.

Latin American

Barlow, Betty M., and Barnett, Harriet. *Hola! Vamos a Cantar* (Teacher's Edition and Student's Edition available, each with recording). Delaware Water Gap, Pa.: Shawnee Press, Inc.

DeCesare, Ruth. *Latin-American Game Songs.* New York: Mills Music, 1959.

———. *Songs for Spanish Class.* New York: Mills Music, 1959.

Guarneiri, Anita. *Brazilian Songs for Children* (recording available). Far Rockaway, N.Y.: Peripole Publishing.

Jacovetti, Raymond N. *Escuchar y Cantar* (Teacher's Guide, Student's Booklet, and album of recordings available). New York: Holt, Rinehart and Winston, 1965.

Johnston, Hugh, and Johnston, Suzanne. *Viva México; A Cultural Portrait.* New York: McGraw-Hill Films.

Krone, Beatrice Perham, and Krone, Max. *Cantemos en Español,* Books 1 and 2 (Teacher's Book and Student's Book available, also recordings). Park Ridge, Ill.: Neil A. Kjos.

———. *Cantemos Niños* (recording available). Park Ridge, Ill.: Neil A. Kjos.

———. *Folksongs of Brazil.* Park Ridge, Ill.: Neil A. Kjos.

———. *Folksongs of Our Inter-Americana Southern Neighbors.* Park Ridge, Ill.: Neil A. Kjos.

———. *Mexican Folksongs.* Park Ridge, Ill.: Neil A. Kjos.

———. *Spanish and Latin-American Songs.* Park Ridge, Ill.: Neil A. Kjos, 1942.

Krugman, Lillian D., and Ludwig, Alice Jeanne. *Little Calypsos.* New York: Carl Van Roy, 1955.

McLaughlin, Roberta, and Stanchfield, Bessie Mae. *Cancióncitas.* Minneapolis: Schmitt, Hall and McCreary.

Mexican-American Heritage, Its Heritage (film). Hollywood, Calif.: Communications Group West.

Perry, Sylvia, and Krugman, Lillian D. *Song Tales of the West Indies.* New York: Carl Van Roy, 1964.

Prieto, Mariana. *Play It in Spanish: Spanish Games and Folk Songs for Children.* New York: John Day Co., 1973.

Richter, Ada. *Sing in Spanish with Pedro and María.* Bryn Mawr, Pa.: Theodore Presser Co.

Westervelt, Marie. *Christmas in Mexico.* Bryn Mawr, Pa.: Oliver Ditson.

Wood, Lucille F., and McLaughlin, Roberta. *Children's Songs of Mexico.* Hollywood, Calif.: Highland Music, 1965.

Yurchenco, Henrietta (editor). *A Fiesta of Folk Songs from Spain and Latin America.* New York: G. P. Putnam's, 1967.

Other American Folk Music

Bacon, Denise. *Two-Part American Folk Songs.* Wellesley, Mass.: Kodály Musical Training Institute, Inc.

Brand, Oscar. *Songs of '76: A Folksinger's History of the Revolution.* New York: M. Evans & Co., Inc., 1972.

Carmer, Carl. *Twenty-Nine Stories and Songs of Our Country's Growing.* New York: Alfred A. Knopf.

Chase, Richard. *American Folk Tales and Songs.* New York: Signet Key Books.

Christiansen, Dr., and Christiansen, Mrs. N. W. *A Trip through Yellowstone National Park.* Melville, N.Y.: Belwin-Mills.

Darion, Joe, and Krasnow, Hecky. *Sing a Song of America* (recording available). New York: Sam Fox Publishing.

DeCesare, Ruth. *They Came Singing* (recording available). New York: Sam Fox Publishing.

Ehret, Walter. *International Book of Christmas Carols.* Englewood Cliffs, N.J.: Prentice-Hall, 1963.

Felton, H. W. *Cowboy Jamboree: Western Songs and Lore.* New York: Alfred A. Knopf, 1951.

Hausman, Ruth. *Sing and Dance with the Pennsylvania Dutch.* New York: Edward B. Marks Music, 1953.

Hitchcock, H. Wiley. *Earlier American Music.* New York: Da Capo Press, Inc.

Lawless, Ray N. *Folksingers and Folksongs in America.* New York: Meredith Press, 1965.

Lomax, Alan (editor). *The Folk Songs of North America.* Garden City, N.Y.: Doubleday, 1960.

———. *The Penguin Book of American Folk Songs.* Baltimore: Penguin Books, 1965.

Lomax, John A., and Lomax, Alan. *American Ballads and Folk Songs.* New York: Macmillan, 1934.

———. *Folk Song: U.S.A.* New York: Meredith Press, 1948.

Luther, Frank. *Americans and Their Songs.* New York: Harper and Row.

Moore, Ethel, and Moore, Chauncey. *Ballads and Folk Songs of the Southwest.* Norman: University of Oklahoma Press.

Reference Sources for Information on Canadian Composers, Youth Orchestras in Canada, and Canada on Records. Toronto, Canada: The Canadian Music Centre.

Richter, Ada. Songs of My Country. Bryn Mawr, Pa.: Theodore Presser Co.

Sackett, S. J. Cowboys and the Songs They Sang. New York: William R. Scott, 1967.

Seeger, Ruth Crawford. American Folk Songs for Children in Home, School, and Nursery School. Garden City, N.Y.: Doubleday, 1948.

———. American Folk Songs for Christmas. Garden City, N.Y.: Doubleday.

Stoutamire, Albert. Music of the Old South: Colony to Confederacy. Cranbury, N.J.: Fairleigh Dickinson University Press, 1972.

Tobitt, Janet E. The Red Book of Singing Games and Dances from the Americas. Evanston, Ill.: Summy-Birchard Publishing, 1960. (Also see Appendix D for other titles.)

Wakefield, Eleanor. Folk Dancing in America. New York: J. Lowell Pratt, 1966. (Also see Appendix D for other titles.)

Warner, James A. Songs That Made America. New York: Grossman Publishers, 1972.

Westervelt, Marie. The American Traveler (song collection). Bryn Mawr, Pa.: Oliver Ditson.

———. Mardi Gras (song collection). Bryn Mawr, Pa.: Oliver Ditson.

———. Rodeo (song collection). Bryn Mawr, Pa.: Oliver Ditson.

Wheeler, Opal. Sing for America (song collection). New York: E. P. Dutton.

Wilder, Alec. American Popular Songs: The Great Innovators, 1900-1950. New York: Oxford University Press, 1972.

AFRICA

African Story-Songs. Seattle: University of Washington Press.

Afro Request: Ghana, Nigeria, Biafra. New Rochelle, N.Y.: Request Records.

Beal, Newton. Pygmies Are People. Far Rockaway, N.Y.: Peripole Publishing.

Dietz, Betty Warner, and Olatunji, Michael Babatunde. Musical Instruments of Africa: Their Nature, Use and Place in the Life of a Deeply Musical People (recording included). New York: John Day.

Folk Songs of South Africa. Chicago: Society for Visual Education.

McLaughlin, Roberta. Folk Songs of Africa. Hollywood, Calif.: Highland Music, 1965.

Marais, Josef. Songs from the Veld. New York: G. Schirmer.

Mbira Music of Rhodesia (stereo LP with accompanying booklet of teaching aids). Seattle: University of Washington Press.

Monsour, Sally, and Land, Lois Rhea. Songs of the Middle East. Marquette, Mich.: Mark Foster Publishing Co.

ASIA

The American Society for Eastern Arts (ASEA). Records of Eastern Asian music, with explanatory notes and photographic documentation.

Bayanihan Series (Music of the Philippines). Rochester, N.Y.: Bee Cross-Media, Inc.

Berger, Donald Paul. *Folksongs of Japanese Children.* Rutland, Vt.: Charles E. Tuttle.

Danielou, Alain. *Northern Indian Music.* New York: Frederick A. Praeger, Publisher. (Published as *The Ragas of Northern Indian Music* by Barrie & Rockliff, London.)

Dietz, Betty Warner, and Park, Thomas Choonbai. *Folk Songs of China, Japan, Korea* (recording included). New York: John Day, 1964.

Holroyde, Peggy. *The Music of India.* New York: Frederick A. Praeger, Publisher, 1972.

Krishnaswami, S. *Musical Instruments of India.* Delhi, India: Publications Division, Indian Ministry of Information and Broadcasting, 1967.

Opera Chinois (Peking Opera Company). San Francisco: American Society for Eastern Arts.

Teaching About Asia. San Francisco: American Society for Eastern Arts.

White, Emmons E. *Songs from Appreciating India's Music* (cassette recording). Boston: Crescendo.

White, Florence, and Akiyama, Kazuo. *Children's Songs from Japan.* New York: Edward B. Marks Music, 1961.

EUROPE

DeCesare, Ruth. *Songs for French Class.* New York: Mills Music.

———. *Songs for German Class.* New York: Mills Music.

———. *Songs for Italian Class.* New York: Mills Music.

———. *Songs for Russian Class.* New York: Mills Music.

Gray, Vera, and Offer, C. K. *Children's Songs of France.* London, Eng.: Oxford University Press, 1964.

Klinck, George A., and Klinck, Jean. *Ecouter et Chanter* (Teacher's Guide, Student's Booklet, and album of recordings available). New York: Holt, Rinehart and Winston, 1964.

Krone, Beatrice Perham, and Krone, Max. *Chantons en Francais,* Books 1 and 2 (Teacher's Book and Student's Book available, also recordings). Park Ridge, Ill.: Neil A. Kjos.

———. *Singen Wir auf Deutsch,* Books 1 and 2 (Teacher's Book and Student's Book available, also recordings). Park Ridge, Ill.: Neil A. Kjos.

———. *Songs of Norway and Denmark.* Park Ridge, Ill.: Neil A. Kjos.

_____. *Songs of Sweden and Finland.* Park Ridge, Ill.: Neil A. Kjos.

Morton, Miriam. *The Arts and the Soviet Child.* New York: The Free Press, 1972.

Regier, Don. *Folksongs of the British Isles.* Park Ridge, Ill.: Neil A. Kjos, 1965.

Spanish Music: From Popular to Concert Stage (film). Hollywood, Calif.: Communications Group West.

OCEANIA (HAWAII AND AUSTRALIA)

Anderson, Hugh. *The Story of Australian Folksong.* New York: Oak Publications.

Introduction to the Hula. Honolulu, Hawaii: Mele Loke Publishing Co.

Kelly, John M., Jr. (editor). *Folk Songs Hawaii Sings.* Rutland, Vt.: Charles E. Tuttle, 1963.

Roes, Carol. *Children's Songs from Hawaii.* Honolulu, Hawaii: Mele Loke Publishing Co.

_____. *Song Stories of Hawaii* (song folio and recording available). Honolulu, Hawaii: Mele Loke Publishing Co.

Tabor, Troy E. *Mother Goose in Hawaii.* Rutland, Vt.: Charles E. Tuttle.

APPENDIX K

KEY SIGNATURE CHARTS
AND TONAL PATTERNS

KEY SIGNATURE CHARTS

(For Use in Later Childhood
to Teach Reading—Not for Singing)

Writing syllables on charts is optional.

EXAMPLES OF TONAL
PATTERNS AND COMBINATIONS

(For Use in Middle and Later Childhood)

Place on chalkboard or flannelgraph. Do not write tonal syllables below notes. They are placed here for your help only.

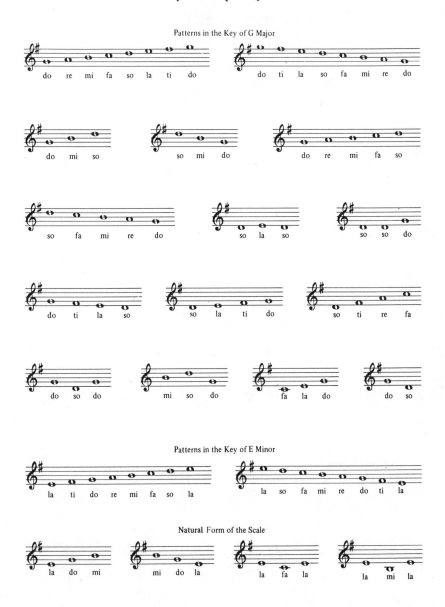

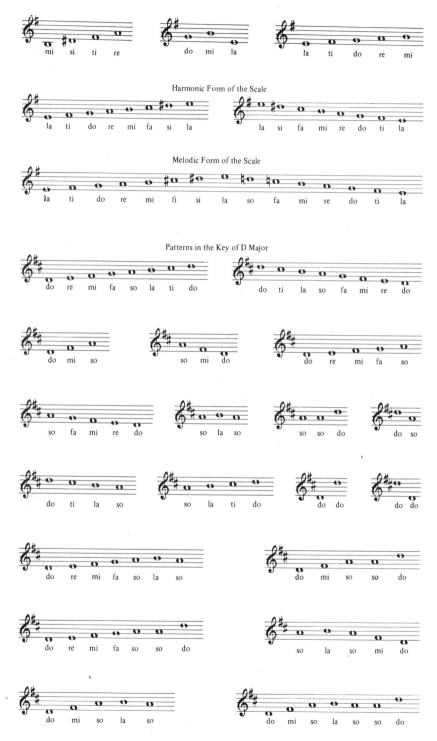

Patterns in the Key of B Minor

la ti do re mi fa so la   la so fa mi re do ti la

Natural Form of the Scale

la do mi   mi do la   la mi la   la fa la

mi fa mi re do ti la   mi si re la

Harmonic Form of the Scale

la ti do re mi fa si la   la si fa mi re do ti la

Melodic Form of the Scale

la ti do re mi fi si la so fa mi re do ti la

Patterns in the Key of F Major

do re mi fa so la ti do   do ti la so fa mi re do

do mi so   so mi do   do re mi fa so

so fa mi re do   so la so   so so do   do so

Patterns in the Key of D Minor

Harmonic Form of the Scale

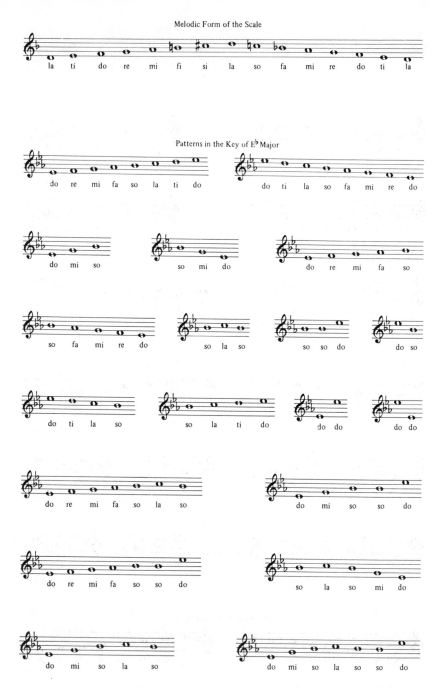

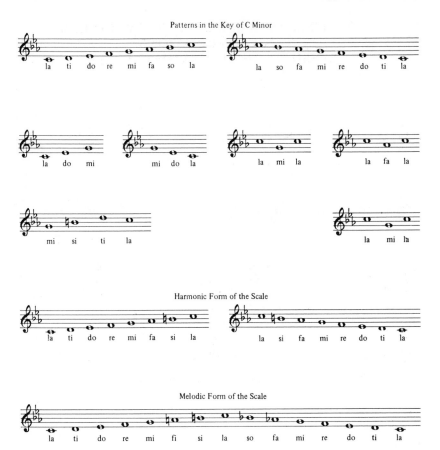

Patterns in the Key of C Minor

la ti do re mi fa so la
la so fa mi re do ti la

la do mi
mi do la
la mi la
la fa la

mi si ti la
la mi la

Harmonic Form of the Scale

la ti do re mi fa si la
la si fa mi re do ti la

Melodic Form of the Scale

la ti do re mi fi si la so fa mi re do ti la

EXAMPLES OF BASIC SYLLABLE PATTERNS
AND COMBINATIONS
BASED ON THE PENTATONIC SCALE

Key of G

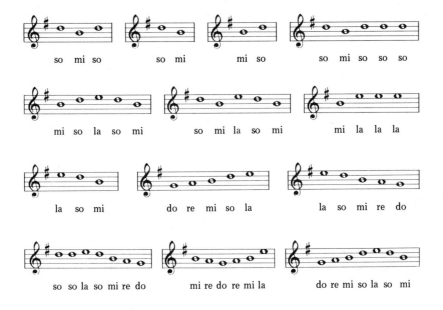

APPENDIX L

ADDRESSES OF MUSIC PUBLISHERS AND SUPPLIERS

Abingdon Press, 201 Eighth Ave., S., Nashville, Tenn. 37202. Octavo music, music supplies, cassettes, filmstrips, and recordings.

Academic Church and Choir Gowns Manufacturing Company, 1125 N. Highland Ave., Hollywood, Calif. 90038. Choir gowns and accessories.

Addison-Wesley Publishing Company, Sand Hill Road, Menlo Park, Calif. 94205. College level text material for music education courses. Also, new Basic Series *The Comprehensive Musicianship Program.*

AIMS Instructional Media Services, Inc., P.O. Box 1010, Hollywood, Calif. 90026. Producer of teaching films.

Alfred Publishing Co., Inc., 75 Channel Drive, Port Washington, N.Y. 11050. Publisher of books by Grace C. Nash, using techniques of Orff, Kodály, and Laban. Choral music in all categories.

Allyn and Bacon, Inc., 470 Atlantic Ave., Boston, Mass. 02210; 695 Miami Circle, N.E., Atlanta, Ga. 30324; Belmont Park, Belmont, Calif. 94002; Rockleigh Industrial Park, Rockleigh, N.J. 07647. Textbooks and teachers' aids. Basic Music Series *This Is Music for Today.*

The American Association of Colleges for Teacher Education (AACTE), 1 Dupont Circle, N.W., Washington, D.C. 20036.

American Book Company, 430 West 33rd St., New York, N.Y. 10001. Music textbooks, recordings, and other educational materials. Basic Series *New Dimensions in Music.*

American Music Conference (AMC), 75 E. Wacker Drive, Chicago, Ill. 60601. Representative of many music companies, especially in the instrumental field. Source of research and assistance in maintaining music in the schools.

American Orff Schulwerk Association (*See* Mrs. Ruth Pollack Hamm).

The American Record Guide, Inc., P.O. Box 319, Radio City Station, New York, N.Y. 10019.

American Society for Eastern Arts, 425 Bush St., San Francisco, Calif. 94108. Source of multimedia material, resources, and reference materials on Eastern Arts.

Angel Records (*See* Capitol Records).

Associated Music Publishers, Inc., 609 Fifth Ave., New York, N.Y. 10017. Carl Orff educational publications, choral and piano music, miniature scores (subsidiary of G. Schirmer).

Association for Supervision and Curriculum Development (ASCD), 1201 Sixteenth St., N.W., Washington, D.C. 20036.

Augsburg Publishing House, 426 S. Fifth St., Minneapolis, Minn. 55415; 57 E. Main St., Columbus, Ohio 43215; 2001 Third Ave., Seattle, Wash. 98121. Publishers of sacred choral, vocal, and organ music.

Bailey-Film Associates, 11559 Santa Monica Blvd., Los Angeles, Calif. 90025. Distributors of records and films.

William L. Bauhan Publisher, Dublin, N.H. 03444. Publisher of *Quick Tunes and Good Times.*

Mel Bay Publications, Inc., 107 W. Jefferson Ave., Kirkwood, Mo. 63122. Guitar class method. Music for the recorder.

Bee Cross-Media, Inc., 36 Dogwood Glen, Rochester, N.Y. 14625. Distributor of multimedia ethnic material.

Bell & Howell, Old Mansfield Rd., Wooster, Ohio 44691. Producers of MUSIcache, basic music library of standard repertoire from 300 major composers.

Belwin-Mills Publishing Corp., Melville, N.Y. 11746. Publishers of *Listen There's Music,* graded elementary music education series, choral music, and song collections. Music representative for J. Fischer & Bro., H. W. Gray Co., Franco Colombo, Halbe, Adler, Jobete, Music Minus One, Schott, Novello, Ricordi, and leading book publishers.

BFA Educational Media, 2211 Michigan Ave., Santa Monica, Calif. 90404. Multimedia materials.

The Big Three Music Corporation (Robbins-Feist-Miller), 1775 Broadway, Suite 715, New York, N.Y. 10019. Vast catalogues of more than twenty-five music publishers.

Billboard Publishing Company, Great Barrington, Mass. 01230.

Billboard Publishing Company, 2160 Patterson St., Cincinnati, Ohio 45214.

Boosey and Hawkes, Inc., Oceanside, N.Y. 11572. Specialists in the contemporary idiom.

Boston Music Company, 116 Boylston St., Boston, Mass. 02116. Publishers and retailers of educational music for kindergarten, nursery schools, and elementary grades; recordings and teaching aids.

Bourne Company, 136 W. 52nd St., New York, N.Y. 10019. Publishers of all types of school music; also *Sound Spectrum Series* of recordings.

Stanley Bowmar Co., Inc., 4 Broadway, Valhalla, N.Y. 10595. Folk songs and dances, rhythms, singing games, square and social dances.

Bowmar Publishing Corporation, 622 Rodier Dr., Glendale, Calif. 91201. Records, books, filmstrips, cassettes, and multimedia materials.

Michael Brent Publications, Inc., 70 Winding Rd., Port Chester, N.Y. 10573.

Broude Brothers Limited, 225 West 57th St., New York, N.Y. 10019. Serves all music needs, including Orchestra Department, Choral Department, and Musicology Department.

Prof. Arnold Burkhart, Ball State University, Muncie, Ind. 47306.

Canyon Press, Inc., P.O. Box 1235, Cincinnati, Ohio 45201. Multimedia educational publications; instructional material for lab Electrosystems; Juilliard Repertory; choral material.

Capitol Records, Hollywood and Vine, Hollywood, Calif. 90028. Distributors of Capitol and Angel records.

Carabo-Cone Method Center, Carnegie Hall Bldg., Suite 862, New York, N.Y. 10019. Preacademic and preinstrumental program for preschool and elementary grades. Also a useful course for children with learning disabilities.

Chappell and Company, Inc., 609 Fifth Ave., New York, N.Y. 10017. Publishers of choral, piano, band, and orchestra music.

Children's Music Center, Inc., 5373 West Pico Blvd., Los Angeles, Calif. 90019. Recommended multimedia music materials for all ages. Experienced staff of trained consultants.

M. M. Cole Publishing Co., 251 East Grand, Chicago, Ill. 60601. Publisher of guitar methods.

Collegiate Cap and Gown Company, 1000 N. Market St., Champaign, Ill. 61820. Choir robes and accessories.

Columbia Records, Educational Dept., 51 W. 52nd St., New York, N.Y. 10019. Recordings of instrumental stories, such as *Tubby, the Tuba,* children's song albums, Benjamin Britten's *The Young Person's Guide to the Orchestra,* and a general catalogue of standard works.

Communications Group West, 6335 Homewood Ave., Suite 204, Hollywood, Calif. 90028. Producer and distributor of ethnic materials.

Concept Records, P.O. Box 524, Bellmore, L. I., N.Y. 11710.

Concordia Publishing House, 3558 S. Jefferson Ave., St. Louis, Mo. 63118. Publishers of sacred and educational music; also *The Concordia Music Education Series,* a basic graded curriculum for Christian schools.

Conn Corporation, 1101 E. Beardsley, Elkhart, Ind. 46514. Activity calendars, music aptitude tests, awards, music room posters, picture albums of famous musicians and music educators, song flutes, rhythm instruments, xylophones, cutout books of band and orchestral instruments.

The Continental Press, Inc., 520 E. Bainbridge St., Elizabethtown, Pa. 17022. Elementary reading and writing music programs based on the Kodály method. Recorder materials and liquid duplicating masters for elementary choruses.

Cooperative Recreation Service, Publishing Dept., Radnor Rd., Delaware, Ohio 43015. Inexpensive booklets for class use and recreational singing; 2,000 songs of 65 nations used by youth agencies everywhere for planning their own special editions.

The Council for Exceptional Children (CEC), 1411 South Jefferson Davis Highway, Arlington, Va. 22202.

Crescendo Publishers, 48-50 Melrose St., Boston, Mass. 02116. Music staff-writer; text, library, and reference books, with emphasis on humanities and ethnic music.

Crest Records, Inc., 220 Broadway, Huntington Station, New York, N.Y. 11746. Custom record pressing and tape duplication from tapes supplied by schools and other organizations; producers of Golden Crest records featuring famous artists.

The John Day Co., 257 Park Ave. S., New York, N.Y. 10010. Publisher of a variety of books and music, particularly for the elementary grades.

DCA Action Aides, 4865 Stenton Ave., Philadelphia, Pa. 19144. Color transparencies with instructional recordings.

Decca Records, 445 Park Ave., New York, N.Y. 10022. Song stories and general catalogue of standard works.

DeMoulin Brothers and Company, 1073 South Fourth St., Greenville, Ill. 62246. Choral robes and accessories.

Oliver Ditson (*See* Theodore Presser Company).

Edith Faunt, 4190 West Eleventh Ave., Vancouver 8, British Columbia, Canada. The Staff-Syllable Method.

Educational Audio-Visual, Inc., 89 Marble Ave., Pleasantville, N.Y. 10570. Large selection of music education materials, including music appreciation, sing-a-long, rhythms, dance, acoustical and biographical recordings, as well as standard classics.

Educational Insights, Inc., Dept. M-39, 211 S. Hindry Ave., Inglewood, Calif. 90301. Creative activities packets with music/art-oriented games and activities.

Educational Media Press, Box 1852, Costa Mesa, Calif. 92626. Suppliers of book *How to Write Learning Activity Packages for Music Education* by Joseph W. Landon.

Educational Productions, Inc., P.O. Box 12138, Atlanta, Ga. 30305. Publisher of *Guitar Magic* and *Keyboard Magic*.

Educational Record Sales, 157 Chambers St., New York, N.Y. 10007. Recordings for classroom or home use.

Educom, Ltd., Box 388, Dept. J, Mount Kisko, N.Y. 10549. Music transparencies with prepared transparency units on symphonic form, opera, folk music, Christmas carols, and theory.

Electronic Music Laboratories, Inc., P.O. Box H, Vernon, Conn. 06066. Synthesizers for educational institutions and professional studios.

Elektra Records, 1855 Broadway, New York, N.Y. 10019. Many ethnic selections and folk songs.

Elkan-Vogel Company, Inc., 1712 Sansom St., Philadelphia, Pa. 19103. Publishers of all kinds of educational materials.

Epic Records (*See* Columbia Records).

Estamae, P.O. Box 1507, Pueblo, Colo. 81002. Rhythm records.

Exploring the Arts, Dept. ME1, P.O. Box 139, Needham, Mass. 02192. Publishers of *Exploring the Arts*, multimedia material.

Faunt (*See* Edith Faunt).

Fearon Publishers/Lear Siegler, Inc., 6 Davis Drive, Belmont, Calif. 94002. *Threshold to Music*, a five-year program for elementary grades based on the educational philosophy of Zoltán Kodály. Publishers of materials by Mary Helen Richards.

Carl Fischer, Inc., 62 Cooper Square, New York, N.Y. 10003. Publishers of all types of music; also flash cards, posters, musical puzzles and games,

Kwalwasser-Dykema Aptitude Tests, music dictionaries, and choral collections by Irvin Cooper, Marguerite Hood, Hazel Gertrude Kinscella, Mae Nightingale, and others.

J. Fischer and Bro., Harristown Rd., Glen Rock, N.J. 07452. Publishers of choral, piano, and organ music, operettas, and cantatas; also specialists in sacred music.

H. T. Fitzsimons Company, Inc., 615 N. LaSalle St., Chicago, Ill. 60610. Publishers of music materials, operettas, and cantatas.

Harold Flammer, Inc., 251 W. 19th St., New York, N.Y. 10011. Publishers of choral music, piano and organ music, and bell choir music.

Folk Harp Journal, Mt. Laguna, Calif. 92048. Magazine devoted to varieties of harps and harp literature.

Folkcraft Records, 1159 Broad St., Newark, N.J. 07114. Recordings for use in elementary schools.

Folkways Records, 701 Seventh Ave., New York, N.Y. 10036. A large catalogue of ethnic, educational, and folk music.

Follett Publishing Company, Educational Division, 1010 West Washington Blvd., Chicago, Ill. 60607. Publishers of music texts with recordings, and professional texts. Basic Series *Discovering Music Together.*

The Footnote, Box 5145, FDR Station, New York, N.Y. 10022. Source for hard-to-find music books.

Sam Fox Publishing Company, Inc., 1841 Broadway, New York, N.Y. 10023. Publishers of music education materials, including playlets, operettas, and rhythm band materials. 16-mm educational films for elementary grades.

Frank Music Corporation/Boston Music Company/Music Theatre International, 116 Boylston St., Boston, Mass. 02116. Choral music, studies, and textbooks; from Renaissance to show tunes and pop-rock-jazz.

Fruhauf Uniforms, Inc., 2938 South Minneapolis, Wichita, Kans. 67216. Band uniforms and accessories.

Galaxy Music Corporation, 2121 Broadway, New York, N.Y. 10023. Publishers of choral, band, and piano music.

General Learning Press (*See* Silver Burdett).

Ginn and Company, 191 Spring St., Lexington, Mass. 02173; 125 Second Ave., Waltham, Mass. 02154; 717 Miami Circle, N.E., Atlanta, Ga. 30324; 450 W. Algonquin Rd., Arlington Heights, Ill. 60005; 1510 Young St., Dallas, Tex. 75229; 250 Hanover St., Palo Alto, Calif. 94304. Texts, recordings, manuals, teachers' editions. Basic Music series *The Magic of Music.*

Golden Records (*See* Simon and Schuster).

Greystone Corporation, Institutional Div., 100 Sixth Ave., New York, N.Y. 10019. Library includes Young People's Records, Children's Record Guild, American Recording Society, and other recorded material for educational purposes.

Mrs. Ruth Pollack Hamm, Executive Secretary, American Orff Schulwerk Association, P.O. Box 18495, Cleveland Heights, Ohio 44118.

Hargail Music, Inc., 157 W. 57th St., New York, N.Y. 10019. Texts and teaching material based on the concepts of Orff and Kodály. Harvard, Corelli, and Purcell recorders.

Highland Music Company, 1311 N. Highland Ave., Hollywood, Calif. 90028. Distributors of *Library of Basic Activities, Library of Folk Dances from Round the World, Library of Music for Dance, Capricorn Records* (music for recorders), and miscellaneous phonograph albums for creative teaching.

M. Hohner, Inc., Andrews Rd., Hicksville, L.I., N.Y. 11802. Manufacturers of several models of the "Melodica" as well as harmonicas, accordians, and organs; electronic keyboards; Sonor Orff percussion and mallet instruments; Contessa guitars.

Holt, Rinehart and Winston, Inc., 383 Madison Ave., New York, N.Y. 10017. Elementary music textbooks. Basic series *Exploring Music.*

Hughes Co., 8665 W. 13th Ave., Denver, Colo. 80215. Kits for dulcimers, Irish harps, balalaikas, lyres, guitars, and kalimbas—many simple enough for children to build.

Institute for Development of Educational Activities, Inc. (I/D/E/A), P.O. Box 629, Far Hills Branch, Dayton, Ohio 45479. Publisher of reviews of current literature and distributor of training films and tapes.

International Music Council, UNESCO House, Paris, France.

International Telecomm Inc., McCormick Rd. and Schilling Circle, Hunt Valley, Md. 21031. Ethnic recordings.

Jam Handy Corp., 2821 E. Grand Blvd., Detroit, Mich. 48211. Color films of the stories of great masterpieces, composers, etc., with related recordings.

Keeping Up with Music Education, 1220 Ridge Rd., Muncie, Ind. 47304. Publisher of curriculum resource bulletin with emphasis on Orff-Schulwerk materials.

Keyboard Publications, Inc., 1346 Chapel St., New Haven, Conn. 06511. Excellent multimedia materials in music and art. Publishers of *Keyboard Junior, Young Keyboard Junior, Man and His Music,* and others.

Kitching Educational (a Division of Ludwig Industries), 505 E. Shawmut, LaGrange, Ill. 60525. All kinds of melodic, rhythmic, and percussion instruments for use in the classroom. Orff instruments.

Neil A. Kjos Music Company, 525 Busse Highway, Park Ridge, Ill. 60068. Publishers of all kinds of music education materials, including the Howard Doolin method, "A New Introduction to Music."

Kodály Musical Training Institute, Inc., 525 Worcester St., Wellesley, Mass. 02181. Source of books, films, and videotapes based on the Kodály method.

William Kratt Company, 988 Johnson Place, Union, N.J. 07083. The Master Key chromatic pitch instrument and removable note selector.

Krauth and Benninghofen, Inc., 3001 Symmes Rd., Hamilton, Ohio 45012. Music stands, conductors' stands, and instrument stands.

Hal Leonard/Pointer Publications, Inc., 5525 West Blue Mound Rd., Milwaukee, Wis. 53213. The Learning Unlimited audiovisual band and guitar programs for individual and class instruction.

Library of Congress, 1291 Taylor St., N.W., Washington, D.C. 20452.

Mele Loke Publishing Company, Box 7142, Honolulu, Hawaii 96821. Music from Hawaii.

London Press Limited, Saint Paul's House, Warwick Lane, London EC4, City 5797, England. Publisher of *Music for Me.*

London Records, Inc., 539 W. 25th St., New York, N.Y. 10001. A general catalogue of standard works.

Lorraine Music Company, 23-80 48th St., Long Island City, N.Y. 11103. Multimedia catalogues.

Ludwig Industries, 1728 N. Damen Ave., Chicago, Ill. 60647. Manufacturers of percussion instruments and accessories. Kitching educational classroom instruments for use with Orff program.

Lyons Band Instrument Co., 530 Riverview Ave., Elkhart, Ind. 46514. All kinds of elementary music materials, educational recordings, awards and pins, rhythm band instruments, autoharps, bell sets, and other equipment. Distributors of Threshold and Orff teaching courses.

McGraw-Hill Book Co., 1221 Ave. of the Americas, New York, N.Y. 10020.

Macmillan Publishing Co., Inc., School Division, 100F Round St., Riverside, N.J. 08075; 539 Turtle Creek South Drive, Indianapolis, Ind. 46227; 8301 Ambassador Row, Dallas, Texas 75247; 255 Ottley Drive, N.E., Atlanta, Ga. 30324; 23 Orinda Way, Orinda, Calif. 94563; Canada: Collier-Macmillan Canada, Ltd., 1125B Leslie St., Ontario, Canada. Basic Series, *The Spectrum of Music,* with related arts.

Magnamusic-Baton, Inc., 6390 Delmar Blvd., St. Louis, Mo. 63130. Agents for Studio 49 Orff Instruments and Royal percussion. Recorder dealers for Adler, Moeck, Schott, Barenreiter, Henle, Moseler, Magnamusic, Trapp Family, Nagel, and Vienna Urtext Editions, also Neupert harpsichords and gambas.

Maher Publications, 222 W. Adams St., Chicago, Ill. 60606.

Mark Educational Recordings, Inc., 2542 Raintree Drive, N.E., Atlanta, Ga. 30345; also in Buffalo, Chicago, Denver, Miami, and Fort Worth. Specializing in "on-location" recording and manufacturing of custom record albums. Educational teaching records and audio equipment for the music teacher.

Edward B. Marks Music Corporation, 1790 Broadway, New York, N.Y. 10019. Publishers and importers of all kinds of music education materials, including operettas and collections by Elie Siegmeister, Beatrice Landeck, Lois Lenski, Walter Ehret, and others.

MCA Music, 445 Park Ave., New York, N.Y. 10022. Publications covering popular, educational, and serious music in all categories.

Mercury Record Productions, Inc., 110 W. 57th St., New York, N.Y. 10019. *The Childcraft-Playcraft* series; also a general catalogue of standard works.

Merson Musical Products, 75 Frost St., Westbury, N.Y. 11590. Univax Compac-Piano (portable).

The Metropolitan Opera Guild, Inc., 1865 Broadway, New York, N.Y. 10023.

MGM Records, 1350 Ave. of the Americas, New York, N.Y. 10019. Selections include children's sing-a-long recordings. Firm also serves as distributor for *Deutsche Grammophon* recordings.

Mills Music Co. (*See* Belwin-Mills).

Mitchell Manufacturing Company, 2744 South 34th St., Milwaukee, Wis. 53215. Stages and risers.

Monitor Recordings, Inc., 156 Fifth Ave., New York, N.Y. 10010. Library includes many folk and ethnic albums.

E. R. Moore Company, 7320 N. Caldwell, Niles (Chicago), Ill. 60648; 110 Voice Rd., Carle Place, L.I., N.Y. 11514; 1641 N. Allesandro St., Los Angeles, Calif. 90026; 1605 Boylston Ave., Seattle, Wash. 98122. Choir robes and accessories.

Multi-Media Learning Co., Box 297, Rapids City, Ill. 61278. Individualized instructional materials and games.

Music Education Group, Garden State Rd., Union, N.J. 07083. Supplier of K-8 musical instruments and accessories. Autoharps, bells, recorders, guitars, rhythm bands, melodicas, and Orff instruments. (*See* Oscar Schmidt-International).

Music Education Record Company, Box 445, Englewood, N.J. 07631. Wheeler Becket's *The Complete Orchestra*, which deals in great detail with the instruments of the orchestra and their functions.

Music Educators National Conference (Headquarters address, as of 1975), 1902 Association Drive Center for Educational Associations, Reston, Va. 22091.

The Music Journal, Inc., 1776 Broadway, New York, N.Y. 10019.

Musitronic, Inc., 1826 So. Cedar St., Owatonna, Minn. 55060. Musitronic Learning System consists of a portable group keyboard system designed to meet music education trends.

National Association for Gifted Children (NAGC), 8080 Springvalley Drive, Cincinnati, Ohio 45236. Publisher of *The Gifted Child Quarterly*.

National Association of Music Merchants (NAMM), Suite 3320, 35 East Wacker Drive, Chicago, Ill. 60601.

National Audio-Visual Association (NAVA), 3150 Spring St., Fairfax, Va. 22030. Publisher of *National Audio-Visual Equipment Directory*.

National Catholic Music Educators Association, 620 Michigan Ave., N.E., Washington, D.C. 20017.

National Federation of Music Clubs, Studio 337, Day Bldg., Worcester, Mass. 01608.

National Instructional Television Center, Box A, Bloomington, Ind. 47401. Publisher of materials prepared by the Agency for Instructional Television (AIT), including the *Guide Book* listing available courses, subject levels, etc.

National Keyboard Arts Associates, University Park, Box 2236, Princeton, N.J. 08540. A structured approach to music literacy, teaching elementary students to read and sing standard notation at sight and to play what they sing.

The National Music Council of the Philippines, 1580 Taft Ave., Manila, Philippines. Papers on Philippine music.

National Music Publishers Association, Inc., 110 E. 59th St., New York, N.Y. 10022. Provides information to music educators about the field of publishing in all its ramifications.

National Record Plan, 28 West 25th St., New York, N.Y. 10010. Distributor of phonograph records, reel-to-reel, eight-track, and cassette tapes to schools and libraries from Schwann and Harrison catalogs.

W. W. Norton & Co., Inc., 500 Fifth Ave., New York, N.Y. 10036.

Organization of American Kodály Educators, c/o Christine Kunko, School of Music, Duquesne University, Pittsburgh, Pa. 15219.

Oxford Films, Inc., 1136 N. Las Palmas Ave., Los Angeles, Calif. 90038.

Oxford University Press, Inc., 200 Madison Ave., New York, N.Y. 10016. Books and music for schools, including folk song materials for sight reading.

Parker Publishing Company, Inc., West Nyack, N.Y. 10994. Books on music and education. Brochures available.

J. W. Pepper and Son, Inc., 231 N. Third St., Philadelphia, Pa. 19106. Supplier and retailer of music of all publishers. Outlets in Atlanta, Ga., and Troy, Mich.

Peripole (See The World of Peripole).

Pioneer Music Press, 975 South West Temple, Salt Lake City, Utah 84101. Songs for preschool, kindergarten, and primary grades by Moiselle Renstrom; also the *Festival Series* by Lorin F. Wheelwright.

Pioneer Record Sales, Inc. (See Folkways Records).

Plymouth Music Company, Inc., 17 W. 60th St., New York, N.Y. 10023. Choral music by Don Craig, Meredith Willson, Don Large, Walter Ehret, and others.

Pointer Publications (See Hal Leonard).

Pop Hits, 3149 Southern, Memphis, Tenn. 38111. *Pop Hit Listening Guide*, monthly guide with teacher's supplement. Permission given for unlimited copying. Monthly recording.

Prentice-Hall, Inc., Route 9W, Englewood Cliffs, N.J. 07632; 70 Fifth Ave., New York, N.Y. 10011; 884 Union Commerce Bldg., Cleveland, Ohio 44115; 222 W. Adams St., Chicago, Ill. 60606; 560 Market St., San Francisco, Calif. 94105. Music books, recordings, and professional books. Basic Series *Growing with Music*.

Theodore Presser Company, Bryn Mawr, Pa. 19010. Presser's musical instrument pictures. See Appendixes D, E, and F for published materials.

Pro-Art Publications, Inc., 469 Union Ave., Westbury, N.Y. 11590. Publishers of all kinds of choral music and kindergarten books.

Radio-Matic of America, Inc., Dept. C5, 760 Ramsey Ave., Hillside, N.J. 07205. Master II Stereo (complete mobile sound center).

Random House, 201 E. 50th St., New York, N.Y. 10022. Publisher of books on music and general education.

RCA Records, Educational Sales, 1133 Ave. of the Americas, New York, N.Y. 10036. Direct suppliers of all RCA records and educational albums.

Recorded Publications Company, 1578 Pierce Ave., Camden, N.J. 08105. Records made from your tapes.

Request Records, 66 Mechanic St., New Rochelle, N.Y. 10801. Specializing in folk music of the world.

Rhythm Band, Inc., P.O. Box 126, Fort Worth, Texas 76101. Manufacturers and distributors of elementary musical instruments including Chrom-AharP, Pianicas, Kalub Drums, Resonator Bells.

Rhythms Productions, Whitney Bldg., Box 34485, Los Angeles, Calif. 90034. Specializing in material devoted to the use of rhythm instruments and recordings designed for this purpose.

Richards Institute of Music Education and Research, 149 Corte Madera, Portola Valley, Calif. 94025. Publisher of Kodály-oriented materials.

Robbins Music Corporation (*See* The Big Three Music Corporation).

Lee Roberts Music Publications, Inc., 760 N. Bedford Rd., Bedford, N.Y. 10507. Publishers of Robert Pace Music for Piano Series, including basic piano music for the classroom textbooks.

Robert Rollins Blazers, Inc., 242 Park Ave. S., New York, N.Y. 10003. Blazers and accessories.

Rubank, Inc., 5544 W. Armstrong Ave., Chicago, Ill. 60646. Publishers of choral collections, piano methods, etc.

G. Schirmer, Inc., 609 Fifth Ave., New York, N.Y. 10017. Publishers of music of all types.

Warren Schloat Productions, Inc., 115 Tompkins Ave., Pleasantville, N.Y. 10570. 35-mm color/sound filmstrips including Folk Songs in American History, African Musical Instruments, History Through Art, and Famous Musicians at Work.

Oscar Schmidt-International, Inc., Garden State Rd., Union, N.J. 07083. Autoharps and accessories, books, and material for elementary grades. (*See* Music Education Group.)

Schmitt, Hall and McCreary Company, 527 Park Ave., Minneapolis, Minn. 55415. Publishers of choral music and educational materials, some with recordings.

Schocken Books, 200 Madison Ave., New York, N.Y. 10016. Publisher of books on music, such as *Montessori & Music.*

Scholastic Audio-Visual, 50 West 44th St., New York, N.Y. 10036. Phonograph records and cassettes covering all grade levels, such as Songs and Rhythms for Children, Jazz, Music Theory, Music Appreciation, and Folk Songs.

Schott and Company, Ltd. (*See* Associated Music Publishers).

Schulmerich Carillons, Inc., Carillon Hill, Sellersville, Pa. 18960. Schulmerich American-made, precision-tuned English type handbells.

Scientific Music Industries, Inc., 823 S. Wabash Ave., Chicago, Ill. 60605. Tone educator bells, recorders, melodicas, etc.

Scott Educational Division, 104 Westfield, Holyoke, Mass. 01040. Jam Handy brand filmstrips, picture/prints, records, and cassettes.

Selmer, Box 310, Elkhart, Ind. 48514. Dolmetsch recorders.

Shapiro, Bernstein and Company, Inc., 666 Fifth Ave., New York, N.Y. 10019. Publishers of educational and recreational music.

Shawnee Press, Inc., Delaware Water Gap, Pa. 18327. Fred Waring choral series and educational materials.

Silver Burdett, Div. of General Learning Corp., Morristown, N.J. 07960; 460 S. Northwest Highway, Park Ridge, Ill. 60068; 435 Middlefield Rd., Palo Alto, Calif. 94301; 4640 Harry Hines Blvd., Dallas, Texas 75235; 3272 Peachtree Rd., N.E., Atlanta, Ga. 30305. Texts and multimedia educational materials; materials for utilizing Kodály and Orff techniques; monthly educational program using contemporary youth music (*Pipeline*). Basic series *Making Music Your Own*.

Simon and Schuster, Inc., 630 Fifth Ave., New York, N.Y. 10020. Library includes *A Child's Introduction to the Orchestra* and other *Golden Records*.

The Society for Ethnomusicology, 210 South Main St., Ann Arbor, Mich. 48108. Publisher of *Journal of the Society for Ethnomusicology*.

Society for Visual Education (SVE), 1345 Diversey Parkway, Chicago, Ill. 60614. Distributor of multimedia material.

Sound Book Press Society, Inc., 36 Garth Rd., Scarsdale, N.Y. 10583. Lillian Baldwin's library of music selections for young people, from *Tiny Masterpieces* to *Music to Remember*. (*See* Silver Burdett.)

Southern Baptist Convention Publishers, Sunday School Board, 127 Ninth Ave., N., Nashville, Tenn. 37203.

Southern Music Publishing Company, Inc., 1619 Broadway, New York, N.Y. 10019. Publishers and importers of contemporary music and Pan American Union publications.

Southwest Music Publications, P.O. Box 4552, Santa Fe, N.M. 87501.

Strayline Products Company, Dept. A, Box 4124, Hamden, Conn. 06514. Strayline safety candles.

Summy-Birchard Publishing Company, 1834 Ridge Ave., Evanston, Ill. 60204. All types of publications in the music field, including methods and textbooks.

Targ & Dinner, Inc., 2451 N. Sacramento Ave., Chicago, Ill. 60647. Distributors of high quality bells, percussion instruments, etc.

Time-Life Records, Time-Life Bldg., 540 N. Michigan Ave., Chicago, Ill. 60611. Extensive catalogue of classical music by periods. Albums include material on the times, with pictures in color.

Tonette, 7373 N. Cicero Ave., Lincolnwood, Ill. 60646. Tonettes and tonette instruction books.

Trophy Music Company, 1278 West 9th St., Cleveland, Ohio 44113. Vibra-Bell recorders.

Twinson Company, 433 La Prenda, Los Altos, Calif. 94022. Lummi sticks, bamboo hop kit.

"Uniforms by Ostwald" Inc., Ostwald Plaza, Staten Island, N.Y. 10301. Uniforms and accessories.

United Transparencies, Inc., Dept. 9ME3, P.O. Box 688, Binghamton, N.Y. 13902. The staff, bar lines, time signatures, flats, sharps, key signatures, dynamic indications, major and minor chords for projection.

Vanguard Recording Society, Inc., 71 W. 23rd St., New York, N.Y. 10010. A general catalogue of standard works.

Carl Van Roy Company (*See* World of Peripole).

Variety, Inc., 154 W. 46th St., New York, N.Y. 10036.

Volkwein Bros., Inc., 117 Sandusky St., Pittsburgh, Pa. 15212. Secular choral music, all voice combinations.

Vox Productions, Inc., 211 E. 43rd St., New York, N.Y. 10017. *Music Master* series, presenting the composer's biography with a background of his best known works; also a general catalogue of standard works.

Wadsworth Publishing Company, 10 Davis Drive, Belmont, Calif. 94002. Books in the areas of music education, literature, skills, etc.

Walton Music Co., Inc., 17 West 60th St., New York, N.Y. 10023. Publishers of Norman Luboff's Choral Series. Compositions by contemporary composers.

The C. E. Ward Company, New London, Ohio 44851. Choral robes and accessories.

Warner Bros. Publications, Inc., 1230 Ave. of the Americas, New York, N.Y. 10020. Instrumental and vocal music—all styles, all levels. Publications include "Sesame Street," *Blueprints,* and *Living with Music.*

Weiss Products Imports and Manufacturing Co., P.O. Box 544, Skokie, Ill. 60076. Recorder flutes and musical merchandise.

Wenger Corporation, Wenger Bldg., Owatonna, Minn. 55060. Manufacturer of risers, acoustical shells, music stands, cabinets, mobile music resource centers, etc.

Westminster Recording Company, Inc., 1330 Ave. of the Americas, New York, N.Y. 10019. A general catalogue of standard works.

David Wexler and Company, 823 S. Wabash Ave., Chicago, Ill. 60605. Music-writer, Model 10 with larger notes, simple operation for school and studio use (produced by Music Print Corporation) and many other educational items. Distributor of Cordova guitars.

Willis Music Company, 7380 Industrial Rd., Florence, Ky. 41042. Dealers and publishers of many educational materials for kindergarten, nursery school, and elementary grades; also autoharps, recorders, etc.

B. F. Wood Music Company, Inc., 1619 Broadway, New York, N.Y. 10019. Choral music and collections.

World Library of Sacred Music, 2145 Central Parkway, Cincinnati, Ohio 45214. Choral music and collections.

The World of Peripole, P.O. Box 146, Lewiston Rd., Browns Mills, N.J. 08015. Manufacturers/distributors of musical instruments for education and recreation, such as drums, cymbals, songbells, resonators, recorders, and Orff instruments. Publishers/producers of related publications/recordings.

Don Wunn Musical Instruments, 313 East Burnside, Portland, Ore. 97214. Owner of CLEF HOUSE—cards, pictures, posters, glasses, musical gifts, and conversation pieces.

The Wurlitzer Company, Dekalb, Ill. 60115. Manufacturer of pianos, electric pianos, organs, The Mobile Music Learning Center, and Key/Note Visualizer.

Xerox Educational Materials, 245 Long Hill Rd., Middletown, Conn. 06457. *News Parade,* a Weekly Reader.

Yamaha International Corp., P.O. Box 54540, Los Angeles, Calif. 90054. Band instruments, drums, pianos, organs, guitars, amplifiers, combo organs, harmonicas, recorders, and audio products.

Young People's Records (*See* Greystone Corporation).

Index

A

Absolute music, 167, 168-172
A cappella style, 196
Acting out songs, 22, 130-132, 134-135, 136-137
Action songs, 138-139, 310-311
Activities:
  for developing awareness of rhythm, 156-158
  with instruments, 243-244, 279-281
  for learning intervals, 103
  for listening, 227-228
  in music reading, 121-124
  in singing, 63-65
African music, 342
Afro-American music, 217, 286, 338-339
"Air de Ballet" (Jadassohn), 134
Alphabet songs, 22
American Folk Songs for Children in Home, School, and Nursery School (Seeger), 23
"Are You Sleeping?", 34-35, 64, 251
Asian music, 343
Assemblies, 44-45
Australian music, 344
Autoharp, 39-40, 126-127, 262-268

B

Bach, Johann Sebastian, 191, 226
Balfe, Michael William, 134
Ballet, 173-174, 220
Band, elementary, 45, 279
"Band of Angels," 84-85
Barbershop quartets, 287
Bartók, Béla, 167
"Battle Hymn of the Republic," 286, 292
"Bear Dance" (Bartók), 167-168
Beat, 92-93, 109-119, 265 (*see also* Rhythm)
Beguine, 189
Bells:
  and creativity, 254-257
  harmonic use of, 251-254
  for learning chords, 103-107
  and melody, 245-251
  types of, 239, 244-245, 261
Bennett, Michael D., 192
Bicentennial program helps, 283-292
Black dances, 188-189
Black music, 217, 286, 338-339, 342
Blues, 288
"Boating on the Lake" (Kullak), 134
Bolero, 188